Family Therapy
Full Length Case Studies

Family Therapy

FULL LENGTH CASE STUDIES

Edited by *PEGGY PAPP, M.S.W.*

Foreword by *SALVADOR MINUCHIN, M.D.*

For
THE AMERICAN ORTHOPSYCHIATRIC ASSOCIATION

GARDNER PRESS, INC.
Distributed by Halsted Press
Division of John Wiley & Sons, Inc.
New York   London   Toronto   Sydney

To My Children, Miranda and Tony

Second Printing

Copyright © 1977 by Gardner Press, Inc.

Gardner Press, Inc.
19 Union Square West, New York 10003

Distributed solely by the Halsted Press Division
of John Wiley & Sons, Inc., New York

Library of Congress Cataloging in Publication Data
Main entry under title:

Family therapy.

    "For the American Orthopsychiatric Association."
      1. Family psychotherapy—Cases, clinical re-
ports, statistics. 2. Psychotherapist and
patient—Cases, clinical reports, statistics.
I. Papp, Peggy. II. American Orthopsychiatric
Association.
RC480.8.F35   616.8'915   77-16641
ISBN 0-470-99355-3
Printed in the United States of America

Contents

FOREWORD   vii

PREFACE   ix

1   THE FAMILY THAT HIDES TOGETHER   1
Frank S. Pittman, III, M.D.

2   "OK—YOU'VE BEEN A BAD MOTHER"   23
John H. Weakland

3   THE IDENTIFIED PATIENT   35
C. Christian Beels, M.D.

4   GENERATION AFTER GENERATION: The Long-Term
Treatment of an Irish Family with Widespread Alcoholism
over Multiple Generations   47
Elizabeth A. Carter, M.S.W.

5   IT'S 10 PM—DO YOU KNOW WHERE YOUR PARENTS
ARE?   69
Ian Alger, M.D.

6   THE ANATOMY OF A THERAPIST   101
Harry J. Aponte, A.C.S.W.

7   THE DIVORCE LABYRINTH   117
David V. Keith, M.D. and Carl A. Whitaker, M.D.

8   FOLLOW-UP TO DIVORCE LABYRINTH   133
Augustus V. Napier, Ph.D

9   THE FAMILY WHO HAD ALL THE ANSWERS   143
Peggy Papp, M.S.W.

10   IN-LAWS AND OUT-LAWS: A Marital Case of Kinship
Confusion   167
James L. Framo, Ph.D.

11   ON BECOMING A MYSTERY   183
Marianne Walters, M.S.W.

12   "SOMETIMES IT'S BETTER FOR THE RIGHT HAND NOT
TO KNOW WHAT THE LEFT HAND IS DOING"   199
Richard Fisch, M.D.

Contributors

IAN ALGER, M.D.
New York Medical College

HARRY J. APONTE, A.C.S.W.
Philadelphia Child Guidance Clinic

C. CHRISTIAN BEELS, M.D.
College of Physicians and Surgeons of Columbia University

ELIZABETH A. CARTER, M.S.W.
Family Institute of Westchester

RICHARD FISCH, M.D.
Mental Research Institute

JAMES L. FRAMO, Ph.D.
Temple University

DAVID V. KEITH, M.D.
University of Wisconsin School of Medicine

AUGUSTUS Y. NAPIER, Ph.D.
University of Wisconsin School of Medicine

PEGGY PAPP, M.S.W.
Ackerman Institute for Family Therapy

FRANK S. PITTMAN III, M.D.
Emory University

MARIANNE WALTERS, M.S.W.
Philadelphia Child Guidance Clinic

JOHN H. WEAKLAND
Mental Research Institute

CARL A. WHITAKER, M.D.
University of Wisconsin School of Medicine

Foreword

Psychotherapy has suffered since its inception from a major blind spot in conceptions of the therapeutic process. Psychotherapists who have spent the equivalent of centuries in observing people and have written thousands of books about their patients have, through some twist of pride, been slow or unwilling to observe themselves in the process. During an era in which scientists study the influence of the experimenter on the experimental field, we have gone on talking as if the patient exists in a dimension of time and space quite different from ours. Explorers and explainers of the labyrinth of other people's minds and behavior, therapists have not paid enough attention to their own input to this labyrinth. This blissful state of affairs allows therapists to explain objectively the "essence" of the personality of their patients or the characteristics of the social system that remain after all resistance has been dissolved and the idiosyncratic context of therapy has been neutralized.

Family therapists should have profited from the observation of the tunnel vision that has affected so many individual therapists. Instead, we have been repeating the same mistakes, talking about the family or the therapeutic process as if the therapeutic system has a black hole occupied by an invisible therapist who is not affected by the feedback process, and whose operations are not part of the system itself.

This book comes to challenge this mistake by the use of a simple procedure. Peggy Papp asked a group of prominent family therapists to discuss a case from beginning to end, and to describe their idiosyncratic ways of putting theory into practice. Reading their explanations of the therapeutic process, the reader finds him-or herself moving slowly from the explanations to the explainers. At one level, you come to understand the difference between Whitaker, Papp, Aponte, Pittman, and so on with respect to their ways of being therapists. But inevitably, as the reader moves through the series of explanations, he or she shifts to a superordinate level of understanding. First, one may pay attention to the family dynamics—to the dyads and triads, to coalitions, scapegoating, and so on; then to the therapeutic techniques—to paradoxical tasks, processes of joining, utiliza-   *vii* tion of cotherapists, videotape feedback, and so on. But finally, in order to make sense of differences in the explanations, we begin to pay attention to the processes by which the therapists carry the families toward an acceptance of alternative realities that they consider therapeutically helpful. We see that family patterns expand and family members experiment with new outlooks on life and people, accommodating to the therapist. The therapist also accommodates, but his position in this process is central and highly complex.

Each of the therapists explains the nature of change, and their explanations are diverse. Because their descriptions are cogent, and because they are all competent healers who help families, we cannot escape the nagging feeling that we are dealing not only with Explainers but with Convincers. I assume that many of the therapeutic operations presented by each of the convincers are, at formal levels, isomorphic, but we do not yet have a generalized conceptual framework for integrating their various approaches. This is the direction of the future. By showing us the different ways in which some of the best family therapists understand and explain their therapeutic interventions, this book offers the basic material from which a unified conceptualization of the therapeutic process can develop.

Salvador Minuchin, M.D.

Preface

Peggy Papp, M.S.W.

This book includes eleven full length case studies by leading family therapists. Its purpose is to give the reader a step-by-step account of the thinking process that takes place in treating a family over a period of time. It emerges from a conviction that therapy is a process of trial and error, and therefore the most truthful and effective way of describing it is by following the personal trial and error process of the therapist. Rather than the more common approach of describing general theory illustrated with selected interventions or separate interviews, contributors have been asked to discuss a case from beginning to end describing their idiosyncratic way of putting theory into practice. This process is usually left out of professional articles and training tapes. The actual therapy experience is sifted through a conceptual refinery where it is packaged, embellished, edited and polished for publication. While this is instructive in presenting a general framework, it is deceptive as it leaves out the myriad accommodations which are required in putting concepts into action. It is analogous to buying a "put-it-together-yourself" toy which appears simple from the picture on the box but when opened you discover 357 pieces with instructions that don't fit the pieces. To your dismay you end up with an airplane with one wing, five tails and no engine. The same kind of bewilderment and frustration often occur in attempting to follow theoretical instructions in putting a family together. The novice is left with a disquieting sense of inadequacy—why don't the methods work as illustrated in the articles and on the training tapes?

Occasionally a therapist will present a transcript of an interview and discuss the interventions. While this is more helpful, it does not give the reader any idea of the progress of the therapy over time. What happened after that one interview which turned out so well? How did the therapist maintain the change; meet the next crisis; handle the new problems produced by the change; keep from getting bored, angry or feeling frustrated?

With the growing acceptance of family therapy as a major treatment modality comes the enormous problem of conceptualizing and teaching it. The shift from the individual to the family as the unit of treatment makes concept-tualization more difficult because of the complexity of the system one is dealing with. There has been much written on the intricacies of the family system, its homeostatic mechanisms, patterns of interaction, cycles of feedback and basic structure. There has also been an equal amount written on methods and techni-ques for changing this system. But there has been little written on the personal struggle that takes place in putting the two together.

My most memorable experience with this difficulty occured several years ago when after reading an article by Salvador Minuchin on the treatment of a family with an anorectic girl, I tried his approach on a similar family I was treating at the time. It did not turn out the way it was supposed to, and I sat there in the middle of the chaos thinking, "This never happened to Sal Minuchin." In relating this story to him some time later he exclaimed, "Oh, Peggy, what hasn't happened to me! Everything, but everything has happened to me!" And I thought, "It's the 'everything' that would be helpful to know about."

This book attempts to deal with something of the "everything"—the thinking behind major interventions, the unexpected turn of events, the slip between the cup and the lip, the mistakes, doubts, second thoughts and finally the outcome. I am acutely aware that it is possible to record only a small part of this process and that even the struggle and searching are edited.

The book includes a wide variety of families, problems and approaches, with the length of treatment varying from two years to two interviews. Contributors have been chosen not only on the basis of their expertise but on their ability to articulate their personal thoughts and feelings. Creative therapists are always questioning, searching, experimenting and re-formulating their ideas. It has long been my contention that a therapist develops a theory congruent with his philosophy, personality and life style. This congruence adds the flavor to the therapy. In order to preserve this flavor the articles are carefully edited in the hope that the reader will get a sense of the style of the therapist from the style of his/her writing. One cannot read Frank Pittman's article "The Family That Hides Together" without becoming aware of his jauntiness which is part and parcel of his therapy. This jauntiness becomes his therapeutic lifeboat as he cruises through crisis after crisis slyly winking at the family, the world and him-self. He sets this tone in his first session as he wryly comments on the family's need for a victim, "It seems kind of unpleasant to me, but I wouldn't want to change something y'al enjoy so much."

On the other hand it is Chris Beel's superb organization and clarity which allows him to deal effectively with a "borderline personality disorder" in a hus-band. Regarding his relationship with the couple, Beels states, "They expected a kind of friend of the family advisory relationship and this fitted in well with one side of my personality." Making prime use of this side of his personality he gives explicit explanations and instructions which help the family to organize themselves in times of crisis.

Perhaps the most difficult style to capture on paper is the unstructured, existentialist style of Carl Whitaker and David Keith. Whitaker has alternately intrigued and confused his colleagues over the years with his anti-theory theory. In reading "Divorce Labyrinth" one begins to sense what he means by the difference between "doing" something to a family and "being" with a family. "Can I be alive enough to help them grow? Was it too rich? Was it too lean? Did these people ask for something we didn't hear?" are the questions Whitaker and Keith keep asking themselves. As one accompanies them on this "long and growth producing journey," sharing their anxieties, impulses and fantasies one senses the impact of the total therapeutic experience in evolution. Gus Napier further explores this experience from the family's point of view with his probing follow-up.

At the opposite end of the pole from this non-structured method of Whitaker and Keith is Harry Aponte's highly structured approach with a one parent black family in "Anatomy of a Therapist." Working within the structured concept of realigning the family according to sibling hierarchy, he comes face to face with his own personal issues of hierarchy. "The family is black, I am Puerto Rican. They are poor in Philadelphia, I was poor in New York. I felt connected with them and yet, that day, our positions and current circumstances put great distance between us, and I felt it." Aponte's awareness that, "They treated me like a member of the oppressive society that over-awed me as a child" becomes a central issue in the therapy and adds a touch of poignancy to their brief encounter.

It is through the intertwining of the external dialogue with the family and the internal dialogue with the therapist in the following cases that it is hoped the reader will be given a glimpse of aspects of therapy which defy theoretical definition.

1

The Family
That Hides Together

Frank S. Pittman, III, M.D.

The Vocational Rehabilitation counselor specifically requested family therapy for the Meeks family. He told me only that Carter Meeks was upset over his daughter's lifestyle. That sounded simple enough. I had no warning of what lay ahead.

On March 19, the Meeks arrived early, had coffee and cokes in the waiting room, listened to the Beethoven piano trios on tape, and chatted with my wife, who is my secretary. I was seeing a battling couple and was, as usual, 15 minutes late. While the departing couple fought over the next appointment, I stepped into the waiting room, apologized for my tardiness, and introduced myself. As I ushered the family into the group therapy room, I noticed that Mr. Meeks walked with a cane and that the three children were of indeterminate sex but looked just like their mother.

The group room has a large butcher block coffee and foot table in the center and has nine director's chairs in a circle around it. Mrs. Meeks chose the chair nearest the door, Mr. Meeks stumbled through the room to the opposite chair. I sat equidistant from them. The children clustered around their father. The circle had the older girl on my right, her father next, then the youngest child, the boy opposite me, an empty chair, the mother and two more empty chairs between the mother and me. The youngest child pointedly moved her chair almost behind a large *Scheffleria* at the window.

I then noticed the five Meeks. Carter Meeks, the father, was 43. He was a large, handsome, blandly dignified, white-haired, pink-faced man with glasses, in a casual jacket and a stiff back brace. He was in physical pain. Dolores Meeks, the mother, was 44. She had an open, plainly pretty face, sensible clothes and hair, and the appearance of a much younger woman trying to look like a much older woman. Rebecca was 19, and like the other two children, looked physically like her mother. She wore overalls and boots and was flat chested and big hipped. Her blonde hair was stringy and dirty. She had been crying and now looked sullen. Jackson said he was 20, but he looked 14. He was short and very thin, pale and sickly looking, and wrapped up rather warmly for such a nice spring day. He lit a cigarette as I did, and followed me in putting his feet up on the central table. Mary Anne was only 12, but she was about the same size as Jackson. She refused to look at me or the others, as she bundled herself in the corner, making a show of her noninvolvement. She wore clean jeans and a hooded parka. I thought at first that she was a boy.

As I spoke to Rebecca, trying to establish the identities of the children, Dolores began fussing. First, she fussed at Mary Anne for not speaking up. Mary Anne stuck out her tongue and withdrew further. Jackson echoed his mother and Mary Anne stuck out her tongue at him, too. Carter said, "Now, Dolores," to her, which she ignored as she told Rebecca she should have dressed differently. Rebecca fussed at her for fussing, whereupon Mary Anne fussed at Rebecca for fussing back and Jackson fussed at Mary Anne for fussing. Carter again fussed at Dolores, who switched to Jackson and told him to take his feet off the table. He started crying and shouted at her, while his father shouted at her for her unending criticism. She then started in on her husband. Within less than a minute, everyone was crying except Dolores, who said, "See, they're all a bunch of crybabies." I felt as if I were watching a bad TV dramatization of something, so I said so. Each blamed someone else. The blame shifted back and forth, with any four attacking whomever seemed to be losing at the moment.

I tried several gambits to get them away from their performance on to the business at hand. I kept trying to explain that my first task was to try to understand why they were coming to see me now. I commented that I could understand it better if they'd all stop fussing long enough to catch me up. I asked if they acted this way at home, always seeking a victim to blame, and was told that they had for years. Carter was sure it was Dolores' fault, etc. I said something like, "It seems kind of unpleasant to me, but I wouldn't want to try to change something y'all enjoy so much. But why are you seeing me now?" Jackson said it was his mother's idea and Dolores said her husband had been depressed. For once, there was no disagreement, as Carter finally got a chance to tell his story, with persistent corrections from Dolores.

Carter had a bullet lodged in his spine from Korea 25 years before and had had intermittent pain. He had been on partial disability, had gone to school to become a typesetter, had married Dolores, and had been largely unhappy at home all these years, feeling that Dolores disliked everything and everyone, including himself, and distrusted all pleasures. This had not bothered him because he was busy with work and church activities, until 4 years ago, when his back pain had gradually become so severe he had submitted to surgery. After four operations, he was now unable to sit long enough to work, was in constant pain, and had one numb leg. Seeing that he couldn't return to work, Delores decided to return to school while Carter became a house-husband. Her increasing independence angered him, as did her babying of the painfully shy and asthmatic Jackson. Carter tried to impose the same efficiency and order he had used in his work and received universal opposition. He begged for approval and got none. His life had been guided by two needs: to be nice and liked, and to be orderly. He did both at work, but couldn't do both at home. Dolores didn't like him. The bickering became intense, and Dolores repeatedly threatened to leave but didn't.

Rebecca had been school phobic and socially isolated throughout high school, but had now gone off to college in Alabama. This was her second year. She identified with underdogs and planned to be a veterinarian. Rebecca was an anxious girl, often depressed, preoccupied with her small breasts and the belief that no man would tolerate her unless she gave him all his heart desired, including a hefty share of her parents' meager finances. A month before, she moved in with a boy who had just flunked out. She began requesting more money with which to live and to support him. Carter, though he disapproved, tried to give his children anything they wanted and was willing to increase her allowance. Dolores was furious, as she disapproved on religious grounds (she's been raised a hard-shell Baptist) and on a variety of personal grounds. She resented the financial outlay. She thought he was a fool. She thought her efforts to raise Rebecca right had failed. She disliked Rebecca's boyfriend. At this point in the story, they all started crying and shouting again, stating a variety of familiar principles and slogans and commandments. As usual, I was somewhat less interested in anyone's feelings than in what they were doing and how they affected one another, whether their actions acheived their goals. I suggested that it seemed to me that it was up to Rebecca to decide how she would live (though she seemed to be settling for very little), but up to her parents to decide how they would use their money. This satisfied no one. I decided to find out more about Jackson and Mary Anne.

Jackson had been severely asthmatic, sickly, withdrawn, antisocial, and often depressed, even suicidal. He had quit high school, at which he did poorly, and was going to welding school but couldn't lift the heavy items to be welded. He had never dated. He had a few friends, who mistreated him. Dolores felt as distrustful of them as she was of Rebecca's boyfriend. Carter wanted Jackson to move out on his own, but Jackson cried whenever he suggested it. Dolores disliked the marijuana plants he grew on the back porch. He cried about that, too. When he cried, both parents became his slaves. I was amused by this and said so, whereupon he cried some more, and then slyly winked at me.

Mary Anne was seen by both parents as their one potential success. She had been severely school phobic, but made straight A's. She had temper tantrums if she didn't. She had no friends and said she couldn't bring friends home because of the constant bickering. Each parent blamed the other for that.

As the hour ended (by now I was running over a half hour late and was clearly uncomfortable), I tried to spell out what I thought I had heard. Ideally, I like to come up with a clear and simple (often unavoidably and deliberately simplistic) definition of the family crisis. My focus initially may be more on the situation that has precipitated the family crisis than on the people in the family. Despite overwhelming pathology in this family, it had functioned in a way everyone tolerated, however marginally, without outside help until Rebecca moved in with her boyfriend and all hell broke loose. This was not completely accurate, of course. There had been many problems for 4 years, since the change in Carter's functional state, physical condition, and family role had led to complementary changes that had been poorly tolerated all around. Perhaps the family could have been considered dysfunctional from the beginning and had been overtly pathological since Jackson's asthma and Rebecca's school phobia. In taking a history, I prefer to go from present to past rather than to start at the beginning. My preference was to focus on the current crisis of Rebecca's roommate. I like to define the problem, then elicit or point out the obvious solutions. These solutions will, almost invariably, require a change in the family rules or role assignments, a change in its view of its past or future, or a change in one or more individuals. Therapy may then consist of negotiation of the resistance to change. Individual inflexibility may then be examined as it interferes with the specific changes required. It is akin to peeling an onion from the outside rather than from the core. This approach seems efficient, and has the added virtue of respecting nonconflictual uniqueness. Many people settle for far less than total mental health. I could conceivably have treated this family without ever dealing with their incessant bickering, if no one was unhappy with the bickering process and each was unhappy only with his win–loss ratio at the bickering game.

So, in summary, I suggested, rather tongue in cheek, that the problem seemed simple enough. Rebecca had become the first member to break the family rule of total noninvolvement with the outside world. She had friends now. Jackson wanted to do so, but was afraid. Mary Anne was under pressure to do so, but was afraid. Dolores was being forced to do so, but saw it as sinful and dangerous. Carter had previously done so at work, and now wanted to do so, but only if Dolores accompanied him. I congratulated Rebecca on overcoming the family phobia and asked if the others would like to follow suit. Surprisingly, all but Dolores agreed that this was the real problem. Mary Anne said she wanted to have friends but couldn't because of the family bickering. Jackson said he wanted to date, but no one would have him. He suddenly got support from all four. Carter said he would like to ask Dolores to go out with him, but she wouldn't go. Dolores agreed, talked about sin, and said she wanted to leave him. They all ignored it again. I found myself irritated with Dolores. On top of everything else, she insisted on talking about solutions, often drastic, without clarifying what problems she wanted to solve. I told her that no one seemed to believe she would leave, but that no one was stopping her. She smiled coyly and said she just might do so if Carter financed Rebecca's immorality.

I told them I knew how to solve the problem. Then I assigned several tasks, explaining that the defined problem could be solved if (1) Rebecca would figure out how to support her roommate without Carter's help, (2) Jackson would ask for dates until he got one, (3) Mary Anne would ask friends to the house, (4) Carter would ask Dolores to go out with him, and (5) Dolores would choose a place she felt morally comfortable going. Then I got up, leaving Rebecca and Dolores furious, Carter triumphant and lecherous looking, Jackson a bit scared, and Mary Anne fussing at her parents for fussing. As they protested, I told them we'd discuss it in a week and gave them an appointment.

When I assign tasks, I don't quite expect them to be performed. The tasks represent the direct sensible actions healthy people can take to correct the unpleasant situations about which they complain. Occasionally, someone will not take such action because it has never occurred to him. Sometimes, the act is not taken because of fear. In those cases, my casual endorsement of the act with the promise of support and the direction of family support may then be sufficient to overcome the fear. More often, the rational act is avoided for more complex reasons and its refusal may have great symbolic importance in either an internal or interactional conflict. This conflict becomes clear as the failure to act is explored in later sessions. The reduction of issues into tasks simplifies the problem solving process.

People get bogged down in the complexities of how they feel and begin to think that their feelings have some concrete importance. They forget that what happens to them is determined not so much by how they feel, but by what they do. In general, if they do things differently, they will feel differently about themselves and other people will treat them differently. This generalization is not quite true of the more marked extremes of mood disorder, either mania or depression, which seem to be treated most efficiently by a combination of biochemical methods and the appropriate actions to reinforce the desired moods as the medicine makes them chemically possible again. The generalization is true of schizophrenia, which seems to be a biochemical defect that produces decompensation under stress and therefore leads, to the intolerance and avoidance of stress and action characteristic of schizophrenics. On phenothiazines, most schizophrenics no longer decompensate under stress and can begin to unlearn the bizarre self-protective maneuvers they have needed when biochemically vulnerable. Some schizophrenics prefer their psychosis, with the protection from reality it provides, and may even try to override their phenothiazines with large amounts of hallucinogenic drugs to restore the psychosis. This is the extreme of living within one's feelings rather than in the world of goal-directed action and interaction. For the rest of the world, feelings are to be understood and respected (so many problems are a direct result of the effort to eradicate rather than to accept undesired feelings), but then transcended.

It may seem that I don't value feelings. I do, but I don't always consider feelings the best determinants of action. Change must precede insight and often must even precede motivation for change. Even if the coordination of feelings and action is one's long-term goal, such a goal is rarely achieved by day to day, moment to moment, feeling-determined actions, which ignore long-range realities. So at the same time that I am trying to bring about an identification, understanding, and above all, acceptance of feelings, I am pushing people to act, perhaps against their feelings, toward their independence, their expanded range, and their long-term goals—*their* long-term goals, not mine for them.

I, as a therapist, even more than as a person, must have a strong reality base, which includes a knowledge of how to get from one point to the other, and some idea of the odds of something working out, to counterbalance those people who only act on sure things or who believe in luck and are always willing to bet everything in life on longshots. If wisdom is the ability to make decisions on part knowledge, that willingness is a necessary ingredient for efficiency of treatment. There are few great risks to testing out some appropriate action that doesn't totally work out—it at least expands functional range and we may learn something from it. Sometimes the prescribed action may be to take no action at all. When I prescribe no action as a task, it is not because of incomplete understanding on my part (which is always there) or because someone's feelings aren't right yet (which will usually be the case indefinitely), but because I think it will work best to let things happen without that person's efforts at controlling the situation.

In the tasks I assigned to the Meeks family, I asked the parents to take no action about Rebecca's love life, but I also asked them to take no action about her roommate's finances and Rebecca could then pursue her stated goal of independence, both social and financial. I told Mary Anne to take no action about her parents' bickering, but to pursue her stated goal (of having friends over to the house) despite their behavior. My tasks for Jackson and Carter were straight counterphobic recommendations' to face the feared females, tasks assigned offhandedly and optimistically. Dolores' problematic task (to state her preference on entertainment) was an effort to move her out of her protected defensive position in which she controlled her family by being blameless (because she never asked for anything for herself) but dissatisfied. I asked her to take charge of getting what she wanted by asking for it. I did not ask Carter and Dolores to stop bickering because neither expressed the goal of a bickerless relationship—that might come later. In assigning tasks, the therapist cannot direct the settlement of conflicts unless the weight of reality is overwhelming on one side, in which case it is the reality, not the therapist, to which the combatants are bowing. The therapist's trick is to demonstrate the ease with which each person can achieve stated long-range goals without anyone else changing his goals.

In assigning tasks, I am not authoritarian. I try to maintain my posture as a friendly consultant, personal, concerned, and gently amused by the absurdity of it all. It is clear that my tasks are presented as challenges, not between me and them but between their goals and their feelings, which keep interfering with one another.

I could have made other choices with the Meeks family if we had defined the problem differently. Had the family come in a few months earlier or later, reacting to a different crisis than the issue of Rebecca's independent lifestyle, the bickering might have seemed more prominent than the family-wide fear of the outside world. Or perhaps Dolores' standards, always unachieved, could be seen as central. I have seen some families through a series of peripherally related crises years apart. The Meeks family, however, like most chronically dysfunctional families, had a central core defect that tends to make the routine processes of change more difficult. If the tight boundaries were not *the* core defect, at least they were *a* core defect related to the current crisis and therefore open to examination and change. The initial definition of the problem does not have to be accurate but it does have to be relevant. My misperceptions and misformulations will be corrected soon enough, but, meanwhile, all the family members need some changes of their own to work on, to distract them from their demands on one another to change.

MARCH 29

On March 29, 10 days later, the family arrived for their second appointment. They looked happy. They took the same seats as the time before, with one exception. Mary Anne now sat beside her mother, away from me and next to Jackson. They kept these seats thereafter. Rebecca had returned to college. I began by asking about her. All enthusiastically reported that she was very happy. The family had decided they would not object to her decision to live with her boyfriend. Jackson again stated his jealousy of her, but it was free of bitterness this week. He could hardly wait to tell me, with great pride, that he had asked a girl for a date and she had accepted. He had liked her and would date her again. All except Mary Anne joined in the sexual innuendoes and encouragements for him to immerse himself in the mysteries of overt sexuality. Surprisingly, Dolores led this encouragement, totally abandoning her piety of the week before, which was replaced by Mary Anne's complaints that we were being disgusting. Jackson was triumphant. The other three had done less well with their tasks. Mary Anne refused to have friends over because her parents continued bickering. The battle was ostensibly because Carter gave Rebecca some money, which angered Dolores, so she refused to go out with him when he invited her. He pouted and she defended, but no one cried or took the battle seriously. Dolores was determined to tell me about Jackson's severe depression last year after losing a job. She then told me about his mistreatment at the hands of all the neighborhood boys, whom he persisted in courting despite their cruel bullying of him. Jackson was feeling too good to be bothered by this, though Carter defended his passivity against Dolores' call to arms. Mary Anne tried to stop the battle and we had a light, comic opera replay of last week's impassioned battle. I felt overwhelmed and confused by the change in Dolores, who seemed determined to be the opposite of whatever I had seen her as being previously. I said so, and Carter explained angrily that Dolores would do anything to be right. I tried to explore her concern with money and found that there was quite enough, so I dismissed this as another nonissue, like the moral one. I suggested that they all pursue the previously assigned tasks. Carter then attacked Dolores for her lack of love. He accused her of other men, which everyone decided was absurd. He then broke down in tears and expressed suicidal thoughts. More exploration revealed his severe depression which predated the episode with Rebecca. He was sleeping badly, waking early, eating poorly, and losing weight. He had even given up his volunteer work at a hospital and, more significantly, given up his metal sculpture, his great source of identity since his disability. I prescribed imipramine 100 mg/-day for him, feeling the depression had gone past the point of being psychological and was of biochemical significance. All seemed relieved and Carter seemed grateful. Was Dolores' strange behavior a reaction to Carter's depression, as she claimed? I doubted it.

I should have picked up on the severity of Carter's depression at the first visit. Too much was going on. I found myself viewing Carter as a tragic hero, crippled and somewhat castrated by his disability, and pleading for love and reassurance from his heartless wife. I began to see her as the villainess. She confused me. I said so.

APRIL 5

The next week, Mary Anne was missing. She had chosen to have a friend at the house while the family came to the session, thus performing her task while defying me. I was to discover later how this typified Mary Anne generally. Jackson was much closer to the girl he was dating and was having some fear of his sexuality with his more experienced girlfriend, whom he had desired but feared for 3 years. He was also physically ill. There was a battle over whether he would see the family doctor for his cold, but he poutingly refused. Dolores asked me to examine his lungs; I was willing and Jackson was willing. In my other office with Jackson alone while I found my dusty stethoscope and he removed layers of underwear, I noticed that he was not only clearly past puberty but well muscled, a secret hidden by his bundling clothes and his childlike face and stature. I commented on his well-developed body, assuming this was part of the reason for his and his mother's desire for me to examine his perfectly clear chest. I assured him in passing that he was well equipped for the sexual task he feared. He seemed relieved. This all took less than 5 minutes while Dolores and Carter chatted amicably. When we returned, Carter attacked Dolores again for not loving him. Jackson supported his father in believing the whole family suffered from her inability to love, which she attempted to rectify by overcriticizing and overprotecting. Dolores agreed, to my surprise, and acknowledged that her attacks must be efforts to make up for this hardness she felt inside. She thought Carter's expectations of her were excessive because he had been deprived as a child. As she tried, rather awkwardly, to explain herself, with a minimum of defensiveness, Carter continued to pathetically attack her for her failure to make him feel the way he had hoped a woman could make a man feel. Jackson joined in tearfully, relating his fear that his girlfriend would fail him, too. In a few minutes, Dolores was again as defensive and hard as she had been previously. I could now see what Dolores was up against. I assured Carter the medicine would be working better in another week and encouraged him again to risk asking Dolores for a date, but to be sure he was ready to appreciate her willingness to risk getting close again. Dolores denied that she had revealed anything she had revealed about her fears of being insufficiently loving. Carter attacked again and they left bickering.

In this third hour, I wish I had gotten more history of Dolores' background. Not until a year later did I do so. It might have helped me understand her relationship with Jackson. The history I got on Carter's family was helpful. He had grown up in poverty, neglect, and chaos, while he sought love through hard work and rigid goodness. I'm glad I examined Jackson. It helped me see him as a man rather than the boy he appeared to be when dressed. It also furthered our relationship. I have no objection to physical examinations of patients, though I don't do it routinely, or even often. I tend to avoid examining my female outpatients for minor complaints, as I fear it may be misunderstood, and they usually avoid asking me to do so, probably for the same reasons. Appropriate physical attention from a physician, even a psychiatrist, seems appreciated. I prudishly avoid anything seductive, or even potentially so, when it extends beyond the verbal.

APRIL 12

I was feeling good about the Meeks family as I anticipated Session 4. Mary Anne was present, defiantly refusing to describe her new friends. She disliked me, seeing me now as the cause of changes in the family. She was angry at me because Rebecca was off with her boyfriend, because Jackson was too busy dating to pay attention to her, and because her parents were going out at night without her, a new experience. Dolores confessed that she'd enjoyed it, Carter confessed that she'd made him feel good. Both confessed that sex had been reestablished and was welcome. Jackson confessed, aside to me, that sex had been successful for him. I was openly enthusiastic and congratulatory, even realizing that Mary Anne's anger at me was her way, learned from her mother, of showing love and appreciation. All four responded to my observation. I thought my job was near completion.

The next day, I got a frantic call from Carter. Jackson was distraught, threatening suicide, and refusing to discuss it with anyone but me. I'd had a cancellation and was able to see him alone. He was profoundly depressed. His girlfriend had moved with her family to another state. How could there be sex without intimacy and commitment? When it meant so much to him, how could it mean so little to her? The abrupt move, of course, had nothing to do with him. Within a few minutes of my calm support, he was enthusiastically looking forward to new seductions and new paths out of his isolation. I was amazed at how little support it took to turn him around. The rest of the hour focused on his newly developing pride. He was quite different away from his family. It helped me see how little support he got at home. I wondered if I should have pushed him so rapidly into sexuality for which he was prepared physically, but not emotionally. He seemed to feel overall that it had been a good thing.

APRIL 26

Session 6 was nearly 2 weeks later. All was well. Carter was having side effects from the medicine but was feeling good and was more active than usual. He and Dolores were having fun. Mary Anne was having fun. Jackson was about to finish trade school and was job hunting. I gave support, we talked about reality issues, and they praised me a lot.

MAY 3

Session 7 opened with Carter showing me a rash on his chest and back, for which I prescribed benadryl. Jackson was still withdrawn but was job hunting. He wouldn't ask any girls out, though Mary Anne assured him that all her new friends thought he was cute. Rebecca had visited and seemed happy, though her boyfriend was still unemployed. Carter gave her more money, Dolores complained, Carter pouted over her lack of total satisfaction, and they had skipped sex all week. The usual bickering was low key, but Mary Anne complained about it. Dolores saw Carter as needing to please everyone but her. Rebecca had become part of the outside world for her, a world she still distrusted, and Carter's support of his older daughter was a betrayal of the family and evidence of rejection of her. The old patterns kept threatening to break through.

MAY 17

I had contracted with Vocational Rehabilitation and with the Meeks to see them ten times. I wasn't sure we could do the necessary work in that time. At the sixth visit it appeared that the original goals would be achieved, at the seventh visit it appeared unlikely. The decision was much in my mind at the eighth visit. There had been changes. The originally assigned tasks were being performed, the initially defined problems were being solved. Jackson was still depressed and would probably need much more therapy, but should it be group, family, or individual, or some combination? Mary Anne was socially active and happy but still had some phobias, and I knew school phobia recurs. The marriage was better than it had been, but the constant bickering was still there. I don't know why I thought I could back out at this point, but I tried to do so. My effort was to wrap things up in one further problem definition which could give them all a direction that could be pursued without me. I focussed on the family perception of Dolores' unlimited supply of love, wisdom, and strength which was seen as being withheld. She reinforced this by implying she had the warm milk, but they hadn't earned it. As I gave her much gentle support and attempted to correct the misperceptions of her magic and wean them all from her, the milk began to flow. The more she gave, the more they all attacked her for not giving more. In the end she could only reward pathetic behavior. I hoped this problem could be understood, if not solved right away.

MAY 27

I then saw Jackson alone for what I expected to be the final time. He was on antidepressants now.

He felt good, seemed to enjoy being with me, brightened with support, and had no real problems except a fear of asking anyone for a date. He didn't see himself as undesirable anymore. He saw women as treacherous. He didn't want to talk about his family. He just wanted to be with me, as if I alone shared the secret of his masculinity. I felt he'd adopted me. I did not discourage the transference. I realized I had slipped almost inadvertently from short-term to long-term therapy. I was part of the ongoing structure of the family.

My approach to family therapy, rooted in crisis intervention, should work well in short-term treatment and should make it easier to keep the treatment limited. In practice, I have the same problems as all other therapists. People who need long-term therapy may want quick patch jobs, and people who can solve their problems briefly may prefer talking about it interminably. I try to define the problems succinctly, outline the most immediate changes, and then keep up gentle pressure until people risk change. It is hard to predict how long that will take, but it is not dependent on the extensiveness of the pathology or the number of changes to be made. This family, with so many problems, might have changed far more quickly than it did. I couldn't know until I got some idea of how many risks they were willing to take.

In several previous papers with Langsley, Kaplan, Machotka, Flomenhaft, and DeYoung, we talked about four kinds of crisis, the Crisis of Development, the Bolt from the Blue, the Caretaker Crisis, and the Crisis of Exacerbation. Simply, the Bolt from the Blue is that rare crisis which occurs in a functional family through unexpectable forces totally outside the family. The Crisis of Development is that common crisis which occurs when a somewhat rigid family has difficulty adapting to one of its unavoidable developmental phases. The Caretaker Crisis is one of the many recurrent crises inherent in a family's dependency on someone outside the family, such as a therapist, in-law, or social agency. The Crisis of Exacerbation is another in the relentless series of uproars that a crisis-prone family uses to keep from changing its dysfunctional patterns.

The Meeks family fell within three catergories. The disability resulting from Carter's surgery was a Bolt from the Blue, but that had been handled fairly well years before, and while the new role assignments weren't totally satisfactory, they were workable. Initially I had tried to see the Meeks' crisis as four or even five overlapping Crises of Development. Increasingly over the first few visits it became apparent that this was a crisis-prone family, in which changes didn't take place smoothly even when the necessity for change was made apparent. The background noise was so intense that only the most dramatic gestures could be heard. Crises of Exaccerbation can be handled over and over again, to everyone's satisfaction, but they will continue to recur until the crisis-prone family can learn to make little changes without dramatic gestures, until the background noise is reduced to a level that will permit calm, orderly negotiation to be heard. This requires long-term therapy, as the family is led through the expectable series of life's crises until they learn to handle them without disorder.

Long-term therapy with crisis-prone families is not easy. They might prefer a lifetime series of crisis interventions which would keep the family together without permitting any change to take place. The crisis-prone family can be seen as one which, at all costs, must keep some unworkable pattern unchanged. It may be that all people enter therapy to avoid change, not always in the "look how hard I'm trying" sense, but in the sense that reality seems to be requiring a particularly undesirable change and they would prefer using therapy for finding a more congenial compromise with reality.

At the time I decided (or was forced to realize) that treatment would be long term, I did not totally understand what the crisis proneness was about, what the family was protecting. My formulations changed from time to time, and I consistently threw my ideas at them.

Usually my formulations centered around Dolores. Her standards were unrealistic. No one tried to meet them, though all felt defeated because they couldn't meet them. As they gave up on the real world and expected all life's rewards to come from Dolores, she felt drained, angry, and inadequate. She became a bitch, justifying her failure to love by focusing on the imperfections of others. I sometimes call this the Sleeping Beauty syndrome, in which someone must hack through miles of bramble forest to get a kiss. Or I may call it the Turandot syndrome after Puccini's opera, in which a prince is given three riddles to determine whether he gets to marry the princess or have his head chopped off. Bitching is not sex linked, is a two-handed game, and is characteristic of guilty dysphoria. Once it is defined as a problem, it arouses my sympathy rather than my wrath—"as unpleasant as it must be for others, it must be far more unpleasant for you."

Her style of communication was tricky. A typical example:

Dr Pittman (cheerily): What's up?
Dolores (pouting): I don't have a viewpoint on it.
Carter (hostile): She has a viewpoint on everything.
Dr Pittman (to Carter): I don't think she means she doesn't have a viewpoint. I think she
    means no one cares what her viewpoint is.
Dolores (still pouting, but agreeing): It's irrelevant.
Dr. Pittman (to Dolores): What's the situation as you see it?
Dolores: I don't see it.

Dr. Pittman (laughing and leaning toward her): Dolores, you're pouting.
Dolores: No, I'm not. I came just to cooperate. It doesn't bother me anymore when Carter
    etc., etc. (long list of grievances). It doesn't bother me. I can rise above it. I can
    make a world of my own.

I spent much of my time trying to translate her to herself and to them.

MAY 31

Jackson fought with Dolores over all her rules and cried over any criticism. Mary Anne refused to go to school. Dolores preached and shouted. Carter tried to calm the three defiant combatants. I made the error of assuming that the whole issue was termination, and kept trying to deal with that. Nonetheless, I agreed to continue the therapy, in part because of concern for Jackson, but in part because Dolores still confused and fascinated me.

A few days later I got another frantic telephone call. Jackson had wired himself with dynamite and threatened to blow himself up if Rebecca didn't go with the family to Florida on their summer vacation. Rebecca refused to go unless her boyfriend went, too. Dolores refused to sleep with Carter if he paid the boyfriend's way on the trip. Mary Anne refused to go if the boyfriend went at all. Carter couldn't find a way to please everyone and had cancelled the trip, which infuriated all of them. The call came while I was seeing another family almost as wild, so I tried to direct a quick decision, which sometimes works out well and sometimes badly. I got them all on the phone and told them to go and to take the boyfriend. They all calmed immediately and did as I said, except Mary Anne, who ran away until Jackson caught her and dragged her to the already loaded car. This was an error on my part. I had displaced Carter by assuming it was a true emergency rather than a typical day in the Meek's household. I should have ignored Jackson and supported Carter's decision to postpone the trip (which everyone wanted to take) until everyone cut out the histrionics. That would have bypassed Carter's effort to be good and pleasing, and strengthened his authority. Then a decision could be negotiated without dramatics and uproar.

JUNE 11

For the eleventh session, Carter was at home sick with a severe sunburn. Dolores and Mary Anne were only slightly less sick. I couldn't avoid laughing. Everyone was furious with Rebecca and her boyfriend, who had borrowed money from each member of the family. Jackson was totally over his depression and Mary Anne liked me again. The trip and the boyfriend were so bad, the family felt united and decided it was all absurdly funny.

Therapy proceeded over the next 2 months with the focus primarily on Jackson, who got a job, became physically ill under the pressure, lost to 107 lbs, and quit the job. Carter blamed Dolores for all problems as she and I urged him to stop his bitching by taking charge of the pressuring process on Jackson and Mary Anne. Dolores was both fiercely protective of her pathetic family and fiercely attacking of their inadequacies. She was seen as unloving and got no love in return. She was too defensive to be warm for long, but it seemed to me that her efforts at loving were always seen as insufficient. Increasingly, Carter's passivity was seen as the roadblock, as he never forced action, only bitched at Dolores for failing to do so nicely. As always I urged them to risk taking certain actions that were in conflict with their feelings.

On August 28, the next major crisis occurred. Dolores called at 8:00 a.m. about Mary Anne's refusal to go to the first day of school. She had done this annually for several years. Carter was not at home. I told her to take Mary Anne to school, even if she was kicking and screaming. Dolores thought it up to Carter, not her, to do so. I agreed, but Carter wasn't at home. Dolores called him, he reluctantly came home and, passively and protectively, he assisted. After another call, from Carter, who was reluctant to force her, they got her to school. I called Mary Anne that afternoon to congratulate her. She was barely verbal. The next morning, I called to make sure all was well. Mary Anne had said she didn't feel like going and Carter had almost given in, but Dolores prevailed without much protest. Dolores was angry with Carter for his weakness with the children. She brought up the issue that was to occupy us for over a year. She wanted Jackson to move out.

This episode was the major turning point in the first course of therapy. Perhaps the crisis of Rebecca's boyfriend could have been, if I had understood Dolores at the first interview. Dolores never asked for what she wanted and never meant what she said. She was trying too hard to avoid being the martinet. So I didn't realize that her moralistic posturings were an effort to mobilize Carter with issues that had more meaning for him than for her. Dolores was pleading that she couldn't love Carter if he forced her to be the tough parent, if he protected his "nice guy" posture while criticizing her for being his hatchet man. This was too subtle for me at the time. I was too rushed and irritated on the day of Jackson's dynamite crisis, before the Florida trip, to help Carter understand what Dolores was requiring. I merely told him what to do. Even though it worked (any action on his part would have worked), it did not result in his understanding one of the keys to Dolores' love. The crisis of Mary Anne's school phobia did lead to Dolores' acknowledgement of her wishes, and Carter's understanding of them. She then wanted the final test of his willingness to take the assertive burden in helping the children emancipate from the anxious, isolated family. This understanding did not solve all problems immediately, for the change required in Carter was to be an awkward one. Also, this was not the only key to Dolores' heart. We had neglected the history of the relationship. Each time some item from the past came up, it was so controversial and produced such defensive withdrawal in both partners, it could not be enlightening. I could never get any agreement on what actually went on between them in the past. That may not be important. I don't like to convey that past feelings are justification for current behavior. The patterns are important because people gradually adapt to the situations they are in. However, it may be sufficient to bypass a full understanding of how the patterns got that way and simply acknowledge that past behavior is part of the old pattern and does not necessarily indicate the only possibility of which the participants are capable. This is an optimistic attitude, usually accurate, which keeps the focus on health, with its constant options and potentials for change, rather than on the compelling pressures of the past, which justify pathology as inevitable and therefore unchangeable.

A month later, Carter took action again. He arranged a job interview for Jackson. Jackson got the job. His depression lifted. Carter's active involvement in Jackson's job hunt changed everyone's assessment of him. I became an observer to a process that was going well without my help. I'm never comfortable in that position for very long. I attempted to focus on the marriage. I began to pick up on Carter's complaints about Dolores. She would playfully offer divorce and the complaint would be ignored. I would pick up on Dolores' dissatisfaction and she would dismiss her complaint and dramatize her martyrdom. She was protecting him and he was letting her, and I couldn't break into the sheltered marriage. If I got close, Mary Anne would fight me. I could only succeed in stopping the divorce banter and thereby taking some pressure off Mary Anne. I knew the marriage would eventually be examined, but no one else was willing to open it up yet, so I let it ride.

I try to restrain my tendency to stamp out disease. I tell myself that I work at protecting everyone's uniqueness, even their cherished areas of unhappiness. I tell myself I don't produce change—change comes from crisis, and there will always be another crisis and another chance for change. My impatience still shows, and I can and do drive people out of therapy by threatening to solve a cherished problem. Before I could drive them out of the therapy there was another problem to be solved, Jackson's fear of asking for a date. This was not my choice of the next problem to be approached, but the family wanted it solved first. It was much later that Dolores could tell me that she couldn't open up the marriage to change until she was sure the children could make it in the world. She feared the children couldn't survive outside an intact family, and she feared that any effort to examine the marriage would destroy either Carter or the relationship.

On October 18, for Session 28, Jackson and Dolores came in. Carter and Mary Anne were out playing. Jackson was proud of himself, but he was lonely. His mother was trying to teach him how to seduce girls. He ridiculed her. At that point, I did a spontaneous and unusual thing. An 18-year-old girl, beautiful, lonely, drug soaked and spacey, was in the waiting room with her parents. They had come an hour early. I invited the girl in with Jackson and his mother. Each had similar problems in making contact with the opposite sex. The girl flirted wildly with Jackson as she described the drug culture to Dolores. Her bizarreness was lost to both of them. Jackson smiled seductively but seemed unable to respond verbally. She frightened him as she excited him. Dolores was unbelievably charming. She seemed on the verge of tying the girl up and dragging her home for her son. She was marvelously supportive of Jackson, too. It had been a good move. It cleared up any doubts I had about Dolores' jealousy and it demonstrated Jackson's fear of girls. Incidentally, the girl thought he was cute.

A month later, Jackson found a girlfriend, a girl he'd longed for but had been afraid to approach. Meanwhile, the family battles developed more shape and focus, as they all listened more and respected one another's calm opinions. Therapy was a bit diffuse. Random combinations of family members came to the sessions; Jackson came alone at times; Mary Anne missed more than half the time; Rebecca came rarely. I see whoever comes, without question, unless the immediate problems concern someone who is avoiding the sessions. I might ask for a particular combination to work on a specific problem, as the marriage, or Jackson's sex life. If someone seems to be avoiding something, I'll call him.

By January 30, there was a Caretaker Crisis. Vocational Rehabilitation wanted to stop payment as it became apparent that Carter would not be vocationally rehabilitated. All was going well. Jackson was referred to group therapy at a mental health clinic and everyone else was comfortable with termination.

I saw Jackson alone for a final visit. He was sad and acted pathetic, which he hadn't for several months. I felt confident that all would go tolerably well.

Two months later, Dolores called wanting to pay for individual therapy. She was furious at Carter and threatening divorce. I knew divorce threats were opening gambits, but decided to see her. In passing, she told me she didn't "really" love Carter, and hadn't for years, since long before his disability, and felt guilty about it. I frequently encounter people who think of love as a permanent, concrete solid that is either absolute or nonexistent, rather than as a liquid solution of varying dilution, or an evanescent gas. Even people who can see other feelings dynamically, as situational, temporal, blending, vacillating, and ambivalent, sometimes expect love to be absolute. They forget that it is the emotional commitment which must be absolute rather than the emotions themselves. Dolores' commitment to Carter was unwavering, as I knew. Her commitment to the children was equally absolute, though it was now directed less toward protecting them than toward assuring their independent functioning. I knew that she was finding in herself not only the tenacity and endurance that had always been there, but also a new set of longings for life outside the tight, phobic closet of anxiety. For this, she needed Carter to be stronger. She didn't need protection or security from him. He was resourceful, conscientious, and clever and that was good enough. I had made the mistake of assuming that she needed only for him to protect her from being the bitch in her efforts to wean the children. I overlooked that because we'd talked about it many times and I continued to believe her when she told me it was there. I, in effect, gave her permission to feel what she felt. That relieved her. I then made the error of listening to what she said, none of which really explained why she felt so guilty. I was easily sidetracked to the issue of Jackson and her anger at Carter's passivity there.

Jackson's girlfriend, who did not get along with her stepfather, had been spending the night at the Meeks house, at first on the couch, but now in bed with Jackson. She wanted Carter to take action. He assertively refused, pointing out that Jackson was doing great. I pointed out that Carter's stand was an action. I requested a family conference. Dolores failed to arrange it, saying she felt better about it.

MAY 21

Session 42. Two months passed. Carter then arranged for more Vocational Rehabilitation sessions. A major crisis had occurred. Jackson had stopped payment on a check he'd paid for a car which blew up the next day. Dolores had advised him to do it. Jackson came alone. He was furious with Carter for opposing this action and was pouting. He had also injured his wrist in a skate board accident. My son had had a similar injury months before, so I referred Jackson to my son's orthopedist. Jackson and I were both more concerned with the wrist than with the crisis of the car. As it turned out, the seller of the car pressed charges over the cancelled check, but it was Carter, not Jackson, who got into trouble. Carter wound up spending a night in jail. Dolores felt guilty, Jackson defensive. Carter, after the initial blow to his dignity, realized he had survived the ultimate indignity of jail.

Therapy had begun again. A crisis with one of the children had brought them back, but this time the focus was to be quite different. Dolores could see sufficient health in her children now to risk some concern with her own feelings. I'd tried many times to focus on the marriage. Dolores denied problems, but flirted with the idea that they were there; Carter tried to maintain the idea that the marriage was ideal despite Dolores' bitchiness.

This time I asked, almost routinely:

"Dolores, what has this done to you and Carter? He's considered the kids' feelings important enough to let them do things neither of you approves of."
Dolores: I like him letting them lead their lives. We can't live the way we always did.

From there, Dolores said, rather softly, to me:

"You've always misunderstood me. You don't give a damn. You think I'm prudish and Victorian. I'm not. I'm flexible."
Dr. Pittman (agreeing): You've tolerated a lot that you disapprove of.
Dolores: Not graciously.
Dr. Pittman: Do you think you're loosening up some?
Dolores: I was always loosened up. I just never had the opportunity, but I'm not drinking or smoking pot. I went to a Greek sex play—*Lysistrata*. I laughed more than anyone there.
Dr. Pittman: You really used to get to me. I found out that you need love as much as anybody else.
Dolores: I do. I get it as a nurse. I scare people. I'm bossy, but somebody has to be.

The next week, Dolores said, as she attacked Carter for his severe social phobias:

"All those years, I stayed home and my life revolved around the children and the house. I had anxieties about going out, so I didn't push it. I'm not blaming anybody for that, my life was wrapped up with three children. I see how foolish I was. I've come to see what boring people we are."
Carter objected, saying: She's got to be right about everything.
Dr. Pittman: Carter, she's inviting you to come out and play.
Dolores: No, I'm not. There's no enjoying anything with him. I don't have to wait for him to drag me out. He's afraid somebody will be out in the yard. I can go out by myself.
(Carter walks out, enraged.)
Jackson (screams at his mother): Damn you ... etc.
Dolores: I don't know why everything I say comes out humiliating and degrading. It's just my way of being humorous.

Carter, when younger, must have been much like Mary Anne, like Jackson had been a year before, so sensitive to rejection or criticism that all encounters were painful. If he felt love and approval, he was confident and capable. Dolores must have given it most of the time, until right now. She was just as determined to get him past his phobias as she had been with the children. He could not see the love in this and neither could she. Dolores had to resort to action. She did, as we later discovered, and it worked. She was finally trying to get what she wanted, rather than to defend herself. She was no longer the bitch. Rather than blaming others for her unhappiness she was actively seeking happiness, not for others, but for herself.

Somehow Jackson understood this. After months of passive resistance, he now asked Carter to find him an apartment and help him move out. Carter did so quickly. Jackson whimpered and pouted as Carter moved him out. Dolores cried and Mary Anne fought to prevent it, but Carter was stalwart, as if he had learned something from Mary Anne's school phobia. Within a few days, everyone was delighted with the move.

For 4 months we worked on the marriage. Other crises occurred. Dolores' invalid father died and she became closer to her mother and sisters. Carter broke down at the funeral and Dolores had to support him rather than vice versa. Jackson exulted in his independence but brought home his laundry and his appetite. Rebecca married and moved away. She asked for two wedding presents— mammoplasty and a truck for her husband. Carter arranged the surgery but refused to give the truck. Carter found a part-time job. Jackson made the decision to break up with Lulu and begin dating other girls. Mary Anne had a few days of school phobia, which Carter handled effectively while Dolores gave support from the sidelines.

The major focus was the marriage, despite the many distractions. Dolores generally approved Carter's handling of crises and the uproar was no longer present. There was good communication and increasing closeness and optimism.

The couple usually came alone. With delicate but often forceful structure, I kept Carter calm as Dolores explained her lack of feelings. She meant that she didn't feel the love she thought she should feel. She saw Carter as strong, without her help, but still afraid of social situations. To her, Jackson and Rebecca were grown and healthy, and better off without her. Mary Anne was doing well, and seemed to do best when she left her alone. She saw no role for herself in the family and no point in staying with Carter. There was some mourning for her father, but more mourning for her mother who had been married to a joyless man and had never lived. She did feel anger at Carter for his weakness at her father's death, but her depression dated back a year to the time of Carter's emergence as strong and competent. As I translated Dolores' indirect manner of expressing herself, I found that Carter could understand what she was talking about. He could see that she had retired as the family bitch and now wanted to be his playmate. I urged him to seduce her. She beamed. She did the housework nude, became young and sexy again, and identified her former self with Ma Joad in *Grapes of Wrath*.

Gradually, she felt relief from the burden of guilt for not loving Carter enough. There was much pleasure now and good sex, though she felt something would still be missing between them until they could go out with other people. He would try, but it scared him. She was optimistic about overcoming what she saw as the final, but original, family phobia.

Should the marriage have been saved? Certainly it didn't offer Dolores or Carter a life of nonstop euphoria. Many in Dolores' position, or Carter's, chose to end their marriage rather than to settle for some degree of frustration or boredom. Not many people achieve such maturity that they can get pleasure from what they do, independent of someone else's response. Reasonable expectations and a shared determination to both give and take make marriage possible, and that seemed achievable here. The marriage was not destructive—it was not the marriage that kept either Dolores or Carter from having fun in life. They had never seriously pursued pleasure together—that had never been something either had considered possible. As it turned out, it was possible.

Reviewing the 60 visits, I can't see the therapy as a complete success. The initial crisis was simple enough. As with all developmental crises, the central issue is whether the change in the maturing member is within normal limits or is an indication of a problem. The therapist, who is supposedly an expert at what is normal, must make this judgment. The family could accept Rebecca's behavior as normal, but then they wanted to be normal, too. Dolores, having spent 25 years protecting her husband and children from the world, decided she wanted them to overcome their fears. The crisis of Carter's disability had reversed their roles at home and had given her an opportunity to see that the world was more fun than hiding in a closet full of phobics. I was enlisted in her effort to bring this about. She couldn't do it herself, as she was far too prickly and confusing. I accepted the challenge, seeing quickly that it was a long-term job. Jackson had an initial success, then failure which reinforced his fear and paralyzed him for another year. Eventually, he was as successful as Rebecca had been. Mary Anne was partially successful, but she required repeated crises and is not out of the woods yet. This process with each of the children lurched forward from crisis to crisis as Dolores and I taught Carter how to handle each phobic child in turn. I'm not sure Carter ever quite caught on to the underlying principles. No matter how often things were explained to him, it was only near the end that he noticed much beyond the degree to which he was being smiled at or frowned at.

I was seduced by the early successes with all five of them into believing that Carter and Dolores were healthier than they really were. I got sidetracked briefly into seeing Dolores as so overwhelming that all would be well if she resigned. She did, and it soon became clear that she had been protecting Carter all along. I could get Dolores past it, but not always. I couldn't get Carter past it at all. Phobic individuals (and I include Rebecca, who feared losing her boyfriend if she didn't give him everything he wanted) are not that hard to deal with if those around them don't share or fear the phobia. Dolores had only recently and incompletely overcome her phobias. Even if she did not have the power to get the other four past each phobia as it came up. So it was slow.

I wonder what I could have done differently. My one effort to provide non-family therapy for someone, the group for Jackson, failed because he could not yet see anyone outside the family as a member of the same species as himself. A group may eventually be useful for all three of the children. I think the family format was right. However, I'm glad I held each of the individual sessions. Perhaps I could have met alone with Mary Anne at some point, as she hardly had an emotional existence apart from her mother. I never did get close to her. Some therapist will probably have to do so some day. I kept hoping that health in the parents would free her, too.

The basic format of what I do as a therapist is quite simple. I simply define the problem, find simple solutions, and tell people to take those simple actions to achieve their goals. If they don't take the actions, I then explore with them why they don't, and try to overcome whatever resistance there is. With the Meeks family, we went through this process many times until they were doing with their lives what they wanted to do. Often I had to be the reality tester, though each of them could veto me at any time. Jackson spent a year vetoing my belief that a girl would go out with him if he asked her. A strange girl in my office convinced him otherwise. I did refuse to give Jackson any legal advice about the check for the car. I am an expert in many areas, but not law. Above all, I must know and make known the limits of my expertise. As a physician, I treated two rashes and one case of influenza, and diagnosed a broken wrist and a case of pneumonia. That was almost as incidental to therapy as my suggestions about movies, but it did further the relationships. As a psychiatrist, I treated two severe depressions in what I consider the appropriate manner, with antidepressants. I treated an uncountable number of phobias with reality testing, support, and the enlistment of the family in providing irresistible pressure to face the phobic situation. The easiest job I had was in letting them see me clearly and in making sure they knew my view of everything relevant. At times I had to be quite personal in exploring why my view differed from theirs. The most difficult task I had was to teach Carter and Dolores how to tell one another what they felt, what they liked, what they wanted. They learned to do it tolerably well with me, with the children, and with the outside world. They couldn't quite learn it with one another. It apparently takes less time to unlearn one's native tongue.

The real problems in the marriage were revealed late in the treatment, when Dolores came alone. The initial marital pseudoproblem, the constant bickering, was problematic for me and for Mary Anne, but not for Carter and Dolores. It was painful for Dolores to reveal her dissatisfaction with Carter's social phobias, and both saw her revelation of them as a betrayal of the marital commitment. Perhaps Carter's phobias should have been dealt with much earlier, but Dolores and I were distracted by Jackson's more overt fears. Throughout the nearly 2 years I've spent with the Meeks, I've often wanted a team of therapists to help me drag them each out of their dark closets. The results might have come quicker and might even have been better. A different approach might have been used with somewhat different results. It might have helped if I had gotten a fuller history from Carter and Dolores at the beginning, if the marital conspiracy to protect Carter from revelation of his fears could have been broken.

Therapy with me is not usually a gentle process. I try not to protect people from the pursuit of their goals. This can be frightening, as it was to Mary Anne and to Carter at times. But, despite my warm and loving nature, I've had little success with coddling people out of phobias. I've also had little success in changing everyone's life with my clever insights and brilliant interpretations. I don't know how to proceed except rationally, methodically, tenaciously, directly, one problem at a time. Therapy is not an act of love, or an act of genius, but a plodding process of impatient practicality.

2

"OK—You've Been A Bad Mother"

John H. Weakland

My specific ideas, actions, and reactions in dealing with this case—involving a 15-year-old boy with school and behavior problems as the identified patient, and his divorced parents—can only be understood in relation to their context, the general approach developed at the Brief Therapy Center of the Mental Research Institute over the past ten years. The basic ideas and procedures involved in this approach have been described at some length elsewhere (1, 2). Here, I hope a brief summary of these will be adequate for orientation to the case material to follow, which in turn may clarify the general approach by concrete illustration of its application.

How one conducts therapy—and evaluates the outcome—depends greatly on one's general view of the nature of problems. In common with other family therapists our Center views problems as interactional—that is, not something residing in a particular individual, but an aspect or a resultant of interaction between individuals in a family, or in some other ongoing system of social interaction and communication. Along with this, we view problems as behavioral in nature—that is, as consisting of behavior by the identified patient, which is stimulated and shaped by behavior of other persons involved (or sometimes by other behavior of the patient himself). Accordingly, we see problem resolution as requiring behavioral changes by those involved in the system of interaction, and the essential business of the therapist as one of promoting such change, which the members of the system have not been able to accomplish on their own. These views too are common enough among family therapists. We differ from many family therapists, however, in our concentration on the presenting problem, in our focus of intervention and our goal of treatment, and in our means of promoting change. For the most part, these differences rest upon pursuing the interactional view of problems, in concept and practice, further than is commonly done—even when our practice appears oriented to one individual.

If one really focuses on behavior, any problem—of the kind people bring to therapists—may be defined generally as consisting of a) some observable behavior, which b) is characterized as undesirable (distressing, difficult, deviant) either by its performer or by some other concerned person, but which c) persists despite efforts to get rid of it. Accordingly, our treatment begins by inquiring what the problem is, in behavioral terms—what is the identified patient doing and saying that constitutes a problem. This includes, unless it is obvious, how this constitutes a problem. That is, we see the behavior as itself the problem, not as "the tip of the iceberg," the outer sign of more fundamental inner feelings, nor even necessarily a manifestation of some deep and pervasive disarray in the system of interaction. On this basis, we next inquire not about the nature of interaction as a whole in a family, but about behavior immediately related to the problem behavior—namely, what is being done to try to handle (prevent or resolve) the problem, by the identified patient or others concerned.

Both a general view and concrete experience underlie this focus. The interactional view of problems implies a cybernetic rather than a linear concept of causation. On this view, not the origin but the persistence of a problem is central for understanding and treatment (3, 4). That is, what behaviors function to maintain or reinforce the performance of the problem behavior, although this is defined as undesired or undesirable? Ironically, in our experience it regularly appears that while people's attempts to handle the existing problem usually are well-intentioned and often apparently logical, something in them constitutes the reinforcing behavior: "The 'solution' is the problem."

In other words, problems consist most basically of vicious circles, involving a positive feed-back loop between some undesired behavior and inappropriate efforts to get rid of it. In our approach several things follow from this view. Our general treatment aim is to interrupt the vicious circle maintaining the problem behavior. Our specific interventions are therefore aimed primarily at interdicting the misguided solution being pursued. This often may involve the substitution of some other opposite or incompatible behavior, but this is a means of insuring change, not the essential change itself. Also, an apparently small but strategic change in problem-handling may serve to initiate a beneficent circle leading to progressive further improvement, so that long-term treatment and heroic changes are not required.

In making such interventions, since our aim is behavioral change rather than intellectual understanding—which in family therapy as in individual treatment may produce no change in actual daily behavior—we do not devote much effort to clarifying and describing the interactional situation to those involved. Instead, we depend most on behavioral prescription, and on reframing the situation so as to make different problem-handling behavior seem logical and appropriate to the participants, in terms of their own pre-existing ideas about people and problems. Finally, since we take the idea of interaction in systems seriously, we believe that it is possible to influence an entire system through appropriate change in any member. Therefore, rather than always seeing all the members of a family, we often concentrate our treatment attention and effort on whoever seems most ready for change, or possesses the greatest leverage in the system.

The Z Case

I first heard of Jacky Z by a phone call from his mother. She told me that Jacky was doing poor work in school and being truant, as well as being difficult to handle at home, and both his high school counselor and the learning disability teacher in the special school he attended two days a week suggested me to her as a family counselor.

On the phone, Mrs. Z did not go into the specific difficulties much, but filled me in on the family background, which she saw as involving possible obstacles to treatment. Mr. and Mrs. Z had been divorced for 4 years, Mrs. Z having legal custody of the children. (Jacky at 15 was the youngest of three teen-age children. His older sister and older brother were described as no problem, and I never saw either of them.) The father had remarried shortly after the divorce, but still lived in the area, and maintained some contact with the children. However, Mrs. Z described him as a proud and rather stubborn man who had not been keen on the idea of family counseling when she had called him about it.

On hearing this, I told her that, while I would be glad to see Mr. Z also, for the way I work this would not be essential, at least to start with, and if he were urged he might well become more resistant. Therefore, I suggested, she might call him and say she was coming to consult me about Jacky and would be glad to have him come too if he wished, but she should avoid any appearance of pressing him. She sounded receptive to this, and said she would do so, and call me soon about a time to meet—since she wanted to leave this open to fit his schedule also. A few days later she called again, to report the whole situation had changed. When she called Mr. Z and made the proposal, his response was that no family counseling was needed, because the main problem was just that she wasn't handling Jacky right. Therefore, he would have Jacky come to live with him, and would soon have him squared away. Mrs. Z, apparently at her wits' end in trying to deal either with her son or his father, had agreed to give this a trial.

Reviewing this phone call, I had two thoughts. First, that I should have called Mr. Z myself, rather than leaving this to her. This, in fact, is what I would ordinarily do. I do not have any note as to why I did not in this case, so I cannot be positive, but it is highly likely that I was not especially eager to see the father anyway. Since the boy was living with his mother, I saw her as the key figure, and since she had seemed very receptive to my initial suggestions, I was confident I would be seeing her in any event. Second, that this confidence was a mistake; in all probability, Mrs. Z had not approached Mr. Z as I had suggested, and certainly she had acceded to a course of action different from what we had agreed on without consulting me. It will be evident later that I should have kept this indication that her readiness to agree did not mean equal readiness to act accordingly more in mind. But I did not, probably because after this call I mentally wrote off the inquiry as one of those things that might have been ,but didn't develop.

Quite a few months later, though, I was surprised to get another call from Mrs. Z. She said that his father had not got Jacky squared away; instead, things were worse, including lots of difficulty between father and son, and Mr. Z was now willing to give counseling a trial. I made an appointment to meet with the two of them, stating that it would be desirable to get the basic information on the situation from them before seeing Jacky himself.

When they arrived, because of the previous phone contact and the lapse of time, I began by asking "What is the problem *now*?" I addressed this question first to Mrs. Z, since she had been the prime mover in instituting treatment. She began by reporting an incident that apparently was the precipitating event for seeking me out again. About a month before, Jacky did not return home to his father's house one evening. Instead, he called and said he was at his mother's house. But he was not; in fact, he did not show up at either house all night. Next day at school, the counselor found out that he had stayed over night with a friend. Since then, he had been coming home late on other occasions, and cutting school. Mrs. Z also said, more generally, that at the time Jacky went to live with his father he was completely out of her control. I asked "In what way?" to get more concrete behavioral information. She replied that he was also cutting school then, also he was smoking pot, and he had stolen and dismantled a bicycle. Also, without my asking, she volunteered some information on how she was trying to handle all this, saying "When I ask him what's the matter, why does he do these things, I don't get an answer—he just doesn't communicate." This remark started me thinking that probably Mrs. Z was doing too much asking, in ways which defined her position as weak and ineffective, rather than telling her son what she expected of him, and taking some appropriate action to ensure compliance. I made a note of this, but no comment, at the time.

I then asked Mr. Z what the problem was, in his view. His style of response was positive and definite—only his statements were varied and contradictory: At the time of the bike theft, he had asked for Jacky to come and live with him, because "I've always felt he needs a man's company." Moreover, the school counselor had reported that once Jacky broke down and said "I never see my father." So, "Maybe Jacky felt abandoned by me. But, when I try to, he won't talk to me about it." On another front, Mr. Z reported that Jacky had been noted to be hyperactive in school some time ago. He had been put on Ritalin. However, some of the kids teased him about this ("You're taking dope") and recently the doctor had said Jacky has reached an age where he needs to learn self-control, not medication. Mr. Z also said Jacky is only doing third grade work, has no interest, can't sit still, is small for his age and people treat him like a baby; he has bad companions and no sense of responsibility. Mr. Z also said that Jacky doesn't talk, just keeps everything inside. But when Mrs. Z apparently agreed with this—"When I ask him if he knows what's right and wrong, he just answers 'Yes' and has no more to say"—Mr. Z then said "He's not just silent, he's full of excuses." This concluded the initial session, which I felt was rather emotional and chaotic, full of anger, anxiety and confusion, despite my attempts to structure it according to plan.

On reviewing this session a few days later, however, both the problem and its handling appeared clear enough, at least in main outline. Jacky was behaving badly both at school and at home, with acts both of omission and commission. Both father and mother were trying to handle this mainly by talk. Since each of them seemed to alternate frequently between the view "He's bad" and the view "He's sick," this talk similarly alternated between lectures and anxious inquiries, with the later probably predominating. They were persisting in such talk although it was getting nowhere—Jacky giving minimal answers and obvious excuses. Also, though this point was not really clear to me at the time, this persistence probably was being reinforced by the school counselor and learning disability teacher, who were indicating that Jacky had problems, that communication was the answer to this, and that Jacky did talk to *them*.

A week after the first session, Mrs. Z called to tell me that Mr. Z had backed out again ("He's always been leery of psychologists"), and—in obvious contrast to his "Let me handle things" stance—had asked her to call and cancel the second appointment that we had set up. Added to this was a report, though, that he had gotten firmer with Jacky, and the boy was behaving better now. My impression of her call was that she really felt powerless—that nothing could be done without Mr. Z's active cooperation—but was trying to maintain a hopeful stance: He's taking charge and Jacky's better. My own view was quite different, but I try not to argue with the client. I therefore told Mrs. Z, "Mr. Z does not have any full veto power over the therapy; some useful things by way of review and considering what may come next can be done without him. However, I can readily understand that you might feel like relaxing for a while. Jacky seems better right now, even if this should prove only temporary—and to go on now would mean acting without Mr. Z, perhaps even in some opposition to him. So think it over, take your time; you can always call me if you want to talk further."

At that point, while I certainly thought the Z's needed help, given the difficulties already encountered, I was quite uncertain if I would hear further from them. However, I also thought that to take the tack just described, of apparently backing off rather than pressing for a further meeting, would maximize the probability of further contact. I had my doubts as succeeding weeks went by, but in about a month Mrs. Z at last called me again. She reported that Jacky had been having further school difficulties, had been cutting school, and was finally suspended. His father had now agreed to cooperate further, though somewhat reluctantly. The main thing they had in mind, though, seemed to be that "Jacky might talk to you; he won't open up to either of us." This struck me as a further example of the idea "Communication is the answer," which I doubted as already noted, plus some note of "Fix him up and then send him back." However, I did want to get on with treatment, there was nothing to be lost by seeing Jacky, and perhaps something to be gained by first-hand observation, even though I believed that from the parents' descriptions and my experience with similar problems I already had a rather reliable image of the boy. Therefore, I told Mrs. Z, "I don't know if he'll talk to me, but let's see. You bring him in—there's no use at this point, when it's not essential, to draw on Mr. Z's limited store of cooperation."

When Mrs. Z arrived with Jacky, I thought that he looked about like any 15-year-old boy, except that he was rather guarded in manner. I began by asking him "What's your understanding of why you're here?" He did not reply immediately, and after only a very brief silence his mother—always a rather nervously quick woman—began to press him: "Go on, answer the doctor, Jacky." This plainly irritated him and made him more reluctant to talk, but finally he said "I don't go to school, but no problem outside it." Within moments mother and son were involved in a running argument: "You and my father always hassle me." "That is not so, you have a lot of freedom." "No, I don't." "You were getting into a lot of trouble, so something had to be done: I'm trying to explain why you were sent to live with your father." Very quickly the pattern was plain, and consistent with my expectation from the initial session: The boy makes brief complaints or accusations (or just silently looks pained), the mother responds with lengthy, defensive explanation or argument, and so on and on around the circle.

A small sample of this seemed plenty, so I asked Mrs. Z to wait while I talked with Jacky alone. My ideas in doing this were a) it would be easier than having more redundant argument, b) it would help my standing with Mrs. Z by complying with her expressed wish that I talk with him, and increase credence for any recommendations I might later make about dealing with him, and c) though I had in mind working primarily with her, some useful intervention might be made directly with him. Once we were alone, I found that when asked a plain question and given a little time, he was reasonably forthcoming with answers. I began by asking if he thought he had any problems. "Just school—it's a drag. I don't want to go, but I have to." For the rest of the session, I deliberately took a stance as much as possible opposite to what I felt sure everyone else must have told him, over and over. First, I suggested that he really didn't *have* to go to school; people might threaten or exhort him, but they couldn't actually do much. I asked if he thought he had a learning disability. He said no, plainly, and went on to say he was getting C's as it is, and could get A's if he really tried. I suggested that probably he shouldn't, at least not anytime soon: since both his parents and teachers thought he has a learning disability, his getting A's would confuse and rattle them too much. He also mentioned that his parents' hassling him was a pain. I agreed, and asked how he handled this. He said "I try to do what they ask." I pointed out this might be a difficult, or perhaps impossible task, since it seemed to me that their demands might be unclear, inconsistent, and conflicting. He agreed. I wondered if he might make some headway in such circumstances by apparent agreement; that is, by saying, "Yes, yes" to whatever they asked. He gave it some thought, but was uncertain. I thanked him for coming, and sent him out, saying that we probably would meet again later, if only to help cool his parents' concern and hassling some by putting on the right appearance. In my thinking, this was both a further intervention—the opposite of "You've got big problems, and really need therapy"—and laying some ground work for getting him to come in readily if I should wish to see him again later. But I never did.

Mrs. Z was to call me about a further appointment, but again it was about a month before I heard from her. She had, however, been in the hospital for a minor operation during part of this time. She reported that Jacky was back with her; Mr. Z had thrown up his hands on dealing with him. Mrs. Z said that Jacky was all right—except that he was cutting school, smoking pot, stealing, and driving her up the wall. She raised the idea of a private school for him. Or, along the same line, what about sending him to summer camp—only the likely ones are full of his pot-smoking friends. At this point, I realized that while I had gained a rather definite view of the problem and what kept it going, so far as treatment and change were concerned we had mainly been going around in circles, and seemed about to continue with more of the same. I therefore interupted her to say that I understood from what she was saying that the problem still existed, and was quite serious—in fact, so serious that I thought it would be a mistake to try to give her any advice off the cuff in a phone conversation. Instead I proposed that I should review and think over the whole matter, and then call her back in a few days with some better recommendation on what should be done.

I did go through such a review, focusing my thinking mainly on how I might get her more firmly involved in treatment and more ready to follow any advice I wanted to give her on how to deal with Jacky more effectively. I then called her, and began by reemphasizing the serious and difficult nature of the situation. Since this was something she herself had been saying in various ways here and there, I assumed she would agree strongly with my statement, which proved correct. On similar grounds, I next stated that on the basis of my review of the problem, it appeared quite clear that as Jacky's mother she herself was the only one sufficiently concerned and influential to be in a position to give Jacky the help he needed so much—not his father, the school personnel, or even myself; though I would offer some advice, I was not important to Jacky and she was. Then, to block her from backing away from the problem again, I said that even though she was the only one in a position to really help Jacky, since he had given her a long hard time, I certainly could understand if she wanted to wash her hands of him instead. Mrs. Z, as I had hoped, responded "No, I'm confused and struggling, but I'm still ready. I'd like to get clearer how to deal with Jacky." I suggested that then it would be most appropriate for just the two of us to meet, and talk about that specifically; she agreed readily.

When she came in, I had one specific aim in mind: To get her to stop getting involved in defensive arguments with Jacky. Hoping to locate a specific initial target area for such change, I began by asking about her priorities—what was the main current difficulty, or what would she most like to see changed in Jacky's behavior. Her answers, however, were rather lengthy and rambling. She mentioned that he was going to school but not to classes, that she wanted to establish better communication, also more cooperation, but at one time he might talk and be helpful, then at another be silent and just do as he pleased. I attempted to shift the framing of "communication" from talk toward action by asking "Am I correct that at least part of the communication problem is that you can't tell what to expect from Jacky?" She agreed, and I went on to suggest that the basic problem seemed to be that Jacky needed to learn to be more responsible for his own behavior.

Then, in order to get more information on her own views—her "language" as we usually call it—I asked "What is your best guess as to the reason for Jacky's behavior problem?" She said that there had been a lot of fighting between herself and Mr. Z at the time of divorce, repeated the report from the school counselor that Jacky had complained "I never see my father," and wondered if her involvement with another man had had an impact on Jacky. Almost at once, though, she went on to a different theme, "I really feel Jacky wants discipline."

Since this last remark was in line with my own thinking, I picked up on it immediately by saying "It does sound like things go a bit better when you say what you want from him more flatly, without much discussion or argument— and it might go still better if you could even be somewhat arbitrary." But, since I now was anticipating that she would probably retreat after any move toward taking more firm charge with Jacky, I went on to add "I don't really expect that, though. You are very frustrated by his behavior, but your hands are tied because you are carrying the blame for his problem."

At this, Mrs. Z burst into tears and said "I want a life of my own, but I have to supervise him." I considered that this ratified the picture of the situation I had been formulating on the basis of her answer to my question about her view of the cause of the problem—that Mrs. Z was feeling very guilty toward Jacky, and this got in the way of her taking more effective measures in handling him; therefore I needed to deal with this before anything else could be done.

To do so, I then took the steps which, in my estimation, constituted the turning point in the therapy. First I said "As I see it, the most important question is not the past, but where do we go from here." She agreed. I went on "However, the past is important, in that it keeps getting in the way because it remains unsettled. You may be taking on too much of the responsibility, because Mr. Z and the school people and even Jacky himself may be responsible in part for his problems. But I don't see *any* way to ever judge reliably just how much blame and responsibility really belongs to everyone involved. So, in order to get this over with, suppose we do like lawyers do on some issues and just stipulate 'It was *all* your fault.'" She agreed to this, but with the beginning of a smile. "All right, *now* you are the crucial one if Jacky is to change."

Mrs. Z asked, "But how do you get through to a kid like that?" To me, this signaled a small but critical shift away from the problem itself, and the "why" of it, toward how to take useful action on it. This was confirmed when she went on to report an action she had already taken. "Jacky is still coming home late at times—but I've stopped going out to look for him." I replied "OK, but I don't know whether you could take the next step—if he is out late after you've asked him to be in by a certain time, lock up the house and go to bed at that time; then when he arrives, let him wait a while, finally let him in, and apologize for forgetting he was out." "I *could* do that—though he'd just go to a friend's house." "Perhaps, but even so you'd be giving him an important message, non-verbally, that home is a valuable place." "That's right."

It appeared that Mrs. Z was now getting with my moves toward less talk, less anxiety, and less defensiveness, and more effective—even if unusual—action. But not completely, as she went on to ask "But what about the daytime?" "Well, we have to take things one step at a time. But in general, I think when you want him to do something, you would be further ahead to say simply 'I'd like you to do such-and-such. But I can't make you do it. If you don't, I don't know what I'll do about it.'" Mrs. Z really encouraged me by the way she picked upon this: "That might be good with Jacky; if he knows what's coming he can handle or evade it." However, I continued to take a doubting position, saying "Yes, but my bet is you won't be able to really do it. Jacky knows how to push your buttons—especially your guilt button—and get you involved in explaining to him. So you say you'll get with it, but I'll be ready to say 'I told you so' when you don't do it."

We set up another appointment, but just before that time Mrs. Z called to say she had car trouble and couldn't make it. However, she reported trying some things I'd suggested—mainly avoiding getting embroiled in arguments with Jacky—with positive results. But it had not been an easy week. "I certainly did not suggest or expect it would be easy. In fact, though I'm glad to hear you made some progress, I'm mostly surprised I don't get to point my 'I told you so' finger at you. But it's not easy to keep it up, so let's meet next week, and maybe I'll be able to point the finger then."

When she came in a week later, I immediately said "Do I get to point the finger at you?" (It would have been better to have said "I'm sure that now I get to point the finger.") She replied "No—he's been really good. Of course, I've backed off, not nagging so much (she had never recognized her talk as nagging before this)—though not perfect of course." In addition, she reported, though Jacky was still difficult in some ways, he was doing the jobs around the house willingly, and had voluntarily owned up to some matter involving taking money without asking: "He's so good I'm nervous, wondering what will happen next." "I expect probably the next little thing he does, you'll slip and blow it all." "Well, if I can just keep my temper—he really likes to get my goat."

Again I felt she was making considerable change and progress, so I moved to consolidate this, not by reassuring her but by asking "What might be the real acid test of his getting to you?" She said this would be if he went out and didn't come home, or even call—but went on to indicate that maybe she had already passed this test: She reported that he had stayed out late one night, and she had locked him out as suggested. When he did get home and she finally let him in, Jacky revealed that he had encountered a "weirdo" on the dark street and been scared; he was plainly glad to be home and safe. "Well, all right, you've handled that, but what about his smoking pot?" "I've backed off on talking about that—and Jacky has told me he only smokes it once a week now; when he's busy, he doesn't need it."

By this point, Mrs. Z was indicating positive changes and increasing confidence, loud and clear, and I was thinking about terminating treatment at the end of the session—since in my view she had made a basic change in her interaction with Jacky, and this should lead to further positive developments without continuing therapeutic intervention. However, in the time remaining, rather than shifting to a stance of optimism and congratulation, which might set her up for a discouraging let-down as soon as she encountered any difficult situation—which inevitably would occur—I kept on the same track of pointing out that she would meet further difficulties, but there were ways by which she might handle them. I suggested that, especially since Mr. Z had really gotten involved in the therapy, some problems between him and Jacky, and also Mr. Z and herself, probably would still arise. She agreed. I proposed that she could help improve the relationship between father and son by telling Jacky that she knew from much personal experience that his father was a difficult man, rather than defending him, or otherwise indicating that Jacky really should get together readily with his father. Several ideas underlay this apparently negative recommendation: 1) Most important, previous efforts at encouraging them had not worked. 2) Such a change gets her out of the middle and out of an undue responsibility for their relationship. 3) It moves her toward a realistically equal or one-up position vis-a-vis her ex-husband via justifiable criticism of him, and thus away from her previous guilty and one-down status. 4) It presents Jacky with a realistic challenge, to which he is likely to respond better than to "Why don't you get along better with your father?" which implies that this is no difficult matter, and therefore he is an incompetent failure if the relationship does not go well, easily and at once.

As to Mrs. Z's own relationship with her ex-husband, I suggested that if and when Mr. Z should again get on her case, especially by stating or implying that Jacky's problems were her fault, she could really blow him out of the water just by verbally agreeing with his accusations. My underlying idea here was that with Mr. Z, as with Jacky, Mrs. Z had been stuck in a position of overt defensive argument which only fed and prolonged her underlying feelings of guilt; verbal agreement would cut the argument short, while her own reaction to making such an overt statement would be "Really, it's not all my fault."

And finally, I suggested, when Jacky returned to school and met difficulties there, as he inevitably would, she could help him best not by direct encouragement, but by saying "I expect you to work at your studies, but even when you do, after all the mess-up you've been in before, I'm not at all sure you can hack it." Again, my aim was to get her to stop an approach which had been getting nowhere, and to substitute a challenge to which Jacky might respond—if only (but in a way that would require constructive efforts) to prove her wrong. I then dismissed her with the message—still maintaining my doubting or pessimistic stance—that of course she'd have more tests to face with Jacky; I was not sure whether she'd pass them or not, but she knew where to call me if she did not.

I did not receive any further calls. Seven months later I called her and asked how things were going. She said that while there were some ups and downs, generally things were much better; it seems it was right to bring Jacky back to live with her. To this I agreed. She also mentioned that she recalls some of the things I told her, and uses them at times, though "I may feel I have a bleeding tongue"—that is, she has to bite back some of her old reactions. I agreed that it is often an effort to do the right thing, she thanked me for calling, and I hung up feeling that some significant change had been initiated in our assorted phone calls and four actual sessions.

References

1. Weakland, J.H., Fisch, R., Watzlawick, P. and Bodin, A.H. "Brief Therapy: Focused Problem Resolution," *Family Process 13* 141–168 (1974).
2. Watzlawick, P., Weakland, J.H., and Fisch, R. *Change: Principles of Problem Formation and Problem Resolution.* New York, Norton, 1974.
3. Maruyama, M. "The Second Cybernetics: Deviation—Amplifying Mutual Causative Processes", *American Scientist 51,* 164–179 (1963)
4. Wender, P.H. "Vicious and Virtuous Circles: The Role of Deviation Amplifying Feedback in the Origin and Perpetuation of Behavior", *Psychiatry 31,* 309–324 (1968).

3

The
Identified Patient

C. Christian Beels, M.D.

One of my reasons for wanting to describe this case is that it is an example of working with a patient and family in which the patient has a specific liability which can be diagnosed and described. In much family therapy literature and practice, there is an aversion to labeling the patient as such—indeed, the "identified patient" is a term unique to family therapy. It implies that such an identification is a provisional feature of the referral to treatment, and that soon the therapist will de-label the patient and show that the pathology is really a function of the communication system of the family—that it belongs to no individual. Alternatively, it adheres equally to unsuspecting other family members who are seen as "just as sick," or it is a rotating function in which the family members express symptoms in turns, as one after another gets better: a sort of conservation-of-the-illness law of the family system.

I think this concept applies—or is useful—in some families and not others. It applies, for example, to marital therapy of balanced or complementary personality dynamics in each partner. It often applies to adolescent problems which present as an extreme degree of behavior disorder in the adolescent "patient," responding to conflict at the parent level.

On the other hand, this useful idea has given some family therapists a hesitation to talk about diagnoses for fear of "labeling" or "scapegoating" the patient. This hesitation puts them at a disadvantage when dealing with someone like the patient in this case who (a) has experiences of being out of control at times, which are the more terrifying because he has no label for them (he had in   35 fact labeled them as part of his seizure pattern and developed a whole mythology to explain them), and (b) has intelligible characteristics of his own malfunctioning, the identification and reduction of which can be part of the therapeutic contract, and (c) is surrounded by family members who think the fearful worst of him because they have no way of talking about his behavior.

In this case description, I will also try to show what I think I do and the way I think about it. The work is really sorting through a mixed bag of tricks, a cut and dry method rather than a grand design, and the way is visible a week or a month ahead, at most.

At the end I will include some quotes from an interview with Gus and Mary in which I asked them what they thought worked, and finally I will raise a number of questions to which I do not know the answers concerning this case and others like it.

The Case

I got a telephone call from a woman one evening who said she was calling me because a colleague of mine had told her I was the right person in New York to help her husband. She told me at length over the phone about his struggles: he had had some sort of seizures all his life, but had a brilliant career awaiting him as an entrepreneur in the export-import business which he and his father conducted from New York. The family had emigrated from a South American country. From her description he sounded quite depressed, with a disturbance of his sleep pattern, weight loss and apathy. He attacked her physically from time to time. He had dropped out of business activities completely and stayed at home, never going out of the house. He talked occasionally of suicide. She wanted to be sure I could see him because they had both had bad experience with doctors, and she was not sure she could get him to come.

I arranged to see them for a first interview, which lasted about two hours. They brought along their eleven-month-old daughter, who stumbled charmingly around my office during this and all subsequent interviews—individual, couple and family. I learned about and diagrammed the following complex history:

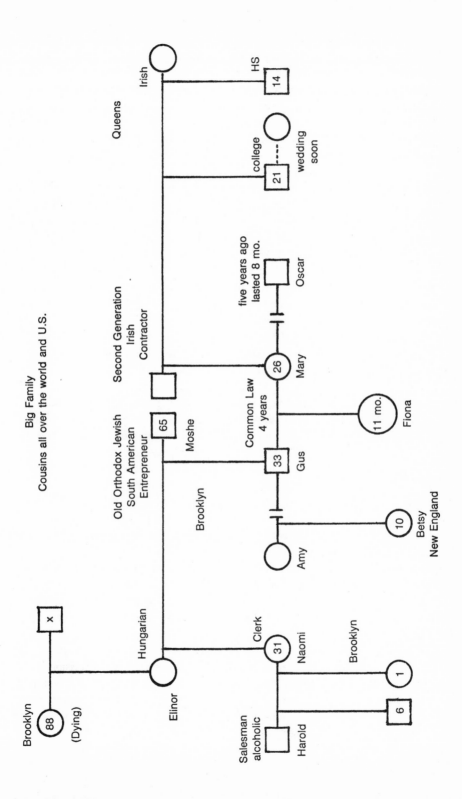

Big Family
Cousins all over the world and U.S.

Gus's family had emigrated to New York when he was twelve, after his father, Moshe, had become concerned that Gus would become too involved with the revolution that was brewing in the capitol city where they lived. Although Moshe preserved the complex family network on which his business depended, he settled into almost complete social isolation in Brooklyn. Gus went to college and while still an undergraduate Gus married his first wife, Amy, when she became pregnant with their daughter Betsy. That marriage was always somewhat unstable and dependent on Amy's family nearby, as Gus found work at a boarding school as a language teacher. He divorced Amy after three years of this kind of life, and returned to New York where he lived a bachelor's existence in Manhattan, doing various jobs and becoming gradually more involved in his father's business. He was occasionally on business trips for his father to Europe and South America. Four years ago he began to live with Mary, who a year previously had had a brief marriage to Oscar, of whom her family disapproved. Her family disapproved of Gus for religious and personal reasons but Mary became quite attached to Gus's family—even more so when she and Gus moved in with them after she became pregnant with Fiona. To summarize, then, the elements of the situation that found expression in Gus's depression, which were evident in the first interview or two:

Gus was the only and favorite son of a patriarchal and successful, though reclusive Jewish family—he represented in many ways the reason they had come to this country. He had two children by two relationships, each of which was marginally acceptable to his family, and from recent performance, his succession to his father's business and his work prospects in general, were in doubt.

Mary was the oldest and most adventurous of a rather closed Irish-Catholic blue-collar family. She had taken on Gus as a fascinating rescue operation—she believed in their love, in his potential for success—to "be a man," as she repeatedly said—but she was getting exhausted from constantly urging him on, mediating between him and his family, explaining him and his father to each other, and advising him on his complex relations with his sister and former wife. Mary was the caretaker and go-between in the situation, and she had just about had it. Mary's family was constantly, sometimes publicly, urging her to leave Gus and come home with Fiona.

Diagnosis: It was clear that Gus had had some transient psychotic experiences which could be distinguished from his seizures—though in talking about them he tended to refer to all his altered states of consciousness as "seizures." He had night-time grand mal seizures, focal episodes leading to tremors of extremities while awake and conscious, and (of a non-organic nature, I assumed) fits of rage accompanied by partial amnesia in which he would attack or at least threaten people, especially Mary. In addition to his depression, there were periods in his life which sounded at least hypomanic. My working diagnosis which I shared with him early in the work, was borderline personality disorder, with possible temporal lobe seizures in addition to some other seizure disorder. He said he was not seriously suicidal, but I was worried about what he might do impulsively.

Harold and Naomi: Gus's sister and brother-in-law were envious contenders for favor in the family and throughout my work with them, Gus and Mary were concerned with whether to compete with them for a share of the family business or strike out on their own. Naomi envied Gus his college degree, of which their father was enormously proud, and she never missed an opportunity to point out that she and Harold were the good hard working ones while Gus, for all his advantages, was a wastrel.

Moshe and Elinor: Both of Gus's parents are part of large, far-flung international Jewish families with very complex caretaking and financial obligations holding them and their cousins together. Elinor was at this time preoccupied with her dying mother and with Moshe, who was very depressed about how badly Gus was doing. Everyone was worried about Moshe's health, as he had had one heart attack. In Gus's opinion his mother was also "driving my father crazy" but exactly how was not clear. Theirs was the kind of family where no amount of strain would ever lead to an open break between the older couple, since they were held together by so many other concerns. Both parents found Gus and Mary's life style and habits of dress incomprehensible. I was never able to form a stable impression of the alliances between Elinor, Moshe, Gus and Naomi, since they seemed to shift constantly, but throughout it all, it was clear that Gus was his father's favorite and greatest disappointment, and that the corresponding feelings of omnipotence and uncanny frustration in Gus were Gus's lifelong preoccupation. Elinor often seemed to be the isolate in the family, and was sometimes seen by Gus and Mary as in league with Harold and Naomi.

Style: Gus and Mary made it clear that they had never consulted a psychiatrist before, and were willing to do so now only because they were desperate. They expected a sort of friend-of-the-family advisory relationship and this fitted in well with one side of my personlity. They were both very attractive, lively and humorous people and I found it easy to spend a little time playing with Fiona and chatting about things I was interested in, as well as much time laying down the law to them. On the asset side they were people with considerable presence and persuasive ability, which got them readily into trusting relations with others—for Gus this became a liability since his confidence and enthusiasm was often a sort of self-delusion. One had to develop the ability to say, "Gus, that's bull-shit," without losing him. Having Mary present at these times was invaluable.

Contracts—The Opening: Following are the beginning contracts I made with Gus and Mary, and their immediate consequences.

(1) *Gus will see a neurologist.* He had been experimenting with his medication and didn't like the previous consultants he had seen. I told him I would treat him only on condition that he see my consultant and get a clear picture of his diagnosis and the proper medication. After many missed appointments, he did that. There was an extensive workup available already and in the end the only neurological diagnosis was grand mal seizures, controlled on medication. I made it clear that Gus should talk only to the neurologist about medication and seizure questions, and that I was not going to get involved in whether some of his

behavior was or was not organic in origin. I was going to treat him as if what he talked about to me was under his control.

(2) *Mary will stop threatening to leave.* Mary regarded such threats as her final card in the escalations that took place between the two. Although her threat to leave quieted him down, it also put him one-down, so that his next move (which started the next escalation) would be from a position of bluff and false pride. I talked Mary into a four month moratorium on the threats, and generally tried to convince her that she did not need to be so responsible for what was happening. I explicitly relieved her of the job of being Gus's motivator and caretaker.

(3) *Planning:* Much of the sessions consisted of interviewing Gus about his plans for getting a job, getting out of the house, etc. My objective was to train Gus to talk about his anxieties with Mary—anxieties which he was unwilling to acknowledge, because he felt that "a man" should not have such problems and Mary's urging him to "be a man" did not help. By showing Mary how to listen to Gus as he made plans for the future, I introduced a new form to their communication and also demonstrated to Gus that he was fearful of going out into the world. It was possible to show that this was connected to his feelings about his father: his desire to succeed in his father's eyes, his fear that if he went off on his own he would fail, and lose his father's love, and the protection his helplessness was getting him. I asserted all these things against considerable denial on Gus's part, but I knew they were getting into the system because Mary heard them—(Gus did too, although he didn't acknowledge them)—and they had a very calming effect on Mary.

Finally I convinced Gus that Mary did not want him to go out and amaze the world—both she and I would be satisfied with a single phone call to apply for a job—any sign of movement would do.

(4) *Gus has to learn to get angry.* This was somewhat paradoxical instruction, since he and everyone else in the house was angry most of the time, but he had to learn to measure his anger against his true feelings. He tried not to get angry at Mary "because she is right—except that he would lose control and lock her in a closet to keep himself from hitting her. We spent several sessions on training him in the expression of manageable anger.

In general, I had the feeling while I was talking to them that the working relationship with Gus could blow up at any minute. He was too positive in his regard for me, and his life was too full of other people whom he had once respected but now rejected completely. I wondered constantly when it was going to be my turn to be thrown into the rejection basket. This was an experience Mary had gone through a few times, but on threatening to leave she had been taken back. I knew I was in no position to apply for a second hearing if I was rejected, so I worked with a sort of dogged honesty to the fore, and, as instructed by Otto Kernberg, kept bringing up possible negative feelings he was having towards me.

(5) *Family Sessions Promised for Later.* I secured agreement that Gus and Mary would try to arrange a meeting of the whole family—at least of Moshe and Elinor—with them and me. They were very frightened of what this might

do to Gus and Moshe, who never talked directly to each other. What the two men did was threaten, cajole, strike authoritative postures, attack and defend, and then cry to Mary on the side. Gus and his mother avoided each other. I finally got Gus and Mary to agree in principle to a family meeting. I will describe the family sessions later because they finally did take place late in the sequence, after many promises and cancellations. The awareness that I intended to bring the family together to talk at some point did form an important backdrop to our work, and was an expression of my confidence that communication between Gus and his parents was possible.

I had a fantasy of a vast family meeting where all would be revealed and they would settle their differences after an enormous brawl. I had to keep reminding myself that this fantasy was part of my wish to get out of the whole enterprise without getting too much of myself caught in it.

THE MIDDLE GAME

General Atmosphere: There were frequent phone calls, cancellations for barely plausible reasons, lateness due to travel problems, and postponements of payment. It became evident that they had just about enough money to pay their board at home and although Mary went to work part time in an office to make some money, it was not enough to pay me. I did not think it was a good idea for them to borrow from parents or family since this would emphasize their dependent position. Their indebtedness to me moved me further toward the position of benign substitute father to Gus, which I pointed out to him (see below). I decided to reserve my influence for getting them to come on time and carry out their homework.

I was discouraged and sometimes angry at not being paid for this very hard work, and struggled with the possibility of bringing this up with Gus and Mary. I might have taught them something about the way they put themselves into dependent positions without realizing it—and I might even have gotten a small payment. But I decided just to send them a monthly bill. I have a private and irrational conviction that psychotherapy should be part of a national health service or should be like the services of a priest, and have never been able to resolve my mixed feeling about fee-for-service.

The session usually began with an uproarious and dramatic account of a family battle at home about whether Gus was going to look for work, or whether Moshe, Elinor, Naomi and Harold were planning to make a move in the family business which excluded Gus. At first I spent most of my time teaching them how to talk to each other, to make "I statements" in the manner of Murray Bowen, and to use elementary problem-solving techniques. I got them to spend half an hour together in the evening practicing this.

From the descriptions of conversations at home, it became evident that Moshe was not going to hand the business over to Gus because he didn't trust him, that everyone regarded Gus as too crazy or at least too lacking in organization to take the responsibility, that Mary thought the only way for Gus to prove himself was to become independent of the family. This view of things was evidenced by family meetings and discussions which excluded Gus and Mary, by the delegation of some responsibilities to Harold, who acted like the heir apparent, and was confirmed by Mary's interpretation of family arguments. It was a view which alternated with Gus's view of himself as alone able to rescue his father and the business from these others, and his fantasies of telling members off, of bringing justice out of old misunderstandings. Mary often got pulled into this stance because of her sympathy with Gus.

I wondered what to explore and say about Mary's side of all this: would there be any point in looking at "what she was getting out of," if for no other reason than to prepare her for her sense of missing something should Gus some day stop being her special problem. Clearly she was making some point to her own family by sticking to this very difficult man instead of coming home to them. Clearly her sense of explicit involvement in Gus's family was important to her, though purchased at great expense. I decided that all these things might be true, but that in the present strained state of affairs there would be no way of talking to Mary about them without sounding too academic and speculative.

Goals: I took the position that:

(1) Everyone is trapped inside this family—no one ever goes outside, and the only hope for Gus and Mary was to move out on their own.

(2) If Gus stayed inside the family he would always feel like the little boy. He kept everything—toys, models, drawings—from his childhood stored at home, and he was afraid to break away from all that. We labeled this his "hoarding" response. Intellectually, they both agreed, and we set up moving out as our goal.

I was privately very doubtful that this would work, but felt I had no choice but to move Gus and Mary toward greater independence in hopes, at least, that the strain this would put on them would reveal a new view of their conflict.

The Diagnosis

I told Gus alone and Gus and Mary together that Gus had a borderline personality disorder. I made the following points about it:

(1) Although he was not crazy in the sense of being schizophrenic, he did have transient psychotic experiences during which he was out of control and when his judgment was not good, we would have to work hard to minimize and contain them. It is a serious illness, with violence a real possibility, and was to be distinguished from his seizures.

(2) One of the features of the illness was Gus's way of not knowing what he was afraid of, and instead of feeling fear or anxiety, split people into good and

bad. I used as an example his way of seeing me as always very good and his mother as very bad—although as I reminded him, sometimes a person he thought of as completely good could turn to completely bad, if he distrusted him for a moment—that had happened to his thinking about me while he was sitting in the office one day.

This awareness that he could really hate and distrust me popped out in eerie associations from time to time. Gus differed from other borderlines in that he had acquired from somewhere just enough observing ego to talk about it with me rather than acting on it, as he did with his family.

He had great difficulty dealing with people about whom he had mixed feelings such as his father and Mary; towards them he experienced violently alternating emotions.

The three of us agreed to work together on these serious problems—I think we all felt better for having a definition of it which fitted the facts, and Gus felt on the whole relieved—he had wondered what was wrong with him.

Planning: A large part of the middle game consisted of setting dates by which time certain pieces of planning would be done: Letters would be written, job interviews would be completed, etc. As we moved through this written schedule, Gus became increasingly aware of his anxiety, and fear of disappointing his father. He missed deadline after deadline.

After a while I told them that we had all been urging Gus to succeed—Mary especially, had been doing that. What Gus actually needed was more experience of failure. I demanded that Gus produce some failures for me—specifically I wanted three job interviews at which he was turned down. He produced one, and not long after that was able to move out with Mary to a new apartment.

Two Family Meetings: We managed to have two meetings with Gus and Mary, Moshe and Elinor. These were tumultuous, full of protestations and accusations. Gus was frequently on the way out of the room, saying "I'm not going to listen to this!" in a very manly way, but obviously afraid to hear what was being said. His father put him down for his clothes, his friends, his idleness, and the women tried to regulate the two of them from the sidelines. I persuaded Gus to stay and listen, got his father to recast his criticisms as concern for Gus and worry about him, whereupon the old man cried, and Gus was struck with how much his father cared about him, and loved him. This was a communication which had always passed through Mary before.

Envy of Harold and Naomi: We spent a great deal of time reviewing the efforts Gus's brother-in-law and sister were making to take over the business. Gus and Mary were both very angry at them. Besides labeling this as jealousy (which label Gus at first rejected) I persuaded Gus for a while that his only salvation lay in getting outside the business altogether. Gus compromised by trying to get a job with a branch of the family in a distant state, which offered many promises, but did not materialize.

Pause. I stopped the treatment at this point, since, as we all agreed, the rest of the work was up to them, and they were too much in debt to me to continue without some payment. I told them they could call me any time, and I did hear from them, especially from Gus, by phone, reporting that they had moved to another apartment, and that things were going well.

Shortly after this, fate gave a push to events which proved decisive. Moshe died suddenly one night. The family went into a great turmoil. There were arguments about the burial ceremony, the funeral, the will, the business. Gus called me on the phone and talked to me at length as if I were a member of the family, a brother or indeed a father.

Gus said he still did not think it was necessary to resume therapy: he was going to handle everything. I heard from him about a month later: He had taken over the business, had asserted his right to determine the funeral arrangements (as the oldest son and responsible member of the family). Next he went on a trip to Europe for the firm, and sent me an exultant letter about how well things were going.

Excerpts from An Interview with Gus and Mary 8 Months Later.

Gus: Things are really going great. We learned a lot here.
Chris: For instance.
Mary: I learned about how to listen—about silence. Oh, I learned so much about how to keep quiet and just let him talk.
Gus: We learned to talk to each other—not fly off the handle. (They listed a number of things which they had experienced as specific assignments: Keeping a calendar with dates and deadlines on it as an external structure, the half-hour talk before bedtime, the instruction to move out and throw away the things Gus had "hoarded" from his childhood.)
Chris: How did you feel about the family meetings?
Gus: Well, that was where I really learned that my father loved me—that he cared what happened to me. I remember how much you insisted we have those family meetings and how much I resented bringing these people here and how much I found out how important it was later on . . . to mention that there are so many things I can't remember that went through in this particular room and I can't remember details. Why, I don't know.

I used to be burying myself in books, discussions . . . we are able to wait now, and be able to watch each other's moods and settle arguments.
Mary: Without violence (laugh).
Gus: Yea, without violence. Well, there hasn't been violence for a long, long time.
Chris: How long?
Gus: None, nothing, I could get the angriest and the thing I do is say, well, you know.
Mary: Knowing what your seizures are—that's important.
Chris: OK, so what did the consultation with the neurologist . . .
Mary: Oh, no. You can admit that you're an epileptic. You could never do that before.
Gus: Oh yea, you're right about that.
Chris: So that was important . . . getting the diagnosis and the medications straightened out.
Gus: The medication is still the same . . . but the mere fact that I can say that I am epileptic and not guess at it . . . while I have a cramp, while I have this, well . . . just to say

it and say what I am. I am an epileptic ... whether you understand what it is or you don't understand ... it doesn't matter to me. I am an epileptic. No, I don't swallow my tongue.

Chris: I wanted to ask you about a couple of specific things that I did. One thing I did was to give you a psychiatric diagnosis. Remember that? I told you that you had a borderline personality disorder. Remember that?

Gus: Yes, but I forgot. (laugh.)

Chris: So that shouldn't make an earth-shaking difference.

Gus: Borderline personality disorder ... which is.

Chris: Well, you remember that I told you a number of things about it. One was that you have a tendency to split things into good and bad.

Gus: To extremes, that I always keep in my mind, and I always pinpoint the people I trust who trust in me and I always pinpoint to them ... you know, how extremes are—not bad but it's just not constructive. They don't lead to anything.

Chris: Then we were talking about how you see people as being either for you or against you, right? and instead of complicated views of things.

Gus: Not anymore ... I don't feel that strongly about it, do I?

Mary: No, because you have your energies directed in a totally new area.

Gus: I can't waste my time with it.

Mary: And if you do start to waste your time, then I see it. I see you going into it and then I say wait a minute, you know. Let's talk about this and then it's gone, absolutely gone.

Gus: Right, you're right. You know I could see it happening and get back to work. I got to get back to the office and it doesn't mean as much as it did before.

As they left, Gus and Mary were telling me about two developments which were not the subject of our work, but which must have affected the family dynamics. One was Harold's advancing liver cirrhosis as a result of his alcoholism. Gus said, "The doctor told him he's got half a liver left, and if he doesn't stop drinking, he'll be dead in a year." The other was Mary's brother, who had no sooner gotten married than he and his wife began to have serious trouble. Mary said, "So now we're the big heroes—even though we're not married we're doing better than the ones that are."

Questions

(1) I don't know what to make of Gus not remembering the diagnosis which I explained to him with such care. It does seem to me that he got the general ideas and that he and Mary used them to organize themselves in times of crises. But did all that explanation have its main effect on them or on me?

(2) If the diagnosis is correct, where was the psychotic transference which is supposed to occur in borderline personalities in individual therapy? Was Mary catching all the intensity of the anger at the bad object which such patients direct against the therapist in other therapies? Is couple therapy an insulation against

this sort of reaction to the therapist? It was only fleetingly apparent in Gus's responses to me.

(3) What would have happened if Moshe had not died? Gus went through an intense and meaningful grief experience afterwards. Did the therapy prepare him for it, and was his relationship with me an important anchor in the vicissitude of that process?

(4) Some of Gus's behavior and symptoms suggest a bipolar manic-depressive picture. He refused lithium when I urged a trial of it upon him. He said he had enough medication already. Might medication have made a decisive difference in his ability to control his excitable states?

(5) What are the "active ingredients" in this complex therapy? As I look back over it, I would agree with Gus and Mary that learning how to talk to each other in a different way was the crucial change. I would also agree with followers of Haley and Milton Erikson who would point to Gus's decisive response to my instruction to bring in three failed job interviews. That instruction was also something which Gus remembered and quoted to me afterwards, although by the time of the follow-up interview he and Mary had forgotten it. So much for retrospective analysis.

My baseline tactic in this and other family work, especially with difficult and "un-sightful" people, is to keep asking them to plan the next week. It keeps them talking to each other, and that provides the basis for changing the way they communicate. Such an action-and-future orientation in the presence of another person in the family (who will keep them focussed on plans and promises during the week) is the basic ingredient. It produces change, or revolt, or anxiety, and any of these can be worked with.

4

Generation
After Generation

THE LONG-TERM TREATMENT OF AN IRISH FAMILY
WITH WIDESPREAD ALCOHOLISM OVER MULTIPLE
GENERATIONS

Elizabeth A. Carter, C.S.W.

Introduction

Peggy Papp's invitation to write a chapter for this book initially created something of an "image" problem for me. After all, when you come out in print, you like to look good. But Peggy made it clear that "looking good" was not the point of this book. "I would like each therapist to reveal what really goes on in their heads as they work with families," she said, "the struggles, the doubts, the decisions, and the indecisions." Nevertheless, my first mental sifting of my cases found me thinking about my "successes"—those families where I had had a clear grasp of what was happening in the family, a good handle on the course of the therapy, and a good outcome. Reluctantly, I gave up this train of thought as even mental drafts of such material came out sterile, pat, and not at all instructive. "OK," I thought to myself, "I'll go all the way. I'll write about a 'failure.'" ("And get brownie points from the readers for being so brave," something inside my head whispered.) And so, for several weeks, I forced myself to think about my "failures." Again, reluctantly, I had to give this up, chiefly because the main reason these cases were "failures" was because I had had an inadequate grasp of the family process, or a poor handle on the course of therapy, and, in most of **47** these cases, the families had dropped out of treatment without my knowing exactly why or understanding what had caused the "failure." It is hard to write about something you know you do not understand.

I finally chose this family to write about because it is the case from which I have learned the most in recent years. I was struggling with a symptom—alcoholism—that I had never previously treated successfully; I was trying to absorb new ideas on the treatment of alcoholism in a family framework[1] fast enough to stay one chapter ahead of the family. I availed myself of an unusual amount of consultation, used every technique I had ever heard of, and used a few I had never heard of. I was sometimes inspired by the perseverence and efforts of the family to change, and I sometimes prayed that they would go to another therapist who would know what to do with them. Enough went "wrong" during the course of therapy that I sometimes thought that I was caught in an endless shift-and-recycle without change. Enough went "right" so that the wife said to me after almost 2½ years of treatment: "I am definitely in charge of my life now," and my estimate of the situation is that there has been sufficient change that she will not succumb to alcoholism again and that there is a more hopeful prognosis in this regard for her children.

The Presenting Problem

The Kelley family did not present around alcohol problems and, ordinarily, it might have been some time before I recognized the extent and seriousness of the drinking in the family. At the time they called me, however, Dr. David Berenson, a psychiatrist who specializes in family treatment of alcoholism, had just joined the staff at my place of work and was spreading the word amongst us that alcoholism is as treatable a symptom in family therapy as any other if family therapists would only stop avoiding it. I didn't believe him, having watched alcoholic family cases go nowhere unless the alcoholic was already in Alcoholics Anonymous, but he was insistent enough to at least "raise my consciousness" on the issue.

Eileen Kelley, age 38, phoned me in the fall of 1974 to ask if I would see her 14-year-old son, Brian. Brian had been persistently truant from school for months and the school psychologist had recommended that he receive individual treatment. When I asked if she and her husband would also come in with Brian, Eileen readily agreed to come herself and said she would ask her separated husband, Jim, to come too. The three of them came to the first appointment.

Eileen Kelley was a slim attractive blonde, pale, wearing dark glasses which she declined to remove, and appearing quite depressed and sullen. Her husband, Jim, by contrast, was affable, responsive, charming and cooperative. He launched into the story of Brian's school problems in a frank, concerned manner, his story being periodically punctuated with sounds of contemptuous disapproval from

Eileen and Brian. Brian was a handsome, sullen boy, bearing a striking resemblance to his mother. He sat with eyes downcast or raised to heaven through most of the interview, refusing to respond to questions from me.

Eileen and Jim had separated just a month ago and Brian's school problems, which had been going on for some time, got worse. The immediate concern was that his frequent truancy had now been extended to complete nonattendance. He had not appeared at school at all for several weeks, although he left home most mornings ostensibly to go to school. I then took a brief family history and got some information on family relationships which indicated that Brian, as well as two older brothers not present at the session, had been caught in the parental conflict for years. The oldest son, Danny, age 17, reportedly a "constant gambler," had moved out to live with his grandmother (Eileen's mother) 6 months ago, saying that he could not stand his parents' constant fighting and wanted nothing more to do with them. The parents stated that at this point he would barely speak to them. The middle son, Tommy, age 15½, although doing well in his school subjects, had started staying out until all hours of the night and was battling continuously with both parents. Eileen said he "also drinks too much," which her husband disputed, saying that Tommy just had "the usual occasional beer parties with his friends."

Returning to the presenting problem of Brian's truancy, I recommended, while Brian fumed, that Jim take charge of seeing that Brian got back to school "since, legally, there is no other choice at his age." I suggested that to do this, he would probably have to go to Eileen's house each morning, pick Brian up, and stand outside Brian's classrooms all day to be sure he did not leave. Jim agreed and said that he would arrange to be late or absent from work for as long as it took. The rest of the first session, and a subsequent session a few days later, were devoted to firming up Eileen's reluctant cooperation in the plan. Brian was back in school by the end of the week, without Jim's needing to actually escort him. Jim gave his phone number to Brian's teachers and asked to be informed of any further absences on Brian's part, at which time he said he would be prepared to put the plan back into full gear.

Evaluation of the Nuclear Family

The Kelley family was in the process of exploding apart after years of parental conflict. The oldest son, Danny, was first to leave, followed shortly by the parental separation, in which Eileen insisted that Jim move out. The middle son, Tommy, was staying away more and more. In response to these drastic events, Eileen had turned in desperation to her youngest and favorite child, Brian, leaning on him for emotional support, determined to "save at least him," and making him the recipient of her complaints and grievances against Jim and the two older boys: "You don't want to turn out like them, do you?" Jim retaliated by telling all three boys that their mother was "crazy." The nuclear family triangle in my office had been fixed for years, with Eileen and Brian in the overclose (overinvolved) position and Jim in the distant position. This pattern, mother-child overclose and father emotionally distant, fluctuated with the other predominant nuclear family pattern of parents fighting with each other, not over their own issues with each other, but over any or all of the children. The emotional pressure of his position in the parental warfare had strained Brian's resources to the point where his behavioral problems escalated and brought him to professional attention in a school in the Bronx loaded with behavior problems.

In intervening as I did, putting Jim in charge of Brian, my purpose was to bring about a shift in the triangle by moving father and son into more involve-ment with each other, loosening the mother—son overinvolvement, and bringing husband and wife, at least temporarily, into some form of parental cooperation, however grudging. In addition to this purpose, I always intervene like lightning in cases involving absence from school. I have found that if you take your time and play around with stately progress, waiting for better emotional relationships to develop in hopes that the school problem will diminish, the symptom takes on a life of its own. The longer a kid is out of school, the harder it is for her or him to return because of falling irrevocably behind in work, embarrassment in front of schoolmates, and trouble with teachers. The longer a person is out of school, the more investment he or she has in staying out and the harder he or she will fight returning.

My initial focus and intervention with the Kelley family follows my usual procedure in working with families, which I call "the Minuchin-Bowen se-quence." By this I mean that I generally begin work by focusing on the presenting problem and recommending tasks around that problem, as Minuchin does,[2] and then will either glide into extended family work or make an explicit second contract with the family to go on in that direction, i.e., coaching parents in work on their families of origin, as taught by Bowen.[3]

The Extended Family

In the Kelley family, it was perfectly clear to everyone, including Jim and Eileen, in these first two sessions, that Brian's problems were directly related to the parental conflict and separation, and that the initial success of getting him back to school would not hold up for 2 minutes if some work were not done on the parental relationship. Since the marital difficulties had been discussed quite openly in our first two meetings, the couple readily agreed when I asked if they wanted to do some work in this area now that Brian was back in school. I then took a more complete family history. I included specific questions regarding use of alcohol by all family members since it had been mentioned by them during the previous meetings in various ways, and I was more alert than usual to that issue.

When I looked at the family genograms after this session, I felt almost overwhelmed and asked for the first of what were to be many consultations with my alcohol *maven*, David Berenson. These consultations, and my learning about the family treatment of alcoholism from David, took many forms. Sometimes we sat down together for an hour and discussed the family and the therapy; two or three times, David met with the family while I sat and listened; several times, he came into an interview at my request for a 10 minute check or follow-up on medication; most frequently, I simply collared him in the hallway for a 3 minute crisis consult on my way to or from a session with the Kelleys. In addition to direct consultation about the Kelley family, I was also learning about alcohol and the family in a course I was teaching with David, during his presentations to the staff, and by reading his papers on the subject.[4] It is evident that without this input on the factors specific to alcoholism in families, I could not have continued to work with the Kelley family.

As can be seen on Jim's genogram, he is the oldest of four, with three younger sisters. The Kelley family is Irish Catholic, with all four grandparents having been born in Ireland. Jim's parents, Jim, and the two older sisters and their families all live within a short distance of each other in a predominantly Irish neighborhood in the Bronx where Eileen's family also lives. Only Jim's youngest sister, Pat, moved to Florida when she married and remained there after her divorce.

Jim's father and mother were both the oldest children in their families, although Jim's father had only one younger sibling, while his mother was the oldest of fourteen. Jim characterized his parents' marriage as conflictual and said that all of the women in the family, including and especially his mother, were "man haters." He said that his mother disapproved of his wife, Eileen, and blamed everything wrong in their marriage and the trouble with their kids on Eileen. I asked how this jibed with her being a "man hater," and Jim replied that his mother said that all men were such a "weak lot" that it was up to the woman to make the marriage work and bring up the kids right. Jim's relationships with his parents and sisters were extremely distant. He said he had been expected to "take care of himself and not cause trouble" and he had always done this, and continued to do this, mostly by staying away. He had not seen some of his 52 cousins (52!) in years. He had had a lot of conflict with his father while growing up but felt that lately his father had mellowed somewhat, especially when he was drinking, which was most of the time.

Jim's mother, according to Jim, was "bossy beyond belief." As a young woman, she had given her mother an ultimatum to chose between her alcoholic father or her. Mother's mother had chosen her husband, and Jim's mother had left home. She had subsequently returned because her "younger brothers needed her." She had six brothers, all alcoholics, and seven sisters, many of whom "drank a lot." Once, she had got angry at the drunken behavior of one of the brothers, had thrown him out of the house, and he had wandered down to the

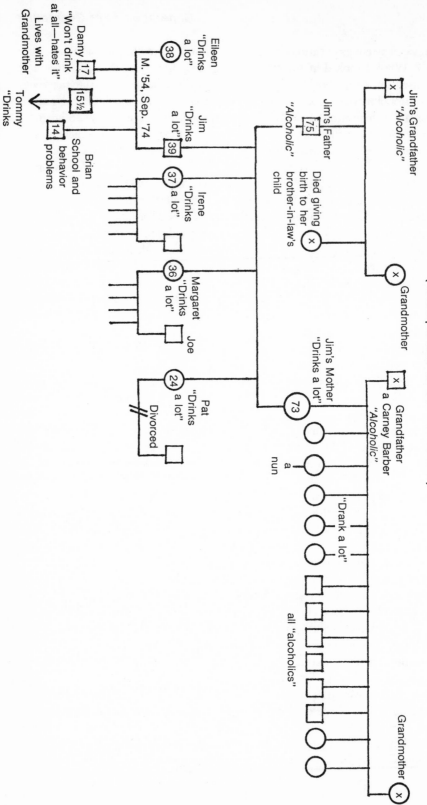

JIM'S SIDE OF THE FAMILY: *The Kelleys*

(Grandparents all born in Ireland)

river and drowned. "When I think about it now, I can feel sorry for her," Jim said, "but not when she's sitting there giving me hell, which is every time I see her. The only way to deal with her is to stay away." Jim could see that this might be how his boys were dealing with him and Eileen and he did not like it.

While giving me the information for the genogram, Jim had characterized all of the males in the family, except himself, as "alcoholics." He had said of the women's drinking, and of his own, that "we drink a lot." This distinction was important to him and was based on his contention that to be an "alcoholic" meant to get "falling down drunk" and/or to lose your job or lose a lot of time from work. He stated firmly that he never came near to losing a job from drinking, could work just as well with a hangover, and although he "could give it up," did not want to since it was "one of the few real pleasures in life." He did state that he occasionally drank "too much" and would now curb that so that he could get a handle on his children's lives. He refused to go to Alcoholics Anonymous because "they make you quit completely."

As can be seen on Eileen's genogram, she is the youngest of ten siblings, of whom nine reached adulthood. Her father died of a stroke when she was 5 years old and she has no memory of him at all. Her older sisters, who remember him well, speak of him as "an absolute rotter, the life of the party on the outside and a terror at home." Her older brother, John, will not speak of him at all. Eileen said that her mother was "always weak and passive, and let Fran, the oldest daughter, run the family." Fran, Eileen said, was "a tyrant whom everyone in the family hates." Mother and Fran now live together and it is "impossible" to have a moment alone with mother. Although not shown on the genogram (for reasons of clarity), all of the siblings are married, except Julia, and have among them many children. Eileen's brother Kevin is married to Jim's sister Irene, making a second linking of the Kelleys and the Hanrahans, and, Eileen added, "just as shaky a marriage as ours."

The Hanrahans are a very enmeshed family. Except for John and Irene, who live "way out on Long Island," and Kevin and his family, who live in New York City, all of them live within walking distance of each other in the Bronx, are in constant telephone and personal contact, and have family gatherings and parties every few weeks or months. Eileen, who said she took part in all this contact "out of duty" said she had a terrible time with her family, felt that they all either "dumped on her" or "ignored her," treating her like "a spoiled brat," "a baby," and even taking Jim's part against her. In general, Eileen said, her family valued the men as important, and all of the sisters "adored" their two brothers. Keeping a good house, waiting on husbands and children, and being a good mother were the supreme values for the women in the family. All of her life, Eileen said, she had been fighting for "recognition" in her family. As a young girl she had "caused a lot of trouble" and rebelled openly in ways that the others had not—playing truant, staying out late, and hanging out in bars with her brother Kevin. Of all of the family, Kevin was and always had been her only friend.

In her discussion of the family's drinking habits, Eileen was very sparing in

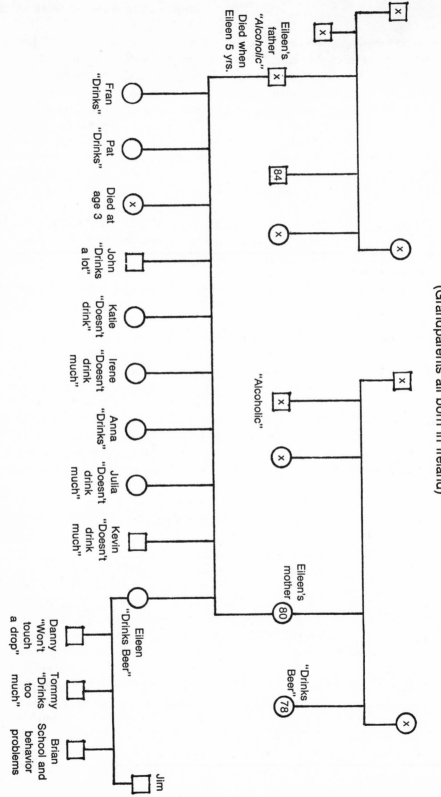

EILEEN's SIDE OF THE FAMILY: *The Hanrahans*

(Grandparents all born in Ireland)

her use of the word, "alcoholic," that label reserved for her father and her mother's oldest brother, both dead. Of her own and her siblings' drinking, she said things like "drinks a little," "drinks a lot," "only drinks beer," and even "drinks most of the time," while denying that any were alcoholics. She did allow that her husband Jim's drinking "might be leading to alcoholism." She freely admitted that she and Jim had done "too much drinking and fighting for years," and that she was worried about her son Tommy's drinking. But an alcoholic, to her, was the stereotyped image of the "Bowery Bum," and she categorically refused to go near Alcoholics Anonymous because it was "full of them," and "I am not in that category." She stated that all of her life, good times and fun had always been connected to drinking and that life without alcohol would be "gray, dull, drab, and boring." She made it clear throughout a good part of our first year of work that she thought I was exaggerating and overemphasizing the problem of drinking in their families.

Making a Treatment Plan

First let me say that, previously, this is the point at which I would have quit with a family like this, stating that if at least one of them did not go to Alcoholics Anonymous I could not work with them. And they would have left. I still more or less felt like doing that but had decided to try something different with David Berenson's help. Luckily I had not yet heard him say that "double drinking" systems (both spouses involved in the drinking) made things really tough, even for him. I therefore brought him the genograms and said something like, "OK, chief, what do I do now? She's the youngest of 10, David, 10! Even if they weren't all drinking all the time, how can the youngest of ten take hold of things? And his mother is the oldest of fourteen, David, *fourteen*! Wouldn't you like to come up against her? And he's got 52 cousins! Do you know how many triangles we're dealing with? You'd need a computer to figure that out!" David (imitating Murray Bowen, I think) kept studying the genograms and saying infuriating things like "Fascinating," "The most interesting family I've seen in ages," etc. He asked what I would do with the family if there were no alcohol in it. "I'd fish around for the most motivated one and help him or her to start reducing the chaos somewhat—first by being less reactive to the spouse and then by taking charge of the kids." "Terrific," said David, "That's what you do here." "But," I said, "the drinking will undermine it." David agreed that it would. "But you predict that to them, and when it happens enough times, one of them will hear you and realize the drinking has got to go." "But that's been going on for 20 years and they haven't realized it yet," I replied. "They haven't been in family therapy before," said David Berenson.

In addition to the above, which made my heart sink, David went over with me the basic concepts for working with alcoholic systems, that is, families organized around drinking. The idea is not to stamp out drunken behavior, which is serving a functional purpose in the family,[5] but to help the family members to include this (a modification of the drunken behavior) in their repertoire of behavior without having to drink. One functional purpose of alcohol in the Kelley family, for example, was "to have a good time." All fun and recreation was associated with drinking, and Eileen could not imagine a party without it. I had a hard time imagining Eileen having a good time under any circumstances, since whenever I saw her, she was grim, depressed, and sullen. When I mentioned that to David, he assured me that if I wanted to see what she was talking about, I should have her come drunk to a therapy session and videotape it. I pretended I didn't hear that, and we went back to our discussion of the functional purposes served by drinking. Jim, ordinarily soft spoken and affable, gets angry and belligerent when drunk. When called to task for it later, he is all apologies, blaming it on "the drink." Eileen also has problems expressing anger when sober and, instead, gets locked into sullen withdrawal. When drinking, however, both of them are able to start out "having a good time," express tenderness and affection that is rarely expressed while sober, have sex, with which they otherwise have difficulties, and/or express the anger and bitterness that they otherwise avoid and store up. This certainly does not get problem areas dealt with functionally, but it does get them expressed and ventilated. Simply stamping out drinking, in this framework, would be also stamping out good times, affection, sex, and anger.

The First Year of Treatment

I continued to see Jim and Eileen together, but their three boys refused to come to the therapy sessions. I decided not to make an issue of that since I thought things would go faster and better initially if I spent the time coaching the parents to deal differently with their sons rather than forcing them to come against their wills. From the start, Jim was off and running. Within a few weeks, he had drastically reduced his drinking, was in frequent contact with Brian's teachers, had laid down the law to Tommy, and has asked his father, mother, sisters, and brothers-in-law to gather for a family meeting at his parents' house. I tried to slow him down a bit, especially long enough to make some plans as to how to deal with his family of origin, but he was exhilarated and confident of handling it all. The more exuberant he became, the more sullen and depressed Eileen was, speaking only when spoken to, and then mostly to complain about Jim or the boys. She was drinking more than ever, she said, implying that it was Jim's fault, and if Jim thought he was straightening out Tommy, he could guess again, because Tommy had been arrested for shoplifting. It was clear in these early weeks and months, that any "success" that Jim achieved with the children would be taken as a personal affront by Eileen. Nevertheless, Jim forged on. I had recommended in the beginning to both parents that they not chase after Danny, the oldest son, but rather let him come around in his own time, which he undoubtedly would if he saw his parents making some changes. This had started to happen, and Danny was now at least speaking to them, although he made it clear that he would not return home to live. Jim's family was meeting regularly once a week and Jim said: "It's our own family AA meeting. I keep bringing up the fact that we all drink too much, we do some arguing, but it's OK."

This was the first of several instances, I now think, where I failed to take an important stand with Jim. I knew that his enthusiastic, head-on, unplanned plunge back into his family would have to boomerang sooner or later. I did mutter cautionary warnings to that effect, but I think I was so dazzled by his dramatic, do-it-yourself approach, that I failed to communicate the pitfalls to him clearly, and I did not predict to him, which I could have, that his unplanned efforts with his family of origin would fail. Once or twice, I half heartedly suggested that he bring his parents and his sisters into a session with him, but when he assured me that they would be "well oiled" when they got here, I backed away from the thought of conducting a sessions with that many people "under the influence." In retrospect, I wish I had tried it.

After several months, during which Eileen remained depressed and inactive in our sessions, I remembered David Berenson's crazy suggestion that I videotape her drunk. Cautiously and skeptically, I asked him about it. "Besides showing me something, would it have any helpful purpose for her?" I asked. "For sure," replied David with his usual understatement. "After she stops drinking, it will be a useful blueprint for her of behaviors she needs to build into her sober state." He then went on to describe to me a project which he had worked on at the National Institute of Alcohol and Alcohol Abuse (NIAAA) with Dr. Peter Steinglass.[6]

In this project, they had run a research award for chronic alcoholics and their families, complete with an open bar. Videotapes showing family interaction with the alcoholic both drunk and sober revealed a far higher level of involvement, both positive and negative, among all family members when the alcoholic was drinking. These tapes were then used to help the families increase their level of involvement when the alcoholic was *not* drinking.

With a confidence that I did not feel, I raised the idea with the Kelleys, giving some version of the above rationale. Instead of the flat refusal for which I was sort of hoping, they were intrigued by the idea and agreed. Eileen volunteered to go first, since I had stipulated that one of them had to be sober to drive to and from the appointment.

Words cannot convey the difference in Eileen Kelley when she appeared for the next appointment. She was relaxed, smiling, gregarious, funny, and without the dark glasses which she habitually wore to our appointments. There was absolutely no sign of the "typical drunken comportment" which I had expected—

no stumbling, slurring of speech, etc. When I inquired as to how much alcohol she had imbibed, she replied, "Just two beers," and pulled out a six-pack of beer to continue the process on camera. Now clearly there is not enough alcohol in two beers to support a physiological explanation of her dramatically different aspect and behavior. The change is understandable, however, as a "throwing the switch" phenomenon, documented in the NIAAA study, which showed whole families shifting into their "drinking behavior mode" as soon as the alcoholic uncorked the bottle and started to mix his first drink. As the interview continued, and Eileen sipped along through several more beers, we moved from an initial bantering stage into a thorough exploration of all the troublesome issues in her life. She spoke freely of her long-standing hurts and angers with Jim, of an affair years ago that still caused bitterness between them, of specific difficulties with extended family members, and of her fears and doubts about her motherhood. A later review of the tape, without the Kelleys, showed clearly the "positive" interpersonal impact of Eileen's drinking behavior—not on Jim, but on me. Amused, delighted, and astounded, I was triangled into intense interaction with Eileen, while Jim remained silent and mostly ignored. That was easily correctible, but I wondered how and when Eileen could get to work on those problem areas without drinking. She had not even been able to mention them previously. Since David Berenson advised me not to show her that tape until after she had stopped drinking, I put it away, and the "old Eileen," sober, grim, silent and depressed, returned to our sessions. It was agreed that Jim would next be taped while drunk or drinking, but some crisis interfered on the appointed day and we somehow never got around to it. Again, I ask myself, how did I miss and join in with this evasion?

In the spring of 1975, Eileen suggested that she and Jim switch living arrangements, permitting her some time alone to "get herself together." Jim agreed, saying that if he moved into the house, it would be easier for him to continue trying to "get the boys straightened out." I saw this as Eileen's first move to take hold of herself, and supported the idea. From this point on, in a further effort to help break their stalemate, I started to alternate seeing them each separately and then together. In the separate meetings, Eileen's focus moved somewhat from complaints about Jim and the children to talk about her own life, but in an extremely helpless manner that tugged constantly at the "big sister" in me. I worked extremely hard in sessions with Eileen not to move in with hope, advice, and reassurance. She talked about wanting a job, but couldn't start looking; she said she was dying of loneliness; she was drinking more than ever; and she frequently took her phone off the hook and spent days and nights crying. I asked David Berenson about medication for her, and he said: "Not yet. You've got to let her hit bottom." As I forced myself during those months "not to be helpful," I came to appreciate the dilemma of the much-maligned "spouse of the alcoholic," whose automatic rescue moves have the effect of supporting a continuation of the drinking and preventing change.

Jim, meanwhile, continued to report heroic struggles to deal with both his family of origin and with his boys. Things were not going well on either front, he reported, and he was "getting exhausted." His initial exhilaration at re-connecting with his family had been replaced by hurt and anger as he found himself caught up again in old patterns. He listened politely when I suggested different tactics to him, but I could tell he was writing the family off again. He was more concerned with handling the boys, and we spent an enormous amount of time on one crisis after the other. His sincerity, concern, and good intentions were obvious. What I did not realize, and probably should have, is that he was again drinking heavily and I was simply along on a merry-go-round ride. In the summer, he mentioned a "girlfriend." Since I think that an active affair will interfere with the resolution, pro or con, of the marital relationship, I told Jim that. I reviewed with him the principles of triangulation and the idea that he might focus fruitfully on either one relationship or the other but not both at the same time. Jim said he understood, agreed, and had not at all decided that he and Eileen were through, but "I'm not going to get emotionally involved with this woman—she's just company." I had heard that one before, considered it un-workable, but stopped short of saying that I would not continue to see him with Eileen as long as he maintained the affair. I wonder if it would have made a difference if I had taken that stand.

In the fall of 1975, near the close of the first year of treatment, Eileen decided that she couldn't tolerate the "loneliness" anymore and moved back into the house with Tommy and Brian, sending Jim back to his apartment. I considered this to be a backslide, an indication that she was not yet ready to really work at change but was clutching at the children again for emotional support. She raised this possibility herself, and I confirmed her fear that this was probably a backward, or at most, lateral move. However, she said, it was all she could do at the moment. She and Jim switched dwellings again. Eileen was enraged with jealousy over Jim's "girlfriend," of whom he made no secret, and she went to see a divorce lawyer. Told that she could probably have a divorce within a few months, she then dropped the idea, stating that she "couldn't do it." She tried one or two AA meetings but "couldn't stand them."

In summary, I see the first year of treatment as a constant recycling of the family problems and patterns with me trying to help motivate either one of them to take one really different stand and hold it long enough to initiate the process of change. I thought for a while that Jim was doing that, but his continued drinking undermined his efforts, a factor on which he fooled himself and me. Then I thought that Eileen's switch of living quarters heralded the beginning of a stand, but she was pulled back into helplessness by her fears of being alone and by the triangle with Jim's girlfriend.

The Second Year Of Treatment

As we went into the second year, I said to David Berenson: "Listen, David, nothing is happening. I'm just on a merry-go-round with them. I've got to take some kind of stand myself." I very virtuously did not say 'I told you so.' I said that since Eileen had actually gone to a couple of AA meetings, maybe if I now insisted on that as a requisite for going on with me, she would do it. "What did she do when her last shrink said that?" David asked. I laughed. "She left him. OK, you've got me. What do I do now?" "Well, why not try it paradoxically," he suggested. "Tell her that you know that people with drinking problems take a long time to get down to work, but that you're willing to just sit with her for the next five years while she decides whether to get to work or not." I said this, or words to this effect, the next time I met alone with Eileen. The impact was dramatic. She accepted what I said calmly enough in the interview, but that night at midnight, she phoned me at home and, obviously drunk, told me off roundly. I said I hoped she would come into the office and tell me off sober. The next day she phoned and meekly apologized. I neither accepted nor rejected the apology but repeated my hope that she'd come to the next appointment.

When Eileen came to the next appointment, she said simply: "I guess I do have to stop drinking, but I'm going to do it my own way." She then gave me her own version of a homemade "behavior modification" plan in which she had identified the times, places, activities, and people associated with her drinking and worked out ways to avoid or substitute for them. Eileen then doggedly pursued this plan throughout the late fall and winter of 1975, with at first frequent, and then occasional, slips.

Jim, at about this time, had started missing or canceling appointments. Eileen said he was drinking heavily, fighting constantly with her and the boys, and had started talking about going to his girlfriend's therapist. As soon as she embarked on a serious plan to stop drinking, he dropped out of treatment with me without notification and went to the girlfriend's therapist for individual treatment.

In the early spring of 1976, Eileen told me casually one day, "I'm not struggling with not drinking anymore. I just don't think about it at all. Maybe some day I'll even be able to drink socially, but I wouldn't try it yet." During the six or seven months that she fought the temptation to drink, she had mentioned her progress or lack of it during our meetings, but this had been in no way the focus of our work. As soon as she decided to stop drinking, I had started coaching Eileen on work in her family of origin.

In evaluating Eileen's family of origin and her place in it, I saw as a primary goal for her a loosening of her enmeshment in the family to a degree that she would no longer be driven and ruled by her need for their recognition and approval. I hypothesized theoretically that if she could give up these needs, she would probably eventually gain the recognition and approval as by-products, but, paradoxically, she would have to learn to give sufficient recognition and approval to herself and no longer "need" it, before that would be likely to happen. I knew that a major pitfall would be the temptation to swing to the other extreme and attempt to resolve the problem by cutting off from her family completely rather than hanging in for the arduous process of changing herself in the context of these primary relationships.

I saw that the pattern of conflict followed by sullen withdrawal that she had developed in her family of origin had been carried over to her relationships with Jim and the boys and I believed that in order to permanently change that pattern for her future, she would have to go back and do something different at the source: in the original family. Further serious problems for Eileen, in my opinion, were her complete lack of knowledge about or perception of her father as a real person, rather than as the "black sheep" of family song and story; her blind dependence on her "only friend in the family," Kevin; her acceptance of the family view that she was a "bad mother" as compared to the "good mother," Irene; her emotional distance from her oldest brother; her belief that her mother was helpless, unapproachable, and not able to sustain her end of a person-to-person relationship with Eileen; and the vicious-cycle conflicts over various issues that went on interminably with most of her sisters.

Above all, it appeared to be taboo in the Hanrahan family to openly address or deal with any of these or other important emotional issues, except, of course, when they "accidentally" burst out while drinking. It was clear, also, that if Eileen stopped drinking, and these "accidental" outbursts stopped, the poison of the disturbed and distorted relationships with her family members would be likely to flow inward and result in the worsening of the depression Eileen characteristically exhibited when sober.

In order, then, to bring about useful change in herself (it was *never* a goal to change her family members), Eileen would have to fight and overcome in herself the angry, self-pitying, self-deprecating reactions to them, their viewpoints, and behavior that had always dragged her down. She would have to get out of the "victim" position and learn what part she herself played in initiating or maintaining the dysfunctional patterns and try to change her part. She would have to discover what was good or emotionally important to her in these relationships and to learn better ways of trying to get what she wanted from them. She would have to re-evaluate her expectations, wants, and "needs," from family relationships and give up those that no longer seemed appropriate or functional. In short, Eileen had a big job ahead.

In pursuit of her goals in this work, which we discussed at length, and upon which we agreed, Eileen and I embarked on the "coaching" part of her treatment, which went more or less as follows: Eileen would raise some emotional issue which was currently disturbing her. We would then explore the history of this issue in her family until we had isolated the family member or members with whom it had been most a problem for her. I would usually suggest a task, or strategy, or plan by which the issue could be brought up by Eileen with this person in the present and dealt with in a different, more functional way. We would then look at the repercussions of such a move and Eileen would try to predict the reactions of the "target" family member, and others, to her different stance so that she could be prepared to handle such reactions. Our next session would be an examination of the success or failure of the move, and the raising of the next issue she felt important to be dealt with. This process, of course, was continuously interspersed with crises arising in Eileen's nuclear family, at work, or with family members that she had not expected to have to deal with at that moment. As time went on and Eileen got the hang of the work and absorbed the principles, more and more of the planning of the moves was done by her and was merely checked out with me. Sometimes Eileen understood the emotional ramifications of a task beforehand; sometimes she was surprised and overwhelmed by the emotional experiences unleashed by "simple little changes." Sometimes she accurately predicted the reactions of family members, and sometimes was stunned by their reactions.

One of Eileen's major efforts was to peel her mother away from her oldest sister's protective grasp and slowly open up with her all of the troublesome issues in her life. Much to her surprise, the "helpless old lady" came through with understanding, support, warmth, and even some good advice. Mother revealed aspects of her own life previously unknown to Eileen, and as the exchange deepened, Eileen reported that she no longer felt, nor was treated, "like a baby." Eileen probed her elder sibs for more information about her father, and meeting great resistance, searched out friends who had known him. She made a visit to his grave (her first) in the company of her mother and son, Brian, and reported that it was an extremely moving experience.

Standing up to her oldest sister, Fran, was one of the toughest assignments that I gave her, and she did so at first reactively—with outbursts and tantrums— but gradually brought to the task increasing humor, tolerance, and an understanding of what she herself did to invite Fran's tyranny. She also had several long conversations with her sister, Irene, the "best mother in the family," and decided that Irene wasn't as perfect as she had thought, nor was she herself all bad as a mother. When any of her sisters insulted or baited her during family drinking parties, she learned to laugh and invite them to "tell me that when you're not drinking, and we'll discuss it." Her phone calls and visits to family members were slowly reduced from daily or weekly routines to carefully spaced, carefully planned intervals.

The job of sorting out and understanding the crucial issues and the emotional patterns in the multitudinous interlocking triangles involving Eileen, her mother and aunt, and eight siblings and their spouses, put both Eileen and me to quite a test. She read theoretical articles and learned about de-triangling with reversals and other strategies. Sometimes we were able to look ahead and calmly plan the next move, but more often we examined crises and conflicts *after* they had erupted and got ready for their reappearance, which inevitably occurred.

Her family's initial resistance to the changes in Eileen ranged from scorn to disbelief to amusement, culminating in a gift given to their mother for which everyone except Eileen had been invited to contribute. Although stung by this maneuver, Eileen carried it off lightly in their presence and was able to laugh about it soon afterward. She said this was "the turning point," after which they "could never get my goat in the old way again." And one day Eileen decided that she had become trapped in a childish dependence on her "good brother," Kevin, precipitated a disagreement with him, survived his hurt and anger over it, and announced that she had put that relationship on a "more equal footing."

It is difficult to describe the nuclear family chaos that accompanied Eileen's work in her family of origin during this period. Each week, she reported at least two or three crises involving either Jim or one or more of the boys. But each success with her family of origin made her less uptight in her dealings with her nuclear family. She worked at changing her pattern of alternately slaving for and then rejecting the boys; she learned not to scream back at Jim no matter what he called her; she stopped yelling at Tommy for his drinking and focused on behavioral standards; she took firm hold of Brian's discipline and when he said he wanted to live with Jim, she let him go and laid down firm conditions for his return. She even wrote friendly letters to her old nemesis, Jim's mother, urging her to "take care of Jim, he needs you now more than ever." As is usually the case with reversals, she would embark on such a project in a spirit of mischief only to have it "turn out to be real." She stated to me that there was *nothing* she wouldn't do to straighten out her life, and I was beginning to believe her.

Early in her work on her extended family, I had arranged for Peggy Papp to sculpt[7] (or "choreograph") Eileen in a training group to help clarify issues and triangles in that very large family of hers. This proved very helpful to both Eileen and to me. Eileen experienced directly both the intensity and the patterns of her enmeshment in her family. Watching, I was able to trace the patterns, issues and triangles with a clarity that had not come through verbally. A bonus for the therapy came when Eileen cast me as her oldest sister, Fran. I got the message and pulled way back again. The emotional impact of the sculpting on Eileen was great enough to cause a brief return of her drinking immediately following the event, but that quickly subsided after she examined the experience more intellectually and made plans to work on what she had learned.

When Eileen had been "dry" for about a month and was underway in her family work, I showed her the two videotapes that had been made. As she watched the "sober" tape of the sculpting, she burst into tears at the depressed, frightened picture she presented and said: "No wonder I drank!" Only after she calmed down was she able to study the family patterns portrayed and relate them to actual work done and yet to be done with her family. Although she expressed fear of being embarrassed by the "drunk tape," she actually enjoyed it, and we both laughed and made comments about her openness, warmth, and good humor during that session. Of the serious issues raised later in the tape, she said: "I can't believe I had to drink to talk about those things." By then she had raised most of these topics with various family members.

In the spring of 1976, when Eileen announced that the worst of her struggle against drinking appeared to be over, she entered a period of mourning for the "waste and meaninglessness" of her past life and intense fear of the aloneness that lay ahead. From approximately April 1976 until September 1976, Eileen alternated between periods of intense despair and periods of intense work, change, and movement in her life. My job during that period was to distinguish carefully between these two states so that I could be careful not to offer rescue or proddings when she was in despair, but could be free to offer coaching and suggestions when she was calm and working objectively on her family relationships and her life.

During the periods of despair, Eileen sometimes thought she was going crazy and sometimes thought of killing herself. She stated ruefully, but with some amusement, that drinking would no longer serve the purpose of helping her to escape from these feelings. I was concerned that her "hitting bottom" despair would veer over into a severe clinical depression and therefore asked David Berenson to see her occasionally during this phase. David, assured that her drinking was sufficiently under control to permit responsible handling of medication, prescribed an anti-depressant. Mostly, David and I both told her, she would be able to learn from these black periods if she didn't fight them. We suggested that she get herself emotionally connected at times when she feared being completely overwhelmed. Eileen thus took to calling her mother or her brother Kevin when the despair was too great to bear, and she would then talk over with me in our meetings what she thought she had learned or could use from each bout.[8]

In the work periods during this time, Eileen made many decisions and changes: she joined a woman's group and a political organization to cut down her isolation; she took the first full-time job of her life, and when she was offered a better one after several months, switched her job; she started divorce proceedings; she started dating and broke off the relationship because "he drinks too much, and anyway I'm not ready for a new emotional involvement yet." Above all, Eileen continued working steadily on her relationships in her family of origin, and on the remnants of her reactive anger towards Jim. She no longer blamed Jim for their unsuccessful marriage, and she was prepared to maintain a cooperative co-parental relationship with him for life, she said. Jim, she reported, had quit or lost his job and was living in squalor with his girlfriend, drinking heavily. She did not want to be married to him again, but she mourned the death of their marriage and felt sad about its breakup and about Jim. She hoped, for his sake, that he would "hit bottom" and pull himself together.

In contrast to the lack of assertiveness characteristic of her during the first year of work, she reported at the end of the summer of 1976 that she had "lost her fear of authority and could stand up for herself with almost anyone." She was also proud of the fact that she had been "the life of a Labor Day party without a drink." She said she would never have believed what a difference it made in her life not to drink. She then reported that she occasionally had a drink or two socially, but was careful never to drink with her family, and never to drink at parties. "I'm so pleased to be having a good time without drinking that I'm on a 'high' of my own."

The Last Half Year of Treatment

In the last six months during which I met with Eileen Kelley on a weekly basis, she continued to initiate important changes. Her divorce from Jim became final over Jim's objections and delaying tactics. Brian, who had ping-ponged back and forth between Jim and Eileen until Eileen "let him go," finally chose Eileen to have legal custody of him. She arranged for a full cognitive evaluation of Brian, who had always had learning disabilities, and he agreed to give school another chance if he could be changed to a small private school. Tommy, who had been put out by Eileen for disruptive behavior (mostly occasioned by drinking) and had lived with Jim for a year, now moved out on his own and was applying for college. Danny, whose gambling debt with the Mafia Eileen had refused to pay, asked her to help him start a small business. All three boys by now had a vastly improved relationship with their mother and visited their father regularly.

Eileen began exploring the worlds of theater, art, and music which she "had never noticed before," and she planned her first trip to Europe. She said that there were not enough hours in the day to do the things she now enjoyed doing. She and a woman friend were working on several ideas for a creative business venture so that they would not have to spend their lives working at "just a job." When she announced herself definitely in charge of her life now, she asked to see me at increasingly spaced intervals, and I agreed. This is my usual form of "termination," in which the client's own work continues with less and finally no need to consult with me regularly.

Summary

In the initial phase of the treatment of this couple, I was taken in in a manner all too common in the treatment of alcoholism. When Jim presented himself as in control of his drinking and working hard in therapy, I accepted his good intentions for the fact, because, I think, he did not show the physical signs that I associated with drinking problems. I therefore failed to give him the unequivocal message that his efforts, no matter how strenuous, would fail unless the drinking stopped. To Eileen, who did show the effects of steady drinking, I delivered this message clearly.

Please note that although I saw Eileen alone for more than half of the treatment time, I continued to do *family* therapy[9] with her in that the focus of our work was on action in the entire three generation family system and not on her intrapsychic processes. Her very active work on these relationships is not fully covered here because of my focus on the specific factors involved in working with an alcoholic system.

But what about the outcome for the others? Eileen is clearly in charge of her life, but are they? I don't see the emotional bond between Jim and Eileen as completely broken, in spite of their divorce, and I think that her turn-around will still have its impact on Jim if and when he is able to stop triangling with girlfriends and therapists.

As to the Kelley boys, and the generations beyond them, I don't know. How much change does it take, and who must change, to interrupt a strong intergenerational pattern? Eileen once said: "The only thing I can really give to my children is the way I lead my own life." She wondered if the changes in her life were "in time to save them." I don't know, but surely the odds in their favor have improved. Certainly, Danny, who "won't touch a drop," and Tommy, who "drinks less, but still too much," are actively carrying the loaded issue with them. They certainly won't have a "free ride" on this issue. But perhaps it will make a difference that a pathway back from alcoholism has now been introduced into the system. Perhaps only time, life's stresses, and the work that the boys themselves put into their family relationships will tell.

Some elements in this case are controversial in the traditional approaches to alcoholism. I didn't insist that the Kelleys go to Alcoholics Anonymous; I didn't get into defining "alcoholism" with them, or into labeling anyone as "alcoholic" or not; I didn't get into the "disease vs. psychological etiology" dispute, nor encourage the Kelleys to do so. Alcoholics Anonymous, in my opinion, still does the finest job around on the symptom of alcohol abuse, and fortunate indeed is the therapist whose drinking clients will go there. But the Kelleys wouldn't, and Eileen, at least, found another way. Some will say that she was not "a real alcoholic," because she is able to return to occasional social drinking. Be that as it may. Excessive drinking was destroying her life and now is not. What I did do, with David Berenson's help, was to discover and talk about the functional purposes served by alcohol and encourage her to find a less destructive way of serving these purposes. I think that unless Eileen had actively worked to bring fun, affection, tenderness and anger into her life without alcohol, she would have returned to drinking or remained the grim, depressed woman on the sculpting tape.

A final word about the anxiety aroused in a therapist working closely with this symptom. In my initial learning period, I did occasionally get anxious about where my family and I fell on the alcohol abuse spectrum. If alcoholism is not to be safely limited to "Bowery Bums," then any of us who drink have to take a closer look not only at the amount we drink, but at the purpose it serves in our lives, and in our families. For me, that anxiety subsided after a short while. But what remained to plague me throughout was the obvious direct application to the areas of smoking and eating, which are my addictions. Eileen Kelley and I sometimes joked about it, as she overcame her symptom and I obviously did not overcome mine. But I have very good intentions, you understand, and next Monday . . .

References

1. Steinglass. P., 'Experimenting with Family Treatment Approaches to Alcoholism," 1950-1975; A Review, *Family Process*, Volume 15, #1, March 1976.
2. Minuchin, S., *Families and Family Therapy*, Harvard University Press, Cambridge, Mass., 1974.
3. Bowen, M., "Toward the Differentiation of Self in One's Family of Origin," in F. Andres and J. Lorio (eds.) *Georgetown Family Symposium Papers*, Vol. I, Georgetown University Press, 1974, 77.
4. Berenson, David, "Alcohol and the Family System," in P. Guerin (ed.), *Family Therapy, Theory and Practice*, Gardner Press, New York, 1976.
5. Davis, D. I., Berenson, D., Steinglass, P. and Davis, S., "The Adaptive Consequences of Drinking," *Psychiatry*, 37 (1974), 209-15.
6. Steinglass, P., Davis, D.I. and Berenson, D., "In-Hospital Treatment of Alcoholic Couples," *Family Therapy, Theory and Practice*, Gardner Press, New York, 1976.
7. Papp, Peggy, "Family Choreography," in P. Guerin (ed.), *Family Therapy, Theory and Practice*, Gardner Press, 1976.
8. Fogarty, Thomas, "On Emptiness and Closeness," *The Family*, Vol. 3, isuues 2 and 3.
9. Carter, E. and Orfanidis, M., "Family Therapy With One Person and The Family Therapist's Own Family," in P. Guerin (ed.), *Family Therapy, Theory and Practice*, Gardner Press, New York, 1976.

5

It's Ten P.M.
Do You Know Where
Your Parents Are?

Ian Alger, M.D.

The Visit

It was March, and the wind knew it. I headed my Honda into the Central Park crosstown at 79th Street, and was amazed that the little car was not blown sideways off the road. Rain was driving against the windshield, and I strained to see the curb. The Gormans lived on the West Side, near the river, and I was headed for my first home visit with them. They had all wanted me to come to their home, and I was curious to see it myself. We had known each other now for nearly 10 months, and our therapy sessions had not followed any usual pattern. This would be our eleventh meeting. The first had been in my office, the previous July, when the family had volunteered to be part of a training film on family therapy. That first session had been filmed, and we got to know each other while a cameraman and a sound engineer shared the same room. Every 10 minutes we stopped and chatted, slipping in and out of therapy and metatherapy positions while the film cartridge was changed in the camera. Somehow that experience had bound us together as a troupe, and our second session, which was held in a television studio in New Jersey with the full setup of three camera crews and a director, did not faze any of us. We had wondered if it would be another case of the Louds, but soon decided that the Gorman saga was going to turn out to be quite different.

After that television studio session we had continued to meet in my office until this March night when I was to visit the family at home.

Robert was now 56 and seemed chronically depressed, although socially he presented a suave facade, dressed in a somewhat modish way, and even managed   **69** occasional wit inserted into his somewhat excessive conversational flow. His whole life was a story of seeking and not finding. One business venture or entrepreneurial thrust followed another, success always evading the grasp. So the family had lived in a swirl of dreams and promises, and in a reality of debts and anxieties. Nevertheless the family existed in middle-class comfort. Jane, 10 years younger, had worked through most of the marriage, for several years parttime to leave room for raising the girls, and then for the last 5 years as a teacher, after she earned her certificate by returning to college in 1970.

Although 46, Jane looked drab and worn. There was minimal care to grooming and dress, and her weariness showed through. Under the colorless presentation there flashed an attractiveness and a liveliness, which ignited when she smiled. Her brightness and verbal ease also countered the first impression of dullness and faded life.

Through the rain I saw a small space on Riverside Drive and gladly squeezed my Honda into the spot. The door to the old and once handsome highrise was close, and I quickly strapped my videorecorder over my shoulder, grabbed the bag full of camera and cables, and ran for the entrance. We had videotaped all the sessions from the beginning, so I had promised I would bring the portable equipment to the home visit. I slightly regretted that promise as I struggled through the rain. Riding the elevator, I remembered the story from the first session when Sara, the older daughter, had been locked out of the apartment. "You gave my key to your editor," she had told her father. This had gone on to be a discussion about the lack of communication between members of the family. But Robert had recalled how he had felt locked out in his family, and this had opened a new theme of loneliness and alienation.

The story became more real for me as I approached the apartment door and saw the lock, and rang the bell. Robert answered, and I was welcomed by him, and Jane, and both girls who came from the back of the apartment.

Sara was 15 and still looked somewhat boyish and a little overweight. She smiled easily and moved with an aggressiveness and push which ensured attention. In all the sessions she had been quite open, and most likely to express her feelings directly. These traits perhaps had made her more readily the identified patient at the start. Carol, 3 years younger, was slight and moved with more lightness. Quite pretty, with striking long hair and a captivating smile, she was clearly the little sweetheart of her father. Most of the time she said little and was described by Jane as somewhat shy. This had led her parents to talk recently of their concern for her and, actually, 2 years earlier the family had sought family therapy through a referral from a pediatric unit out of concern for the adjustment of both girls.

As I entered the apartment I was aware that it had a somewhat bare quality to it; but a warmth also came through, and there was an immense amount of space, with the large foyer opening into a dining room, and then the spacious living room opening from the right of that to have its windows overlook the Hudson. As I put the equipment down, Robert took my coat, and Jane offered me coffee. The girls were interested in how the small TV setup worked, so we began together to assemble it; we decided that we would use a tripod for the camera and take a wide shot of the living room. I was struck by how naturally everything seemed to be going. There was to me no sense of strain, and the family seemed genuinely to be welcoming my visit. The wind was still strong, and gusts actually bent the windows in the living room. I exclaimed in surprise, and Robert told me that in the high winds they often bent that way, but none had broken yet.

I had somewhat the same feeling about the family. Over the years it had bent under stress but had not broken yet. Sitting with them in that living room, I felt more comfortable, with a greater sense of unity, but at the same time I had the feeling of incompleteness and partial disorganization. The girls seemed also to sense the same uncertainty, and Sara more frequently took the initiative to relieve tension that showed up between her parents. I had been aware of this from the first session with the family, when it seemed apparent that the parents had the major problem, while the problems with the girls, although real, served also to mobilize the family, and to obscure the chronic dissatisfactions in the parents' relationship

At this point it was Carol who said, "Why don't we have the meetings here? It feels more homey."

Mother responded, "Poor Doctor Alger!"

Robert added, "I told you, you've made an entry into our family, into our marriage."

Jane questioned, "What do you mean, marriage?"

Robert answered angrily, "Just what I said. Anybody else would understand it. What the hell are you embarrassed about?"

"It sounds corny," Jane responded. And at that moment, Sara walked into the room between them and sat down.

Robert continued, "Why don't you talk, then?"

"I'm sorry," Jane apologized.

Robert hurled back, "Don't be sorry, go ahead!" And at that, Sara yawned widely. It reminded me of the same kind of yawn, and the same timing of it in the very first session with the family. Sara kept getting in the middle. But this time it did not distract her parents.

Robert continued, speaking to me, "Jane's made a good transference to you."

Jane asked, "Why?"

"Because I think that."

As if he had not spoken, Jane continued, "I am better able to separate myself from a kind of unproductive dependence on Robert..."

"I can feel that," I added.

Jane went on. "It's a struggle. I still don't enjoy things much, but maybe that's unreasonable ... no place to go, maybe..."

"Yes there is. South America!" Sara interjected.

I could see that Sara was inserting herself again, but I also realized that Jane had been making more efforts to move in her own direction. Robert had been the center of the family for most of the marriage. He had led everyone on a continuing course of financial expectation and subsequent disappointment, followed by last-minute renewed hope and partial recovery, only to have hope dashed again by another unforeseen disaster. Jane had played a special role in this story over the years, becoming entangled in the details, and exasperated by the delays and disappointments, all the while coming up with suggestions and advice which either were rejected or resented. The other part of her role was to constantly provide a sort of maintenance income through her various jobs, both full and parttime. But the dependence which she was now confronting had manifested itself in one way by always placing her in the secondary role, and always downplaying the importance of her needs and her priorities. She did fight for the needs of the girls, but this concern was also a concern of Robert's and he experienced her worry as an attack on him, to which he reacted by withdrawal or angry outburst.

Possibly Jane's new striving for a kind of independence was related to the therapy. I had purposely tried to align myself with her developing of her own interests and competence. From the start she had talked of renewing her studies to complete her master's degree; and even before she could do that, there were requirements that had to be met periodically so she could continue to qualify for the teaching job she now had. But beyond that, I was struck by the drabness of her looks and the lack of care she seemed to show for her personal appearance. Deliberately, over the months, I commented on the contrast between her appearance and the attractiveness that was evident not only in her physical qualities, but also in her liveliness and sense of sexiness and excitement. Whenever I would talk this way, she would flush and become more alive, and Robert would both glow and squirm with some discomfort.

In reacting to Jane's sexuality and life, I usually would include Robert and ask him for confirmation of my own reactions, and he would as a rule affirm what I felt. Both Jane and Robert said from the start that sex was no problem in their marriage. Jane said that it was not an earth-shaking experience, but that it was enjoyable and pleasurable, and that Robert was a good lover. Both mentioned that whenever either of them had felt like sexual activity there had been no hassles or problems. Robert did allow, however, that he would like Jane to take more care of herself and to dress with more style. And she acknowledged that she did not give herself much attention. Over the 3 years of our sessions there was a gradual change in this pattern, and Jane took increasing care with her hair and her dress, so that her immediate appearance was much more alive and attractive. Robert was always well dressed and carefully groomed. From the first session he showed a special knack for style, and although he did not own many new clothes, he was able to assemble his wardrobe in a varied and interesting ensemble and rarely appeared for a session outfitted as he had been in the past.

Sara at first appeared quite boyish in dress and style. She was overweight and seemed to pay little attention to her presentation, although it was clean and in good repair. Carol, 11 years old at the time the sessions began, was very pretty, took a good deal of care with her hair, and dressed in style. After about a year and one-half Sara's appearance began to change drastically. She lost weight, developed a good figure, and began to show a great interest in her dress. She became increasingly attractive, and her roughness of style began to shade into a more mild and tactful approach. During this time she began to date boys and rather quickly and easily moved into a heterosexual peer group.

My flirtation with Jane served to create some competitive feeling between Robert and me, to stir some excitement in Jane, and to absorb the three of us in a little triangle so the girls could step back and become a little less entangled in the marriage. Jane's drabness had been one of the points I had commented on, and earlier in this narrative I mentioned my initial reaction to the drabness of the apartment. This home visit gave me a chance to experience more about the actual living of the Gormans. The sitting room was fairly comfortable, but during the session it seemed that the family did not use it much. I said that I was glad to be able to be together with them. Jane replied, "We never sit in this room."

Sara answered, "That's not true."

"It is true," said Robert.

"Not," retorted Sara.

"Well, I agree—so there!" continued Robert.

At this point I asked Robert, "Is it true you don't sit here?"

Robert said, "No *we* don't."

"Well!" exclaimed Sara.

"WE!" exulted Robert. "WE! We're talking about WE, not YOU."

"I'm not talking about WE," interrupted Jane.

Robert went on, "Mother sits here with Marie, and I sit here with George—but as a family—never!"

"Whenever we have guests, we're all here," Sara interjected, with satisfaction at finally having made her point.

I asked, "This may be the place for guests. Where *do* you come together as a family?"

"At the dining room table, " answered Jane, and her tone conveyed the tiredness that I often detected in both her and Robert when it came to issues of nurturing and parenting.

Jane was born in 1929 in New York, and was an only child. Her father was a businessman whom she "feared and idolized until I was twelve." He encouraged her to be like a boy. Her hair was cut like a boy's, and she was encouraged to disdain "girlish" things, such as dolls, and dresses, and dancing. She said, "I learned to outrun, outfight, and was a better athlete than most boys I knew." The only adult she "knew well" and to whom she felt attached was a black woman called "Nellie." She felt very comfortable with her and perhaps much of the nurturing and caring came from this woman. "She seemed to enjoy spending time with me, and I enjoyed her company very much."

Jane's mother is remembered by her as a depressing nag, caught in an unhappy marriage and plagued by ill health. For most of her teenage years Jane lived with her mother while her father was in the army overseas. She realized he was glad to escape from his family and from his job which he disliked, and after the war he chose further overseas service. In a sense Jane was more responsible for her mother than her mother was for her, and when she went to college at the age of 18 she felt great relief. In her junior year she studied in France and still remembers this as the high point of her life. She was shy but well liked, and she dated boys in high school and college. At 23 she met Robert, and they dated for the next 7 years. He was more attracted to her than she to him, but the romance wore on and she became "more and more attached and dependent on him." It was after her mother's death, when Jane was 29, that she and Robert decided to get married. All through the courtship she had worked as a literary researcher, and she continued work after the marriage. The indicator of financial future soon showed itself when the inheritance from her mother was lost in Robert's business ventures, just before Sara was born by natural childbirth in 1960. Sara was nursed for the first year and was a healthy and alert baby. Within 4 months Jane had returned to work. In 1963 Carol was born. She was placid and developed more slowly, walking at 18 months. Sara was outraged with the coming of the new baby, and the family was advised not to rein Sara in but to let her run free. From that time on the parents felt confused, they say, and think they were very inconsistent in their handling of the children.

Robert was also born in New York, but 10 years earlier than Jane and into a larger family. He was the middle child, the only boy, and says that his older sister was the favorite, while his younger sister received very short shrift indeed. His father was in the clothing manufacturing business, but after the 1929 crash never regained the same position financially again. Robert reports that when he was younger the family consisted of his father, his mother, his sisters, his mother's mother, and assorted maids, cooks, and nurses. The father was busy in business most of the time, and Robert felt that he was put down constantly by his father. He describes his own mother as "infantile," and cannot remember counting on her for anything. Indeed, his memories of life with her are one large disappointment. He describes his feeling that the message his family gave him was to "Look good, don't do!"

School came easily for him, but he recalls that he made no effort to excel. He remembers getting along well with other children and was good at athletics. He became a "lover" early in his teens and was always popular with girls and women. When he was 18 he met a girl whom he married 5 years later. They had no children and after 3 years of marriage divorced. For the next 14 years until he was 40, Robert remained single but had many women friends and, as noted earlier, dated Jane for 7 years before their marriage. He was intensely attracted to

Jane, and to this day affirms his sexual attraction and love for her.

He describes himself as pleased at the birth of both children and liked the idea of having children as part of the family. However, he has said, "I was ill equipped to handle them or relate to them much beyond their infancy. Mainly I don't know how to be a father. I felt I couldn't establish and maintain a morality; I couldn't set an example. I was always willing to help them where I could; bathing, dressing, feeding while they were young. Story telling nightly for years. Helping them with school. But never getting in step where it really counted. My anger frightened them and probably set them a poor example. Eventually I found myself mostly mute with Sara, and rather mundane with Carol."

This self-assessment seems to me to be rather biased and reflects Robert's depression. It is true that he has trouble feeling at ease with his children, but it is also true that both girls demonstrate appreciation and caring for both him and their mother. It seems that the beginning of the teenage years marked a time when both parents felt especially ill equipped to cope with the parenting needed, and that both of them felt their own backgrounds gave them little experience and example of helpful parental care.

So we had come to the point that the family met at the dining room table, and the living room was used when guests were there. I told them that this did not seem so radical but actually had a lot of tradition in it. We all got up and walked into the dining room to get some more coffee. I asked if we could go on a tour of the whole place. Robert showed me how he had scraped the floors, and how he had reconstructed a bed for Sara, because she needed more space when some of her girlfriends wanted to stay over. Sara had a large space, fairly open, next to the dining room. It looked disorganized, but rather fun. The master bedroom was comfortable, although not finished, but it, like the living room, had a magnificent view of the river. Carol's room was the smallest, but it was one she had recently chosen. It actually was a kind of utility and small maid's room. There was little comfort in it, but she seemed happy and had places to look after her animals, which turned out to be an interest of passion for her. The next summer she was able to get her first real volunteer job working in the zoo.

I felt quite happy being with the family. I really had felt welcome and appreciated their letting me so easily look into their lives and share part of an evening with them. The videotape had run out, and I began to pack the equipment, promising Carol, who seemed most interested, that we would watch it together at the next meeting in my office. But the session was not over. Sara and Jane began to talk about Sara's staying over that night at a girlfriend's. There were just going to be some of the girls there. Sara looked very sulky, and I asked, "What's upsetting you?"

"My unreasonable mother," she answered. Then continued, "She just doesn't let me do things. First thing you know, I'll run away, and then they'll say, 'Where did we go wrong?'"

Jane laughed somewhat unconvincingly, and Sara rebuked her, "It's not funny!"

"I didn't say it was!" Jane came back.

I came in to ask, "I still don't understand, Sara, exactly what it is you want?"

Robert turned to Sara and said, "Go back and explain it in words of one syllable."

"Why back?" asked Sara.

"Use three syllables," retorted Robert. And I really felt at this point that he was beginning to enjoy the fight Sara was having with her mother.

Jane went on again, "I don't feel I am being unreasonable. I don't want to be a killjoy. I just don't know. I guess it's all right for you to go."

"Well, what are you anxious about, Jane?" I asked.

Jane replied, "I'm not sure. Maybe I'm anxious about something going on. The group Sara's sleeping over with. No adults at home."

I turned to Jane. "Are the girls' parents friends of yours? Do you know them? Do you talk together?"

Sara interrupted with, "Why is that important?"

"Of course it's important!" I answered.

"Why?" Sara continued. "Nothing bad's happened."

"To find out if those parents are comfortable, and how they plan things together," I explained.

"They feel more than most parents that at 14 you're on your own," Jane said.

Sara was quite involved now. "A lot of people feel that way!"

"But," I said, "a lot of people don't feel that way."

"Well, I think it's all right for her to go, but she has to be taken over there, with the rain."

By now all the television equipment was packed, and I was ready to leave myself. "Would you like me to drop you off on my way?" I asked Sara.

"Sure."

Jane agreed. "It would mean Robert wouldn't have to go out now. Are you sure you don't mind?"

I assured her that it was on my way, and so Sara and I loaded up the equipment and headed for the car. As we drove over to Broadway I wondered about my part in this family decision. I certainly was supporting Sara, and yet Jane and Robert had seemed reassured on their largest concern which had been that they didn't want Sara walking on the street alone that late at night. Sara told me she felt her parents were too worried but that she could understand how they wanted to know where she was going and who would be there. I dropped her off and she thanked me for the lift.

It was just 10 o'clock. I thought of the commercial on radio which asked, "It's 10 p.m. Do you know where your children are?"

The Crisis

When Peggy Papp asked me to write my experience with a family, she said that I should try and convey what it was like for me to treat a family. I should try to show some of the processes I went through, to let others know some of my thoughts and feelings, and to describe the way I decided what I would do next. I chose to write about this family for several reasons. First, I liked the way our original meeting came about, and I'll tell more about that shortly. But also, this was a family I personally liked. I liked each of the members, and I have found in my work that this quality of liking the people is all important for me if I am going to work well. I'm not sure the word "liking" is the best one to describe the feeling. It is more a feeling of comfortableness and a response of really caring about what happens. A third reason I wanted to write about my experience with the Gormans was that I tried many different formats with them. We had met in my office for family sessions, both with and without camera and television crews. We had met once in a major television studio for the taping of a family session. I had met them in their home, and I had met with the parents separately. I had individual sessions with each parent, and with Sara, and the parents had joined one of my couples' groups, and had worked in that for over a year and a half. Finally, I wanted to write about our experiences together because it was a family that was not fresh in therapy. Robert had over 20 years of individual therapy with three different therapists. Jane had been in individual therapy before the marriage for almost 4 years. The whole family had been in family treatment for a year before I met them. In short, even in the modern "era of therapy," this family had received more than their share. The reason this intrigued me was that I quickly realized that no more insights were needed. No more probings of the past were very welcome. The whole reworking of life experience had gone stale, and I would be able to try to focus more on the ongoing struggles of the family, the struggles to pass through a very natural transition period in family life, the teenage crisis; and to help the family work on their communications with each other; and to help each of them begin to find new places for themselves, both as individuals and as members of their family.

As I began to organize my thoughts about the family in preparation for writing, that ride with Sara at 10 o'clock at night came back to me. I began to think that in this family the question might better be put in the reverse: "It's 10 p.m. Do you know where your parents are?" What do I mean by this? Can it be that in our world today parents are having as much trouble, or more, in finding their way than their children are? Formerly the nuclear family provided a more integrated family life, and the stability of that life provided a base for adolescents to move on into their own lives. And while parents had to adjust to this transition, there was a more certain road for parents to travel, and there were more community and family support systems to help. Now there is a shift in the

nuclear family. It has become a much less stable institution. There is fragmentation of the formerly integrated family life. Parents often have multiple job commitments that take them outside the home. Schedules of all family members are
more complex, as many activities previously sponsored by the family are now
directed by other outside institutions and agencies. Travel is complicated and
often difficult. Coordinating meetings of family members is frequently impossible. And the energy required to accomplish even supposedly simple tasks of life is
often not available.

The complications increase at adolescence. What now happens to the inter-
face between parents and adolescents when the teenagers begin to move out into
the world? The boundary between parents and children has become more vague
with increasing emphasis and concern about childrens' rights, and parents' rights.
In a way, parents are now going through a new adolescence of their own as their
children leave. The outside world bombards them. No longer is the road ahead
clear. Many marriages break up at this time, as individual parents now seek new
personal growth. Now there are more options available. Women feel less trapped and are looking for new possibilities. The whole sense of role identity
becomes blurred, and even the value of parenthood itself is often questioned.
Parenthood, once an almost universally noble role, now is under scrutiny.
Parenting involves self-sacrifice, giving to others. Now the question is asked,
"What about me?" Personal growth and self-development are new criteria and
disorient the new adolescent—adult. Explanations for the turmoil come from all
sides, from sociologists and psychologists, from politicians and theologists. The
changes stem from population shifts, with massive numbers of families moving
residence every year. The changes are related to revolutions in communication
and the impact of television, which has shrunk the size of our planet and made a
new yet incomprehensible global village for us all. The crisis is related to population explosions, to the constant threat of the disaster of nuclear war. The turmoil
comes from the inadequacy of the nuclear family to function effectively in the
new corporate society. Such a society demands a new kind of bonding, a
bonding to the job. The first loyalty lies here, and so this society discourages all
other bonding. Small wonder, then, that the personal bonding so needed in the
already isolated nuclear family is breaking apart.

In the Gorman family there had been a history of problems and concerns,
but the crisis appeared when the older girl, Sara, reached adolescence. At this
time the confusion not just of the children, but of the parents became manifest.
Where was each of them going? What was life about? There was confused or no
communication much of the time. Even the way one got keys to get into the
home was unclear. Who was really in charge? The parents would just as soon
have run away as the children. Both parents felt frightened at the role of parent
to adolescents, and the solution of divorce was being gently tested, or at least
quietly threatened. It was in this overall context that the family and I met for the
first time.

The Satellite

Early in 1974 my friend, Bill Douglas at the V.A. Hospital in Salem, Virginia asked me whether I would like to prepare a video presentation. It would be on the topic of family therapy for inclusion in a new experimental program that would be broadcasting medical educational material from a satellite to ten V.A. hospitals along the east coast. The idea of the first family therapy broadcast from outer space was intriguing, and I accepted immediately. One of the families referred to me for this project by the various colleagues I contacted was the Gorman family. They had completed a course of family therapy in a clinic and were looking for a new therapist. Possibly the chance to work with an experienced family therapist was appealing to them, and perhaps the idea of the satellite broadcast also was intriguing to them. At any rate, I explained the project to Robert on the phone, he consulted the family, and later they agreed to take part in the project. Of course, there was no fee involved, and they were asked to sign releases for the use of the material in teaching sessions.

The night of the first interview arrived, and they appeared well ahead of time, obviously somewhat excited. I met briefly with them in the next room and went through the procedure we would follow. The session was filmed with 16 mm color sound equipment. There was one cameraman and a sound engineer. Both of them were in the consultation room, and the cameraman needed free access to move around the circle into which we arranged ourselves. In addition, there was going to be exactly 60 minutes of filming, and there had to be an interruption every 10 minutes, so the film cartridge could be changed. Everyone took in all this instruction, and we were all excited. We shared with each other feelings of some nervousness. I introduced the family and the camera crew and said that we were really all part of one system in the session, and I wanted family and crew to feel equally free to make comments to each other if they wished during the course of the session. (A few times this actually did happen, and once Robert told the cameraman what a great shot he had just missed.)

I also told the family that although this was a teaching demonstration, taking place under unusual conditions, I wanted it to be a helpful session to them if possible. I appreciated their willingness to participate, and one of the possible returns for them could be a new perspective on their family interactions and direction.

The session began with greetings, and with Robert's arranging the seating, and with a fresh exchange of names. I then asked, "What's the deal with your family? What are you looking for?" This is a form I like to use, because it invites an explanation of what is going on with the family, but avoids defining the process in advance as a "problem."

Robert invited each family member to speak, but Jane said to him, "Why don't you start?" This was after both girls had indicated by words and nonverbal signals that they did not want to.

Robert accepted the invitation. He started by giving a survey of the family vital statistics, with details about where they lived in New York and their apartment. He continued:

"We're a family that doesn't feel and communicate with each other too well. That's the first thing. That causes rifts between us, and I feel the children are growing up—Sara is becoming more and more hostile to us because we're not communicating with her, and she not with us. And I feel the same thing with Carol.

"I feel also that Jane and I are very different in many ways, and we could do better if we learned a little more about each other and began to know how to understand each other better."

"How were you feeling while he was talking, Jane?" I asked. "Could you tell me?"

Jane began, "Well, I was, ah, getting ... ahh ..."

"Getting bored?" interjected Sara.

"Getting bored?" I asked.

"I was feeling uptight," added Jane.

I turned to Sara, smiling and said, "Of course, I knew that from you! I didn't have to be too wise to understand that. Do you know how I knew?—that huge yawn!"

"I was tired!" Sara came back.

"Yeah," said Jane. "I was aware of that. I began to get fidgety when he started with where we lived, and our apartment."

Now Carol spoke. "Who cares about our apartment?"

Jane went on, "And I thought, 'Oh, goodness, how long is this going to take?'"

Then I intervened, "But look! The rest of you characters! He originally said, 'You—you—you—'"

"Absolutely!" agreed Jane.

I went on, "So you gave over the whole show to him."

I got a new sense of Sara's sharpness and playfulness when she snapped back at me, "You're not being an analyst for our *apartment,* though!"

"I know, I know," I defended myself. "But once you gave him—You *know* this guy, don't you? I never met him before, but doesn't he go into long lists of things sometimes?" In this way I tried quickly to introduce the idea that something that happened in the family system was a product of behaviors of all the members. But Robert wanted to stay in the spotlight.

"I'm a footnoter," he solemnly intoned.

"A footnoter?" I asked.

"And he's never at a loss for words," Jane put in.

I went on, "He's shoved into the breach, and then everyone's nervous about how he's going to do."

Jane explained, "He's there to do the talking for us when we can't think of anything to say."

Because Robert was so easily put into the spotlight (and accepted the role so readily), I moved to change the focus. I did it by commenting on a nonverbal action but tried to do it in a way that was not judgmental and invited a response. It has seemed to me that working with videotapes and watching sessions repeatedly has sharpened my own awareness of nonverbal behaviors, so that even without videoreplay I am more alert to them. "Do you know what I just noticed while he was talking?" I asked Jane.

"No."

"The way you were holding your hands. Are you aware of how you do that?"

"I'm aware that when I'm tense that I do that."

I went on, "They were turning white, you were squeezing them so hard."

"I was nervous about what he was going to say next."

"About his sort of performance?" I then turned to Robert. "Were you aware of that?"

"I began to watch her occasionally."

Perhaps gratuitously, Jane added, "He's much better than he used to be."

"He's better than he used to be," I added for emphasis.

Undaunted, Robert went on, "We have made a discovery in our family as regards myself."

"You've had therapy," I clarified.

On he went, "One of the things we've discovered . . . where I feel I'd like to talk more with the children . . . I have a tendency to be a lecturer, and, all right, a footnoter . . . I think what Jane feels . . ."

"Jane just gave a big sigh." I noted. "Shall we check. You know what it's about undoubtedly."

"Did you?" Robert questioned.

"There he goes again," said Sara, interpreting the sigh.

I asked, "What was the sigh, Sara?"

"No, the sigh was not just, 'There he goes again.'"

"No?" I responded. "I wasn't sure."

"I was also thinking of what we discovered a little while back," she continued. "About how he feels he has to grab the scene—any kind of action he can grab hold of."

I asked Robert, "Because you feel left out?"

Robert answered, "Yeah. I think that I—" Suddenly his tone changed to one of enthusiasm, as he spoke to the cameraman. "Oh! You missed a great yawn over there!" Sara had yawned again.

"Don't take it personally," I said to Robert.

Sara objected, "I'm tired."

Robert returned to his need for the spotlight. "Much of my behavior is based on, maybe when I was younger they didn't listen to me much in my family."

At this point I felt I had learned something from Robert about his sense of what was going on in the family, and I wanted to check in on each member's perspective. I also had learned that Robert was in the monopolizing role in the family, and I wanted to break up this "lecturing" pattern as quickly as I could. So I turned to Jane and asked, "What's the story in your family?"

"We started [family therapy] out of our concern for the family, especially Sara. Recently we see that centering on Sara may be in part a nice way of deflecting from our own problems."

"This is something you've come to out of therapy?" I asked.

"Yes," responded Jane. "There's not much joy; not much communication— except in situations like this."

I replied, "So this is one value of therapy." Jane continued to elaborate, but I soon turned to the girls, to get their viewpoint.

"Well, let me ask the girls what their feeling is about the family. Because I notice that it's a talkative couple of parents you have here. It isn't just your father who talks, huh? Your mother, she just gave a big spiel—"

"Yeah," Carol agreed.

"She can talk. What about you girls?"

"We don't talk," said Sara.

"You don't talk at all!" I questioned.

"No, at home," laughed Sara.

"But you mean in therapy you don't talk?" I continued.

Sara replied, "We do.—She [to Carol] doesn't."

I turned to Carol. "You don't talk?"

"Not much."

"Not much," I continued. "Maybe that's the smart thing to do in this family ... you have ideas, I bet."

"Sometimes," answered Carol quietly.

I spoke further to Carol. "I just wondered what it does feel like to you to be in this family."

"It's *ok*. We don't usually communicate." And she enunciated "communicate" very slowly and distinctly.

I answered her. "You know, that's become a common thing you all say— but what do you mean by it? And *does* it mean much to you when you say, 'We don't communicate.'"

"I don't know," said Carol.

I went on. "Do you have trouble talking? Being understood by somebody?"

"No."

"What do you mean you don't communicate?"

Carol didn't answer directly but started to talk. "My mother always goes out somewhere at night."

"Yeah," I said.

"She works at night," Carol explained.

"Here I thought it was going to be a much more intriguing story!" (I was making an attempt to introduce further banter, and also the beginnings of some light flirtation with Jane, who was listening anxiously and with a quizzical look.)

Carol continued, "She teaches at night."

Jane broke in, "And how do you feel about that, Carol?"

"Well," responded Carol, "You usually don't stay home at night..."

At that point Sara began to talk, "What we usually do is—usually my mother leaves around five." I started to listen to her, and then realized that it was Sara who had reported that Carol didn't say anything, and yet she was now the one who was interrupting Carol. I stopped Sara in midsentence.

"Something just dawned on me. I *do* want to hear from you (Sara). But I was just realizing that I was asking Carol—and you know, suddenly it just shifted away—and I want to take it back for a minute and ask Carol to tell me. Will you?—about—your mommy going out at night?"

"She doesn't stay at home at all, usually."

"And do you miss the possibilities?" I asked.

"Yeah ... sort of..."

I went on, "What sort of things. We'll make her feel *really* guilty. Tell me—Has this been going on a long time?"

"Yeah ... six months..."

Jane came in. "But even before I did that, do you feel maybe I wasn't around to—ahhh—that I didn't do very much with you?"

"Yeah," Carol mumbled.

Jane bore on, "Do you really feel that? I mean—"

"Sort of..." Carol answered.

"Maybe she *really* feels that!" I said, making an emphasis to highlight Jane's obviously leading question.

"Maybe she does..." agreed Jane, with a touch of embarrassment.

I turned to Carol and asked, "Will you feel free to say anything you want in here?"

"Yeah."

"Just break in if you want," I invited. And I did this because I wanted Carol to know that she did not need to continue to be the shy, sparse-talking child any more. I had demonstrated that I would intervene to help her find room, and at the same time I wanted the others to feel there was space for them too. So it was time to check in with the last family member, Sara, and I spoke to her.

"I want to hear from you."

She had been looking at her father, and did not realize I was speaking to her. Suddenly it dawned on her as the silence grew, and she turned sharply to me, "From me?"

"Yeah," I answered.

"Hear about what?"

"Well," I continued, "You were the start of all this therapy, I gather."

"I was!"

"That's what they said."

"Who said that?"

"Your mother and dad."

"They did?"

I continued, "Yeah. That they were worried about you."

"They should be worried about themselves!"

"They should?" I asked. And at this point I realized that Sara had already done a major piece of work before I had ever seen the family, in putting more of the focus on her parents' relationship, than on herself. And it was not that she was blaming them for difficulties she was having. She was actually saying that she thought they should do some work on their own.

As Sara went on to say that there had been less fighting in the family during the past 6 months, she attributed it in part to her mother's being at work more. There just was no time to fight, she explained! She then went on to talk about the coming summer. "And this summer, I don't know if she's going to be teaching in the day, or at night."

"You don't know?" I queried.

"No, so . . ."

"Talk about communication," I added.

"Yeah," said Sara. " . . .When my sister first started to take piano—I keep thinking about this—and I never knew she was going to take piano—and I came home and I was locked out of the house—and I waited an hour and a half—two hours for them to come home. And I just never knew this was happening—so— no communication!"

"Absolutely sensational!" interjected Robert.

"What?" asked Sara.

Robert answered, "The most talking you children have ever done that I've ever heard since I've known you."

After a little disagreement about this statement between Jane and Robert, Jane said, " . . . but I think what Sara says is true—that we don't tend to com- municate about plans—or else, we do talk about plans and they never take place."

"That's not what I meant," objected Sara.

"Oh." said Jane.

Sara continued, now bringing in her sister to provide further example of how the family did not let each other in on plans, and how the children were affected. " . . . Carol can't ever know [what's happening] until she gets home at night—and then [sometimes] finds nobody home—and where are they?"

"You do get locked out sometimes, Carol," Jane said in confirmation.

"A lot of times," added Sara with some satisfaction.

And so the story of the keys and the feeling of being locked out came into focus again. It was this exchange that had come back to me as I entered their apartment building months later at the time of the home visit. Even more star- tling was the association Robert made about his own past. He revealed that when he was a youngster, from the age of 6 to around 9 years he was locked out of his own home every Thursday. That was the day the help had their time off, and his parents did not trust him to be left alone in the house, so they just locked up the house. When he returned from school, he had to wait around outside for several hours until they returned.

It was at this juncture that another film cassette ran out, and we had to stop the filming of this first interview. Nothing served better than this to demonstrate the impact of context on behavior. Suddenly we were no longer in a therapy session, but were friendly actors taking a break between scenes. We chatted about the way the cameraman was able to move around so easily, and we joked with the sound man, who asked us about the microphones, which were hanging from the ceiling and would get bumped occasionally. Robert and Sara asked me about the plans for the satellite broadcast, and seemed genuinely excited about it. We all behaved like old pros. And suddenly, as if a director called for places, we all returned to the mood of the session, and the sound engineer gave a signal, the whir of the camera began once more, and we were back into therapy again.

The talk shifted more now to the relationship between Jane and Robert, and at one point he said, "She even gets tense when I make a funny comment (when we're out some place)."

I asked, "Do I understand you that Jane gets upset at your performance?"

"For twenty-two years she's been concerned with putting me down constantly."

I reiterated, "Putting you down ..." but then my attention was caught by the fact that as Robert was talking, Sara had begun to hum, rather loudly. I broke off my response to Robert, and turning to her said, "Humming from Sara over there!"

"... I was doing it on purpose to make him mad," Sara confirmed.

I tried to get it clear. "But you were doing something to irritate him then?"

"I think I was."

"Yeah," I said, "I heard you hum ... and I don't know if it's related, but your father and mother were just getting into something that sounds important to me—that he feels put down."

Sara entered a disclaimer. "I wasn't even listening."

"Maybe in the back of your head you heard it somewhere." There was a little further exchange, and a period where Robert got off on some stories about the sea and the Coast Guard. It seemed to me that Sara's disruption had really served to get in the way of Jane and Robert confronting one another. I interrupted the flow by saying, "The humming started—I don't know if it was meant to interrupt you—it had that effect, almost—but—but—you said for years you were put down."

Robert resumed, "My experience with Jane is—although we occupy the same space which is a household, or a home, we are in different time spans—we have entirely different life qualities—and what has kept us together sometimes, I'm not quite sure."

I turned to the girls. "Are you girls aware that there is that kind of tension

... and do you ever think about why they stay together—what in the world keeps them together?" This direct confrontation is important, I believe, because when such a basic issue is present in the family, even though it may be explicitly avoided, it has been my experience that all family members have an awareness of it. Sara's response brought the issue to an even sharper definition.

"I don't think there's any reason to get divorced, though .. At the moment I don't feel like being destroyed ... people say if parents get divorced the kids are usually destroyed."

Now the issue of divorce had been openly talked about, and the children didn't want it to happen and the parents didn't want it to happen, even though they were not thrilled, and perhaps never had been, with the marriage, I tried to find out more about how Jane and Robert felt. He had been so glib, so verbal, that it was easy to experience him as walled off and perhaps impervious to feeling. After he talked about being put down for 22 years, I said that he must have felt very hurt. This simple statement seemed to touch him, and I believe was an important connection the two of us made. Shortly after, I talked to Jane about her frustration. She acknowledged that by not evincing interest in his projects she protected herself against being hurt. As she spoke of her despair tears came to her eyes, and Robert saw them.

From the session, I told the family that I thought the strain between the two parents was where the work lay. It was my belief that the concern about the girls, while having some basis, actually was serving to deflect scrutiny from the plight of the parents. It was because the family had been working in therapy already that I felt I could move this quickly to identify the problem as between the parents.

Another reason I moved that quickly was the pressure of the filming time. The 60 minutes were over, and I know I had been aware as each 10 minutes passed, as each break came and we started a new 10 minute segment that I wanted to capture a flow of the session for the video satellite presentation. Again, it was to me a convincing demonstration of the power of the context in shaping behavior, and in my current work I am continuing to explore this kind of influence. If it could so affect my own behavior when I was attempting to be professional, how much must the context affect all behavior at times when there is no awareness of the subtle cues and signals.

The Gormans and I said goodbye. I had liked each of them. I was drawn to Sara's directness and her vitality. Her desire to grow and to experiment was exciting. Carol was shy yet her tenderness and her sharpness came through, and her beauty and winsomeness were very appealing. Jane looked so tired, but beneath that drab and weary stance was a liveliness, a sexiness, a wit, and a desire to live. And Robert, bogged in his swamp of words and stories, loaded with more information than an encyclopedia publisher could use, still emerged as a remarkable man. Inventive, clever, imaginative, and in the midst of it often terribly boring, he nevertheless showed his own tenderness and vulnerability beneath it all, and his pain at the long history of self-defeats was evident and moved me to want to help not only him, but the four of them.

The Family

As we parted that night, I said I would be in touch with them soon, and they all seemed pleased at this. My original plan had been to see them for this special consultation, and then arrange a referral for further therapy if that seemed indicated. So I was surprised that I had become this involved so rapidly and un-expectedly. A short time later an opportunity arose to videotape a family session in a television studio, and my thoughts immediately turned to the Gormans. It was a chance to meet again, and also their willingness to work before cameras made them immediate candidates for such a project. I phoned, and again Robert discussed the possibility with the others and called me back to say they would be delighted.

The session was scheduled for the PBS studio in Trenton, New Jersey, but the thought of a 2 hour trip from New York apparently did not dampen their enthusiasm. Well before the scheduled starting time they arrived, Robert in a stylish different suit, and Jane in another rather drab outfit. Both girls were tired, but Carol seemed almost asleep. Our second session ranged from problems in ar-ranging family schedules, to the family reactions to Robert's "fake" (as Sara named them) heart attacks. But the session, all of us seated on a raised platform, bathed in spotlights, with three cameras rolling around the murky background, moved us all closer together. I knew we had evolved a therapeutic relationship, and we would be seeing each other again.

During the Fall of 1974 we arranged to meet for family sessions in my office about once a month. The issue of payment came up almost immediately. Of course, the first two sessions were no problem because it was a kind of ex-change of services arrangement. But now the context had shifted again. The family felt the two sessions had been helpful, and they were motivated to con-tinue. I think one factor that may have motivated Robert was his satisfaction at having been able to arrange sessions with me. He was used to trying unusual schemes, and here was one that had really succeeded. I knew the family could afford very little, but I felt it was important to make a contract together. I sug-gested something I have done with other patients and families. It was a standard monthly fee. For a flat fee of 50 dollars a month, I agreed to see the family for at least one regular family session a month, plus any other sessions, family, couple, or individual, that might be decided on by all of us, depending on the continuing situation in the family. The Gormans agreed, and a new phase of therapy was entered.

For the next few months the family sessions moved in focus from the parents' struggles with each other, to problems involving cooperation in the family and concerns about the problems of the girls. As time progressed, sessions with just Jane and Robert were scheduled in between the family sessions. This allowed an opportunity for the couple to concentrate on their interactions, while at the same time the family sessions facilitated the whole group's working on their relationships and goals. I found myself often acting as a model for the parents, and also as a moderator in promoting clearer and more open communication among the family members. Often Robert would move into a somewhat aloof position from which he would pontificate, while Jane and the girls would become embroiled in struggle. Jane seemed especially concerned about Sara and worried about her school adjustment. She was obviously bright, but she found it difficult to concentrate and openly disliked much of her time at school. The problem of Sara's school continued throughout the 3 years of treatment, but gradually a solution evolved through the anguish and the false starts. Perhaps because Sara was entering adolescence first, Jane experienced most anxiety. You may recall what a difficult time it had been for her, since it was then that her own father left for the war, and she had little support from her own mother. Robert's reaction to Jane was usually one of critical nonhelpfulness, and he seemed only too ready to back away and remove himself from the vortex of anxiety.

Late in 1974 one session centered on issues of taking other people's property. Both Sara and Carol had been taking things, although Carol had taken money only from family members, and this seemed more acceptable. Sara had taken some property from neighbors for whom she had been babysitting, and this blew into the open and was of great concern to Jane. In that session I encouraged everyone to talk about things they had taken, and recalled a time when I was young and had taken things, and described how I had felt. This method of sharing some personal experience, as a way of helping others get in touch with their own feelings and also of encouraging others to reveal more details, is one that I find very useful.

By and large, I fostered an attitude of minimizing the disaster quotient in the childrens' development. It was part of a natural evolution, I would explain, for there to be mini-crises and tense issues between parents and young people. Throughout I felt comfortable in this approach and convinced that both girls were essentially strong and developing in a positive way. It is true that I did not have to live with the evolving turbulence of their particular adolescent household, and this was certainly an advantage for me in maintaining my calm. But I was living in my own household with developing adolescents so my input was not entirely from an isolated mountain.

The Couple

Whatever the reasons, and reasons are not easily grasped, the family stayed together, struggled together, and reported that fighting among themselves had lessened. Early in 1975 the sessions with the whole family were put on an *ad hoc* basis, but the parental couple now continued to have sessions with me about twice a month. One of the things that had so struck me was that although the family had great potential energy, it continued to function with a sense of deadness in it. One of my prime goals was to involve myself in the work with the family in such a way that I might induce more feelings of liveliness into its members.

In the early Spring of 1975 I saw Jane and Robert together in one of our regular sessions, and as usual there was some debate about seating arrangements. Also, as usual, Jane did not really care where she sat. During the beginning of the session I got into a rather ridiculous exchange with Robert about voice resonance. It was a characteristic of his style to become lost in words (by his own description, a "lecturer"), and therapists as well as family members could become drowned in his verbal outpour. To counter this I used several strategies, all of them designed to ridicule, or poke fun at, or to lighten the overload. Sometimes I would engage in equally redundant discussion, while at other times I would try and say outrageous things, always attempting to throw the exchange off balance and to create some new possibility for movement.

I opened the session by saying it had been quite some time since we had met together.

"A rejuvenation," said Robert. His voice was usually very deep and full, but this time it literally rumbled in depth and richness.

"I can't talk that deeply," I marvelled.

"Why?" asked Robert.

"It's in the chest," I answered.

"He used to be called 'The Voice'," reported Jane with some suggestion of still being impressed.

"You resonate up here," Robert intoned, pointing to his nasopharynx.

"You can resonate in your chest, too," I said again.

"No," corrected Robert. And we were into a long and ridiculous debate. Robert called on the book written by one of his clients. "He was a proponent of speech," he went on.

"Uh huh," I murmured.

"He wrote a great book, called..."

"The reverberating sinuses," I interjected. And so it went. Finally, I jumped up, went over to him, and grasping his hand, placed it on my chest, as I said, "Listen! Feel it when I talk! It reverberates!"

Robert started up again, and I broke in with, "Have you read *my* book?"

Jane laughed. But Robert hadn't finished. "I have a feeling that the resonation is here," he continued, pointing to his nose. "And this picks up the vibrations—and there's a vibrator attuned to the resonator that..."

"Oh, you can make anything up," I interrupted.

Jane laughed again.

"You're facile and clever enough. You can make it up!"

"He says things so positively you believe it. He does the same thing to me," added Jane.

Now I tried a shift. Anything to break up the pattern. "How the hell *are* you, anyway?"

Robert answered straight off, "Physically, I'm not too well."

"More fake heart attacks?" I asked.

"I don't think they're fake at all!" objected Robert.

"No," I protested, "We went through that once. We have it on tape, so let's not waste more tape on that!"

"At least your teeth aren't falling out," said Jane, now seemingly a little caught up herself in the slight craziness that we were developing.

"Your teeth!" I exclaimed. "One of *mine* did!"

"Jesus!" said Robert.

The bantering continued until Robert said to me, "The way you carry on with me!—and I often wonder why!"

"Because you're fun!" I said.

"No, I'm *not* fun!"

"You *are* fun! ... I see the fun in you, and I feel very few people try and elicit it. They get caught in the seriousness."

"The only people who elicit it are my children—they see the potential of fun."

"I see it ..." I added.

"Lots of people see it," said Jane.

After a few more exchanges Robert concluded, "I live in a fairly isolated world, so I can't tell how I'm fun."

Jane responded with, "You're very witty though—sometimes it surprises me ..." And she laughed. I felt an accomplishment in having stopped the verbal excess, in having raised directly the liking I had of Robert and his fun and playfulness, and in his acknowledging the fun his children often found with him. Jane's defining his wittiness and implying her delight in it was an added bonus. I now turned to her.

"So, what's driving you crazy these days?"

"Nothing," she answered somewhat nervously. "Nothing at the moment."

I went on to say I asked because "... you're sitting here looking so nervous, clutching your hands." It seemed like a little shaky ground, telling Jane she looked so anxious, and depressed. I decided to risk also telling her that she did not seem to look after her hair. It seemed risky because it was so personal, and she looked so fragile at that moment.

"Why don't I take time to be pretty?" she asked.

"You never have," said Robert.

"Lie in a bubble bath for an hour or so, and just soak," I said, adding, "I'm not trying to pick on you. I'm wondering, are *you* concerned?"

"... I'm aware of that. I think Robert looks after himself a lot more. Filing his nails ... the whole world could be falling apart, and he always does ..."

This took the focus off Jane, and Robert grabbed the bait, spiraling the two of them into the old kind of debate. I broke it up with,

"Why aren't you fun any more?"

"It's gone out of our marriage," Robert pronounced.

I then added that the reason I fooled around with him was to try and bring some of the fun back. Jane came in with, "I don't know if it ever was there."

"Can this marriage be saved?" I asked, trying for a little of Robert's resonance.

Jane laughed. But went on, "I can't say it's been gloom all the time."

"So let's start there," I said.

Laughing again, Jane said, "I know it hasn't been gloom all the time."

"Well," I went on, "apparently Robert felt there has been some fun."

"No," disagreed Robert.

"Well," I answered, "you said it had all gone out, so that implies there must have been some in there."

"How much has gone out is very little," answered Robert.

"I see. A grain of fun. Have you ever seen an hour glass with just one grain of sand in it—and that was it—and it ran out *very* quickly."

"It took twenty years!" laughed Jane. "One grain went out very *slowly*!"

Robert mused, "Some picture—one grain of sand!"

I made my point. "Well, it's *never* been a lot of fun. So I think we should realize that... I think *I* should realize that, before I set my sights too high. Because, for Christ's sake, if it's never been too much fun I can't really break my ass trying to make it something it's never really been."

"Could it be?" mused Robert. "...What are the ingredients?"

I responded, "I don't know. You? The two of you? Your family? The people in it? And the options? The possibilities? The networks? The friends? The relationships? These are the ingredients."

The flow had now changed, and the two of them were ready to discuss more seriously the nature of their relationship, and the quality of their marriage.

"Well," Robert accused, "you didn't want to get married in the beginning..."

"Is that right?" I asked Jane. "Where did you get such wisdom?"

"Because I'd been forewarned by everybody in my family," she answered.

"Who?"

"My grandmother—my mother."

"Why?"

"Because they were so miserable."

So the session moved from obfuscation to somewhat brutal frankness, to rather poignant memory. And through this fabric appeared a thread that carried us through the next sessions and that led, later that Spring, to their joining one of my couples' groups.

The Group

There were three couples altogether in the group, and all started in the group together. All were at the further boundary of middle age, and all had children. All six members worked, surely a sign of our evolving society. One was a professional couple, both health workers; the woman in the second couple was a social worker, and the husband was a business man, like Robert. Jane, of course, was a teacher. I had felt that including the Gormans in such a group would be very helpful. First, I knew that it would help them to feel less isolated and would also show them that I felt good about having them work with other couples in my practice. This, I believed, would counter feelings that I thought had developed to some extent in relationship to a specialness about them, related to their having been selected for the video program, and also because they had previously been a clinic family.

Next, I hoped that their exchange with the other couples would help them realize the similarity of problems that all families face in life today. Further, I hoped that all the members in the group would help one another to become aware of their strengths and to learn new possibilities from the experience of the others. These hopes were realized to a large extent in the group, which lasted over 2 years and finally terminated in the summer of 1977.

Robert was well accepted by the group, certainly a different role from the usual insular position he often took in other situations. Henry, the other business man, liked and respected Robert, and the two of them would have intense discussions about business in the coffee breaks, and after the session. Henry told the group on several occasions how helpful Robert had been to him, and how perceptive his ideas were. Robert in turn grew to have increasing respect for the other man, a psychologist, and in a moment of high praise told him that he wished he had been his analyst all along.

Jane held her own in the group and, although more quiet than the others, still was able to express much more than she had been able to when meeting alone with Robert and me. Over the months her appearance changed, and she began to take an increased interest in how she looked. Her concern about too much drinking came to light, and she explored her family history and confirmed her fear that she might be headed for serious problems in this direction. The psychologist, Jim, also exposed his own problem with alcohol, and the family dynamics in both couples were compared, with the result that stigma was minimized and the feeling of concerned help was palpable.

Robert began to discuss his business ventures regularly, and slowly the indisputable fact emerged that he was having more and more "episodes" of success. It also became clear that each success seemed to trigger a wave of anxiety, and the initiation of some self-destructive piece of sabotage. Wonderfully, the group did not attack him at these times but continued to express a sense of optimism that eventually showed itself again as another wave of success on

Robert's part. Jane's perpetual sense of doom and weariness was tolerated by the group and, in that setting, began to feel excessive even to her. It lessened. And with that, Jane showed an interest not only in her appearance, but also in her career. The first barrier was a set course she had to take in order to keep her present teaching qualifications. She managed this. Next, she set about to achieve her master's degree in teaching, registering for courses that would gradually accumulate the necessary points.

All the while the Gorman's concern with the development of their girls would become the topic in the group. This concern was also reflected in periodic family meetings, most often with the couple and Sara, occasional private couple sessions with the parents, and in 1976 several individual sessions with me, at the request of Sara.

The Children

Sara had been the start of it all, or so the story had originally been recounted by her parents. But from the first family session I had tried to minimize any attempts to pathologize her. My early focusing on the couple relationship emphasized my therapeutic direction, and the shift of family sessions to an intermittent basis after a few months gave further support to my intention.

Throughout the first 2 years school problems dominated conversations about Sara. In the second year she was moved to an alternative high school, which was small, and because of a rather idiosyncratic headmaster proved to be a limiting and unpleasant experience for her. The result of this was several months during which she stayed at home a good deal of time. She was not alone, actually because her father ran much of his business from an office there, but she viewed it herself as a period of no small intellectual stagnation.

In early 1976 she asked to meet with me alone for a few sessions. I have no rules about families having to meet as a total group or not at all, so I was happy to arrange the sessions. Sara was now developing into her own person—an evolving and lovely example of adolescent individuation. She had begun to slim down and was showing an exciting abandon with her dress, which was tasteful and yet creatively *au courant*. Her personality had always been alive and exciting, but her physical beauty was now emerging, and she was truly a young woman. She told me that she was running away from home if she were not allowed more freedom, and if she could not go to a boarding school the following semester. She was tired of the constrictions, and the narrowness of her parents; of her mother's wearisome concern, and of her father's sporadic outbursts, alternating with withdrawal and pontification.

In one way of looking at it, family therapy means enlarging the family structure by letting the therapist join the system as an important member. With the Gormans it had really been a question of who was going to parent in the family, who was going to take charge. From the first session I took charge, and began to role model for them. Sara had been bursting into the middle of conversations, had been answering for other people, and had been especially active when there seemed to be any meaningful exchange between her parents. I was the first one to interrupt her and to give room to the others, and she responded almost immediately by being less disruptive. In a later family session when she had left the consultation room in a burst of anger, I followed her and we had a loud argument as I challenged her on this kind of heavyweight maneuver in working on problems with her parents. She came back to the session and struggled with the rest of us in trying to resolve the issue.

As part of the strategy, I tried to convey to the girls that their parents had business to work on as spouses, and that the parents and I needed to resolve the depression that both Jane and Robert felt. In thinking about the dynamics myself, I concluded that when the girls felt that they were going to be destroyed by the divorce (the depression), they had done their best to move in between their parents to try and keep them together.

Later, as Sara began to move into her own adolescent life, the dynamic reversed to some extent, and she began to feel she would be destroyed if she could *not* leave them, and set up a life apart from them. It was because of this struggle between staying and leaving, between loving and hating, that she asked for my help in the individual sessions.

"You see, I cannot honestly live at home. I cannot exist in that house. I'm obviously going to have to go somewhere else to be happy. Everything I like she takes away from me, or wants to, anyway . . ."

"And do you feel they are trying to run your life?" I asked.

"No . . . I live in that house because I have no other means of support. I'm not going to just run away unless they do something to me they haven't . . . Everybody fights—and they've got so many pressures, and they're taking it out on me—never on my sister—she's too quiet, too weak—which isn't true! She's stronger than me! I don't know. They think I'm always lying to them, and I am."

I asked, "What you call, 'Lying,'—is it holding back, or telling just part . . .?"

"It's telling part. And then they find out and call it lying."

"I see."

"My mother I don't like—at all! I love her because she brought me on this earth, and she's my mother—and because I'm a kind person. I can't hate her! But I don't like her. I don't. And it's hard to live with her.

"My father is easy to live with, and he's even stricter than my mother. My mother's a lot more liberal than he is. But he's just so much nicer a person to talk to.

"But sometimes I just can't tell them things. I don't know why."

"Mmmmmmm," I said, wanting to show Sara I was listening, but feeling embarrassed at the therapeutic cliche.

"I can't tell my mother and my father . . . I'm afraid to tell people things to their face. I'm afraid of how they'll react. I'm really very sensitive. I hate being screamed at, because I've been screamed at for 15 years by them. I guess if I can avoid the hassle I will."

"Avoid the hassle?" I queried.

Sara replied, "I don't think I do anything wrong—so I'll do it anyway. So I guess from now on I'll . . . if I make a decision ahead, I'll just tell them, and if they don't like it, they don't like it—that's all. There's nothing I can do about it.

"I'm not saying I won't listen to what they say. I will. I'll listen, and if I think it's right, then I'll respect how they feel—because I have a lot of respect for them. I'm not a totally rebellious kid who's going to do anything. But if I think it's wrong—and they don't listen to me—then, I'm just not going to respect what they say. And that's reasonable.

"My mother'll listen—and she'll change. My father is *so* stubborn—everything has to be his way. He won't change in any way. It drives me up the wall!"

I really felt I was in the midst of this family. Sara could tell me what she was feeling, and I reeled at the swing of her ambivalence. But I realized she was telling me the truth as her feelings veered from anger at her mother to frustration at her father, and feelings of closeness to him, and then feelings of confidence in her mother's flexibility and capacity to change. And out of all this mixture came her growing independence and self-assurance, and what I considered her beautiful statement of self-assertion, tempered with concern for her parent's opinions. She was growing up, and I believed it had been possible because Jane and Robert were growing too. There was no longer the need for Sara to be in the middle so her parents could survive. And now that Sara was moving away, she could safely do it because she felt her parents were solid enough now to provide some support for her if she needed it.

The crisis over boarding school subsided, as plans for a private school in New York evolved. This was feasible as Robert was steadily becoming more successful in his business. From babysitting jobs, Sara moved to providing a part-time messenger service for her father's business, and also later obtained work as an assistant to her uncle. As a messenger for her father she was not always as speedy or without faults as he would have wished. But the mail did eventually go through, and this set up a new relationship with him and provided extra financial independence for her.

Carol had played her role in the family with a very different style. Nevertheless, her shy and quiet behavior also served to keep the parents together, in their mutual concern for her. Robert felt especially close to Carol at the beginning (his little sweetheart), and Jane worried that Carol would have the same problems in reading and learning that she did, and felt that her shyness might mean that Carol would find increasing difficulty in making friends at school.

It was in the first session with the family that I decided to break through the shyness and reserve if I could. I had not let Sara interrupt Carol, but later another instance occurred where I noticed that Carol had tried several times to ask who the name of her father's psychiatrist had been, but each time had been ignored. I finally intervened when Robert answered her on the third try.

"What's her name?" Carol had asked.

"Dr. Morgan," finally answered Robert.

"I was thinking," I said, "about your asking who she, or he, was. And I noticed you asked at least three times, or so it seemed to me. Was that right?"

"Yes," answered Carol quietly, turning to look at me.

"At least three times," I went on. "And the first two times it was as if no one heard you."

"Yeah," she replied, softly, with the beginning of a gentle smile showing.

"Except—I think everybody *heard* you."

"Mmmmmmm," and Carol continued to smile softly.

I went on. "Sooo, the first time—then you asked again. And I thought, 'I wonder if Carol will ask again.'"

Carol was looking at me now, and smiled broadly, with appreciation.

"And you did!" I continued. "And I thought, 'Hey! When you really want to know something, you can speak out.' And you finally got an answer! You had to keep at it though." And Carol was still beaming at me, and I knew we had formed a good partnership and understanding. I concluded, "I was thinking how funny it must feel to say something and have everybody act as if you hadn't spoken."

Carol reacted differently through the remainder of that session. She was more assertive and looked confident. She and I continued to feel close from then on. I saw her in the family sessions, and it often happened through the years of my working with the family that I would speak to her on the telephone when I would call to arrange time for an appointment. We would chat, and she would catch me up on her life. I would usually assure her that I was always available if she wanted to come in and talk. In one of our phone calls she told about a volunteer job she was going to get at the New York Zoo for the summer. It was a wonderful job for her, because she loved animals so much. And she was able to travel independently and to perform well. This was an important transition for her. In one family session the special focus had been on Carol's school difficulties. She was having little success, and Jane especially was concerned that the continuing series of disappointing school experiences could have a permanent influence on Carol's educational and personal future. It was in 1975 that a decision was made that a thorough evaluation of Carol's learning skills and achievements should be undertaken. Jane had the connections through her own work to find excellent resource people, and the study was undertaken. The results showed Carol to have significant learning problems, and a remedial program was suggested. This proved to be of great importance in Carol's development. Her next year at school was much happier. Although she continued to be shy and somewhat reluctant to make friends (especially as compared to Sara who now had become very socially active and was very popular), she developed no marked problems and continued to find her own, albeit quiet, way. She had developed in her adolescence into a very beautiful young woman, and both she and Sara looked forward to being together in the Fall of 1977 in a private school they both liked very much.

So although problems with the girls continued to surface in the family and couples' sessions, the frequency diminished. Eventually, both parents agreed that they were dealing (and dealing more effectively) with the kind of normal adolescent crises that plague every family and that also challenge every family to reevaluate old values and find new perspectives.

The Keys

In July of 1977 it had been a little over 3 years that I had known the Gormans. I found that they had become a real part of my life. I said earlier that I liked them all, so the satisfaction I had felt at their joys and growth is easily understood. So too is the pain at their disappointments and frustrations. On balance the growth of the family, and of its members, seemed to outweigh the rest. Sara was on a trip to California, backpacking with a girlfriend. How wonderful to see the parents' pleasure at her going, compared to those anxious moments in the home visit when they could hardly bear to have her spend the night with her friend.

Carol had gone on a vacation with Jane and Robert, and the three of them had had a marvelous time canoeing together down 21 miles of river.

Robert still managed to skim close to the edge of disaster from time to time in his business, but his successes were mounting in an undeniable pattern, and he was proud that the coming year's tuition for his daughters was already assured. A lecturer still, but less of a lecturer, he had mellowed and dropped some of his aloofness, so more of the tenderness and more of the fun emerged.

Jane had completed all of her work for her master's degree, so new professional possibilities lay ahead for her. She also had a new sense of her own independence, and this was reflected in the way she now took more care with her appearance. She looked and was more open to the world.

It was also in July that the couples' group came to an end. It was a natural ending, but the members had mixed feelings. Jim and Lillian wanted to continue and planned some further family sessions. Henry and Selma were looking for no more miracles and planned to work together on any problems that came up without any therapy sessions. Robert felt disappointed that the group had not penetrated to a "deeper" level. In spite of this disclaimer, the impact the group had on his way of relating was acknowledged by all the other members. Jane felt the group had been of great help to her. She had seen new ways of looking at old problems and had found encouragement to move out more on her own.

I felt sadness that the group was ending and a further loss at the realization that my formal connection with the Gormans was also ending at the same time. We had all gained insights in the group, but the experience of being together as friends had probably overshadowed everything else. A year earlier, the Gormans had issued an invitation to the whole group to join them and some other friends to watch the spectacular parade of ships in "Operation Sail" during the bicentennial summer of 1976. There was no better view in town than through those big windows on Riverside Drive.

Robert had also touched me very much when after learning of my interest in scuba diving he brought in about 40 back issues of "Skin Diver" magazine for me. I remembered things like this as I sat with the group that last night. I had brought a bottle of Bristol Milk Sherry, and a plate of fancy cookies, and we toasted each other, and the future of us all, and the memories. We laughed together, and felt sad at leaving. Jim and Lilly asked everyone to come up to their summer place for a weekend. (I later learned Jane and Robert accepted and had a wonderful time.)

I knew Sara was out west and during the session, Jane said, "She called us last night. . . I think she really just wanted to call us. She couldn't get her sleeping bag into her knapsack, or something like that.(Laughter.) She said, 'It's a long way from home if you have a problem' . . . She's been very nice about calling."

It was tender and moving. Jane who had such little warmth from her own mother was now enjoying warmth from her own daughter, as Sara was able to turn to her and really under the cover of the sleeping bag problem let her mother know she missed her and still needed her.

I suddenly became aware in the group that Jane was playing with a set of keys. "It's almost eerie," I said, "but I remember the first time we met. Do you remember? The keys came up. Sara had been locked out, and she said how she kept thinking about the fact that she didn't know where you were. 'Talk about communications!' she had said."

"It is sort of eerie," Jane agreed. "I have the keys because the reason I was a little late for the group is that Carol lost her keys today and was locked out. She called me at work, so I drove by before the group to let her in."

I thought how amazing it was that the keys came up again. Like a bookend metaphor, the keys in the first session, and the keys in the last session, with the ghost of keys from Robert's childhood drifting in the background. Really the same incident. First Sara locked out, and now Carol locked out. And yet there were such significant differences in the seemingly similar situations. In the first session, Sara was locked out. She didn't know that her parents had taken Carol to a piano lesson; she didn't know how to reach anyone, and finally it turned out that the key wasn't even in the family's possession but had been given to the "editor."

In the second instance, Carol was locked out, but she knew that she could turn to her parents for help. Her mother did have the key, and Carol knew where to call her. It was very clear who was in charge in the family, and there was communication and assurance of dependability. This same conviction was also demonstrated by Sara in her call from the West Coast. She knew she would be able to contact her parents, and she felt assurance that they cared, as she knew she cared.

I realized that when the members of this family knew where they were with themselves, they knew better where they were with each other. and this allowed all of them more freedom to move apart and more freedom to move together.

Near the end of the final group, Jane and Robert asked if I could have periodic family sessions together with the girls and them, if some issue came up that they wanted help with. I really was happy that I may have the chance from time to time to see them all again.

6

Anatomy
Of a Therapist

Harry J. Aponte, A.C.S.W.

For me, the most credible analysis of my activity in an interview comes after repeated viewings of a videotaped session, a *post factum* objectivity. The explanation is teased out through a minute analysis of each sequence and a rereading of my visceral responses in the encounters with a family that are resurrected for me in reviewing the videotape. In a session, I consciously and unconsciously filter these spontaneous reactions along with cooler observations through an internalized theoretical framework that lends coherency to my transactions with the family and gives direction to my behavior. In this writing I will review segments of an interview and comment on how my personal experience in the session, coached in a particular theoretical orientation, guided my understanding and actions with the family.

I will try to say something personal and something theoretical. There is more that I would like to tell about each, but I can't or won't. I will also say it about therapy with a poor family because most people are poor and most of the people who come to our clinics and agencies are poor.

A low socioeconomic family is particularly vulnerable to structural underorganization. Family members often lack contextual support for their individual development and for the elaboration of the interpersonal structure of their family relationships. Families trapped within ghettoized, powerless communities struggle against great odds, not only in dealing with their social circumstances but in developing the basic emotional and social tools for ordinary living. They may well be "underorganized" in the sense that the social structures within the families may be relatively few, relatively inflexible, and relatively discontinuous.

In therapy, the clinician is entering a family's life not as it exists in some one-dimensional diagram of the family's structural relationships, but as it is being lived from day to day. Personality organization and family structures do not exist in static states. They are always in motion, changing and evolving. The conceptual labels that we apply to people and families are abstractions from life. The clinician in therapy does not interact with abstractions but with people in action with him or her at the moment they encounter one another in the context of the interview. The therapist achieves some understanding of a family through experiencing them, their words, their behavior. The therapist's impact on the family and its members is not through constructions in the clinician's mind, but in the actions and the reactions of that therapist to the people in the family.

For a therapist, diagnosis is recognizing repetitive patterns of thinking, feeling, acting, and communicating in the contexts of the life operations that people are asking us to affect. This understanding cannot be conveyed to a clinician just by words as in the relating of historical data. It is too complex and not in the full conscious grasp of a teller. To infer information, a therapist experiences another's experience through himself. A therapist creates a situation that is the same as or that parallels an operation that is a problem to the person or the family. A therapist elicits a transaction between his or her person and a family or among family members themselves in which he or she becomes in some way a participant. In this active context which is created by a therapist and a family, the family members can take the therapist through their own experience of the issue that concerns them.

In the experience, a therapist can perceive the people, consciously and unconsciously, directly and through the mirror of his or her being. If deciphered by the therapist, these direct observations and indirect readings can subsequently be labeled for communication. However, labeling is not required for a therapist to respond purposefully. In the midst of a transaction, the meaning of a family's behavior can be unconsciously "understood" and can be reacted to therapeutically from the basis of this instinctive "understanding." A therapist's theory and training reflexively sift meanings and shape responses.

The Interview

In the following depiction of a part of a session, I will expose as much of my own personal reaction to the encounter as I dare along with my clinical premises. I certainly make no pretense of knowing all that went on within myself as I dealt with this family and they dealt with me. I will describe some of what I observed and thought at the time of the interview and some of what I read into my own behavior after reviewing videotapes of the session.

The family is a low-income, black, single-parent family. There are 12 children in the family; all but three have left the home. The mother, Mrs. Jeffrey, came to the session with the remaining three at our request—Raymond, 17; Daniel, 14; and Stanley, 11, the identified patient.

BACKGROUND

I was to do this interview as a demonstration for a group of clinicians. There were several circumstances that created a stressful atmosphere for the session. The first was that this mother had been reluctant to make the appointment. She informed the intake secretary that the counselor had said her son had problems in school. She, herself, did not have a problem with him at home and was coming in only at the school's insistence. I decided to see the family in the Clinic for the sake of the demonstration. However, I would have preferred to have seen them in the school for the first session because, as presented, the problem was between the school on one side and Stanley and his mother on the other, not between Mrs. Jeffrey and Stanley.

The family arrived an hour early for the interview and I was half an hour late. The waiting added to their perceptible annoyance about being in the clinic. Mrs. Jeffrey gave me a cool reception in the waiting room when we met. I became apprehensive as I anticipated asking them for permission to videotape the session. When we entered the interviewing room, I found myself, to my surprise and discomfort, introducing myself as the Director of the Clinic. I was protecting myself and implying that the request for videotaping was related to the special circumstances, not only of the observing group, but of my position. The tension they felt, particularly the mother and oldest son, and that I was experiencing, is not conveyed in the videotape but was very real in the room. The atmosphere remained tense for a good while into the session.

Therapist: I'm the Director of the Clinic here and what I have is a group of clinicians who can see you here...
Mrs. J.: People who?
Therapist: ... psychologists, social workers, you know [Mrs. Jeffrey makes an expression of displeasure] ... you have an attitude about ... you don't like that?
Mrs. J.: I really don't.
Raymond: I don't either.
Therapist: You don't ... alright. Then maybe I should have somebody else see you because I have to do this for them. This is like ... we have conferences and we show each other the work that we do. It's up to you; I mean, nobody is putting pressure on you.

I was in a bind. They threatened to refuse the taping and I countered with the threat to withdraw myself after having announced I was the director. In the waiting area, they had already threatened me with not accepting me and left me feeling insecure. I felt excluded by them, treated by them as an alien to them and their circumstances. That hurt and irritated me but it did not show. I looked deliberately relaxed and in control as I sipped coffee. A forced retreat would not have brought me any closer to them. They conceded ground.

Mrs. J.: Well, I don't have anything to hide.
Therapist: It won't be ... it's not shown to people outside. This is strictly, you know, among the professional group.
Raymond: Uh, hum.
Therapist: Is it all right?
Mrs. J.: Sure.
Therapist: Okay. All I know is that Stanley has some problems at school, but that he has no problems at home. So you need to introduce me to your family. My name is Harry Aponte and who are the rest of the family?

The family was sitting clockwise: the oldest son, Raymond, mother, an empty chair, Stanley and Daniel. I addressed the mother first. She had been the principal voice of the family's objection to being there. By asking her to introduce her children, I asked her permission to speak to them. In the midst of our tug of war, I was trying to gain her acceptance by acknowledging her power and position. After she introduced them, I addressed the oldest son, Raymond. He was sitting immediately to her right, was conspicuously mirroring her attitude of disdain and impassiveness. I wanted to acknowledge Raymond's position as the oldest. I would proceed to the younger ones only after having touched base with him. The gesture of deference to Raymond reflected a very preliminary hypothesis that was later borne out that the protection of the family's borders against outside intruders in the present context was, in a special way, this son's function.

Mrs. J.: This is Raymond, Stanley and Daniel [she points to each].
Therapist: Okay ... how old are you, Raymond?
Raymond: Seventeen.
Therapist: You're seventeen. You're at home?
Raymond: Uh, huh.
Therapist: And Stanley, you're eleven, right?
Mrs. J.: Will be in May.
Therapist: Will be in May? [then turning to Daniel]
Daniel: Fourteen.
Therapist: And Daniel, you're fourteen. [addressing Mrs. Jeffrey] Okay, these are the only three at home? [she indicates agreement]. Okay ... all I know is that the counselor said that he's got problems and thinks that the kids pick on him at school.
Mrs. J.: Yes, well, this is what she said. You know, he has this tendency to think that everybody's picking on him and nobody likes him. He has this mole on his chin that just grew on there from nowhere, and I took him one time ...
Therapist: When did it grow?

She had an obvious mole on her own chin, too, but I could not bring myself to comment on it—which I might have otherwise done had I not felt cautious with her.

Mrs. J.: About four years ago. And I took him at that time to have it off, but he was frightened and wouldn't let them take it off, so, since then he said the children just teases him and call him "moley face" and all kind of names, you know, and oh, she (the counselor) says it's getting to be a problem in school. So, he is quick to fight and he's quick to, you know, take it upon himself. He is always fighting in school. This is what she says. She feels it's some things that he can overlook, you know, but he doesn't.

Therapist: If he has . . . if he feels this way about kids in school, doesn't he have any of this kind of problem at home? In the neighborhood?

Mrs. J.: Oh . . . yeah.

Therapist: Oh, he does!

Mrs. J.: Yeah, in the neighborhood . . . kids . . . they get into it every now and then, but I don't allow them to fight at home.

Therapist: Who's they?

Mrs. J.: These two. He [pointing to Raymond] likes to pick on him sometimes.

Since we did not have present the school personnel who were making the complaint, I could do little with the report of a problem at school, particularly one to which the mother gave little credence. I needed something that was a problem for them at home, an issue which could be recreated right there in the interview.

Mrs. Jeffrey gave me an opening when she accused Raymond of teasing Stanley. I snatched the opportunity to move toward Raymond. It was a chance to connect with Raymond and approach Mrs. Jeffrey's protectiveness through Raymond. I moved carefully as we were all quite tense and tried to make bridges to Raymond—to his work, school, and other interests.

Therapist: What's your name again?

Raymond: Raymond.

Therapist: Raymond? I would think that you'd be the one who'd take care of him.

Mrs. J.: Uh, uh [indicating no].

Raymond: What do you mean by take care of him?

Therapist: Well, you are the oldest brother. I would expect that you would be the one that they would listen to.

Raymond: [laughing] . . . listen . . .

Therapist: They don't listen to you?

Mrs. J.: No, they don't.

Therapist: Raymond what are you doing . . . do you go to school or do you work?

Raymond: I go to school and work.

Therapist: Where do you go to school?

Raymond: North Philly High.

Therapist: What year are you in?

Raymond: Twelfth.

Therapist: You're in your last year?
Raymond: In my last year.
Therapist: Didn't North Philly win the championship (basketball) or something?
Raymond: Yeah.
Therapist: Are you interested in sports?
Raymond: Just boxing.
Therapist: Just boxing ... how interested are you in boxing?
Raymond: Very interested in boxing. [shifts in his chair, looks with a grin at the ceiling and then at me]
Therapist: I mean ...
Raymond: I want to be a boxer one day ... yeah ...
Therapist: Have you done any boxing?
Raymond: Uh, huh.
Therapist: Where have you done boxing?
Raymond: At the PAL Center on Manchester Street.
Therapist: Have you been in any kind of amateur bouts or are you just training?
Raymond: Just training.
Therapist: Uh, huh ... how much do you weigh?
Raymond: About 195 ... light heavyweight.
Therapist: Oh, no ... you would be a heavyweight.
Raymond: Light heavyweight.
Therapist: Light heavyweight?

Raymond and I, here, find ground on which we can both meet and compete. I, too, am interested in boxing and we dispute each other about whether or not he is a light heavyweight (the light heavyweight limit is 175 pounds). I engage him on this issue. I want him to like me and so we will continue to talk about boxing, but, I want him to respect me, so I am reluctant to back down in our disagreement. This discussion is a metaphor of the struggle between Raymond and myself as I believe he attempts to protect the family. If I can gain ground with Raymond the odds improve to win with the family, but while I try to join him, I must not shrink from him. If I do, I will lose status in my own eyes and possibly his. If I do not feel in control of the situation, I will become inhibited. The tension in me heightens at this point. I struggle between being accommodating and striking back. Being aware of that helped. Did he feel similarly?

Raymond: ... I just started gaining weight, really.
Therapist: Do you think you would be fighting at 175 or something like that?
Raymond: 178. (I let the 3 pound discrepancy pass.)
Therapist: Do you ever go see the fights at the Spectrum or the Arena?
Raymond: Sometimes.
Therapist: When was the last time you went?
Raymond: It was two ladies ... I forget.
Therapist: Two ladies [sniggering]. Oh, I wouldn't have gone to see that. Are you going to see the Briscoe–Hart fight?
Raymond: Ain't that tonight?
Therapist: That's the sixth ... I think that it's next week, next Tuesday night. Are you going?

Raymond: Yeah, I was thinking about going. [he uncrosses his arms for a moment and passes his hand behind his head.]
Therapist: The tickets are pretty expensive ... I thought I was going to go, but I think I am not going to go.

I had kidded Raymond about his going to see two ladies fighting which was joining him in a one-up position. His gesture of discomfort in answering about attending the Briscoe—Hart fight made me think he was not going. I retreated to join him in a one-down position by acknowledging that I probably would not go to the fight because it was expensive, which was true. He conceded me a small smile at the end of this interchange. I thought his defense loosened a bit and I tried to slip through to Daniel.

Therapist: Yeah, that's the camera [addressing Stanley and Daniel who are distracted by the moving video camera] ... Daniel, where do you go to school?
Daniel: Collins Junior High.
Therapist: Collins? What grade are you in now?
Daniel: Eighth.
Therapist: You are in the eighth grade? Are you doing alright in school? Do you have any problems in school?
Daniel: I got no problems.
Therapist: You got no problems in school or at home or any place else ... the only one who has problems is him (pointing to Stanley) ... are you saying yes or no? I said the only one who has problems is Stanley?
Daniel: I don't know.
Therapist: Oh, you don't know anything about it. Okay, well ... cause your mother was saying that Stanley had some kids picking on him in the neighborhood. You don't know anything about that?
Raymond: I don't consider that a problem. I mean, if they're going to pick on him and if he don't stop them from picking on him ... what else you gonna do.

I had hoped that the contact that I had with Raymond would allow me to reach Stanley through Daniel. But, I was getting too close to Stanley and Raymond cut off my move. Tension was up again.

Raymond: I mean, I don't know why they send him to a psychiatrist!
Therapist: Stanley, your brother said it's not a problem? You should be able to take care of it yourself.

Raymond was staring right at me, challenging me. I tightened up, but attempted to deflect his jab and make it an issue between Stanley and him.

Stanley: How?
Therapist: Right?
Stanley: Uh, huh.
Therapist: ... Is it a problem?
Stanley: Yeah.

I had been leaning forward in my chair and for the first time sat back with some feeling of relief as I finally got Stanley to acknowledge a problem. Raymond countered quickly.

Therapist: It is a problem ... how is it a problem?
Stanley (barely audible) They just keep bothering me.
Therapist: What?
Stanley: They just keep bothering me.
Raymond: He's at an early age now, I mean he don't know how to just ignore it ... people always get into a fight. He don't know how to just ignore it and walk away from it ... he can't do that at the moment.
Therapist (to Stanley): He says you should ignore it and walk away.
Stanley: What happens is they come back.
Therapist: Raymond, he says they come back ... what should he do?
Raymond: Are you trying to teach us how to talk, how to communicate ... what we should do at home, or what?

Raymond is too clever. He saw through my strategy and undid it. I felt caught but not defeated. I had already breached the family's defenses and did not experience myself as a total outsider as before. I leaned forward again in my chair and moved in with more confidence.

Therapist: I don't live at home. You're his older brother.
Raymond: I know that I'm his older brother.
Therapist: And he says he's got a problem on the street. I don't know whether there is something wrong with him or whether ... you know ... whether he looks for fights or whether he just simply should be handling himself ... taking care of himself. Like you said; you know, I don't know whether he should be going to see a psychiatrist or not and if it's just a matter that he should avoid the fights and talk his way out of it, then I'm not the one to tell him to do that. You all can do that better than I can.

I am feeling more confident and willing to offer them explicit recognition that Stanley was theirs and even to join their defense against the school. At this point in the encounter, I realized it was all Raymond versus me. I implied here a readiness to disengage rather than continue struggling with Raymond. I sensed the mother's silence and became convinced that she was instinctively watching to see the outcome of my encounter with him to decide her own stance toward me.

Therapist (looking at Raymond and Mrs. Jeffrey): I'm serious .., I mean because all I have to do is just call up the school and say to them, there's no reason for him to be here ... you know ... his family can tell him how to handle himself and that will take care of it ... there is no reason for him to continue to come down here.
Mrs. J.: Well why does that have to be a psychiatric problem because he gets into fights?
Therapist: It doesn't have to be.

I am talking a lot but my refusal to fight and willingness to line up with them draws her out to me. So I pressed my advantage.

Raymond: Well are they trying to say it's a psychiatric problem?

Therapist: You know, you know what I know . . . I don't have it right here [the intake sheet]. I left it in my office. It's like five lines and all I have is what you told the person here [the intake secretary]. Now, I can call the school and tell them this is no psychiatric problem and maybe they'll get off your back, but I don't know anything about it . . . honestly . . . I didn't talk with the school. I only have what you have to tell me, so, if it isn't a psychiatric problem and it's just that, it is something that he should be taking care of himself, then . . .

Mrs. J.: Well, she feels that he, you know, in the class . . . I don't know . . . the counselor feels that the class, not only him, it's quite a few of them that are always into something and uh . . . but he is always down to the office because they're always fighting. That's all. These kids in this one particular class . . . they're just always fighting.

Therapist: Yeah . . .

Mother begins to talk. She reaches toward me. I can relax a bit and lean all the way back in my chair stretching my legs out, still careful however. My voice remains tight.

Therapist: . . . All you have to go on is what the counselor says.

Mrs. J.: That's true.

Therapist: You've never seen it?

Mrs. J.: No. I've never been at school.

Therapist: What does he tell you?

Mrs. J.: Well he tells me the kids don't like him, you know. He told me one time he didn't have any friends in that school because none of them likes him. She [the counselor] feels he has an inferiority complex.

Therapist: Well then, what do you make of that? Let's forget what the counselor says. Your son comes to you and says "none of the kids in school like me, they call me names, they pick on me . . . I gotta fight back." What do you make of it . . . you know your son.

Mrs. J.: Well, I really don't make anything of it. I told Stanley, kids are like this sometimes. I told him too, I didn't think that all the kids disliked him in school and I didn't know the reason why they picked on him. Maybe it's something that he does . . . the counselor feels it's something that, you know . . . it's children that she said causes people to pick on them. I don't know nothing about this. I don't know whether Stanley would cause anybody to pick on him or not. But, he did tell me that the kids didn't like him in school. This was sometime ago . . . and I told him just try to ignore it . . . don't pay it any attention. Some of them likes him because it's a couple of them that calls him.

Therapist: Okay, so you're telling Stanley basically the same thing that Raymond's telling him.

Mrs. J.: . . . Ignore it and walk away.

Therapist: But Stanley isn't buying that.

Mrs. J.: Evidently he's not.

The mother is moving with me. She is allowing me in. I can afford to try to rejoin Raymond here hoping he will reflect and reinforce his mother's beginning acceptance of me. I am feeling less tense, less irritated, less combative, and more in control of myself in the situation.

Raymond: Because they keep coming back and then when they keep coming back, then you have to fight them to make them stay off your back!

Therapist: Okay, now, so then when he fights back...

Mrs. J.: Then he gets into trouble.

Therapist: Then he gets into trouble.

Mrs. J.: With the counselor, the teacher ... right ... then they bring *him* to the office ... right!

Therapist: Right! But he's not able to fight back enough so they don't bother him anymore apparently.

Mrs. J.: No, I guess not.

Raymond: Well ... see ... if he fights back, he's going to get into trouble because of the fact that they have pink slips on him written up that he's always fighting ... he's always fighting. Then if he's right for fighting then he is going to still get into trouble because of the fact that he has those slips behind him. So it's nothing he *can* do *but* fight back!

Therapist: Stanley, can you explain to us ... I mean 'cause your mother and brother are saying you gotta fight back or else try to ignore them.

Stanley (quietly): Most of the people they come up to me and...

Therapist: I can't hear you.

Stanley: Most of the people they come up to me and start bothering me when I be sitting somewhere, they start talking about me and then when I walk away and they come back ...

Therapist: They come back and do what?

Stanley: They start bothering me again!

Therapist: So why don't you just fight them and make them stop?

Stanley: 'Cause I'm scared, I'm gonna get suspended.

Therapist: Have they suspended you from school for fighting? [Stanley shakes his head no.] Have you fought back at all?

Stanley: Yup.

Therapist: And the kids that you fight back do they still bother you?

Stanley Yup ... sometimes.

Therapist: Don't they get scared and not want to bother you?

Stanley: Some of them do.

Therapist: But others keep on bothering you.

Stanley: Yup.

Therapist: Is there any kid in particular who's bothering you?

Stanley: [shakes his head no.]

Mrs. J.: No one special person?

The mother's question becomes a part of my question. She and I are now working together. We are on the same side.

The interview continues in this direction. Mrs. Jeffrey's trust grew and as it did, another level of family organization exposed itself. When she thought the family was under attack, Raymond was employed as the defender of the family perimeter. Later in the interview, as her trust in me continued to increase, she not only joined me in a mutual concern for Stanley but pointedly accused Daniel and Raymond of ganging up on Stanley as much as the neighborhood and school children do. She declared that Stanley is her youngest, the one who has been her baby the longest, and the one whom she has had to protect the longest. With that communication, she exposed the key dynamic to the isolated picked-on posture Stanley assumes outside his mother's umbrage. His closeness to her and dependence on her protection had denied him the development of his own autonomy and strength.

My feeling of success began to turn to guilt as I saw her discard Raymond in the latter part of the interview. He tried to make suggestions for Stanley but Mrs. Jeffrey rejected them all even when he essentially agreed with what she and I were saying. She accepted Raymond's protection in time of trouble but not his counsel when she felt safe.

This is an example of how different family operations will draw out different structural relationships in a family. However, the paucity of structural options and the rigidity of the current patterns in the Jeffrey family were evident as there did not seem to be other ways for Raymond to be included in the family's efforts for Stanley.

I tried to re-engage Raymond as a needed older brother to Stanley but he seemed to have long since accepted the limits of his role and his separation from the family. In the midst of my urging him to give time to Stanley, he revealed that he had been working two jobs for the last four months after school to leave. His mother was startled. She had known of only one. Raymond apparently was earning money for himself in preparation to leave. She made no gesture to hold him back by indicating she needed him at home and he would accept no further responsibility for assisting Stanley.

By the end of the interview, Mrs. Jeffrey acknowledged the need for an older male to help wean Stanley away from her but she suggested Bruce, another son, who was living outside the home. Daniel and Stanley volunteered agreement with the mother about the desirability of Bruce, who had a good government job and was a popular athlete in the neighborhood basketball league. All three viewed Bruce as reliable and available.

Bruce came with his mother and the two younger boys to the next session. Unhappily, but predictably, Raymond did not. The interview itself was anticlimatic. Mrs. Jeffrey had reset her thinking in the previous meeting and had discussed between sessions the basic thrust of the planned changes with her son, Bruce. The second interview lasted little over half an hour. The extent of the distance the mother had traveled in her thinking during the first session was evident in how little effort I had to put into the second meeting. In the latter, Bruce, with confidence and understanding, readily committed himself to take Stanley out from under his mother. She supported Bruce's offer and Stanley happily accepted his new patron. Mrs. Jeffrey had a social life of her own and was not pathologically attached to Stanley.

Reflecting the paucity of structural options to family tasks, Mrs. Jeffrey did not know how to free Stanley without having another child. However, Bruce agreed to do the job. The family indicated no need to continue coming to the

Clinic. Sometime later I attempted a follow-up but did not succeed in locating the family.

The Therapist

The therapist is a mirror of the family in the session. The family's anxiety, resentment, distrust, dependence, respect, aloofness will all be imprinted on the therapist's mind and emotions as they stare at each other, talk with one another, gesture to one another.

The family is black, I am Puerto Rican. They are poor in Philadelphia, I was poor in New York. I felt connected with them and yet, that day, our positions and current circumstances put great distance between us and I felt it. They treated me like a member of the oppressive society that overawed me as a child. I understood their initial resentment and protectiveness but also resented them for not recognizing themselves in me. I knew I had to reach them on their terms but I also could not compromise mine as their therapist and the teacher of a group of clinicians who were observing. The elements for joining the family were all there but so were our respective conflicting positions which were ready to disrupt any possibility of contact between us.

In some way or other I experienced all this as I introduced myself to them in the lobby of the Clinic, walked them to the interviewing room and began the interchange about whether or not they would accept the videotaping. When they agreed to the taping and I continued the session, I knew we were still on tenuous terms. The desire to attack and the inclination to retreat from their attack made for acute tension and conflict.

Did my tenseness reflect the existence of a conflict between the mother's wish for a solution for Stanley and her fear that no one would understand her predicament with him? This woman cared for her youngest son but knew she could not help him grow up. He was her baby, the only one left. But she was not able to tell me all this unless I proved worthy of the confidence. My body and my voice were taut as I saw Mrs. Jeffrey and Raymond stare at me, without seeing me, challenging me to pass the test.

I worried about them, Mrs. Jeffrey and her children. I felt conflicted about the teaching and demonstration that I was attempting to do at that moment. I could fail the family and the observers and myself. I hoped that my ambivalence about the family reflected a clash between their hope and fear and that they did not just disbelieve and distrust. If Mrs. Jeffrey had no expectation of help and only viewed me as an adversary, I would be of no use to them. If her defensiveness, like mine, protected a vulnerability and a wish to connect, there was hope. It was on this premise that I proceeded. I maneuvered for openings guided by my intuition about them.

My eyes kept going back to Mrs. Jeffrey and Raymond. I was protecting myself against them and I felt challenged to reach them. I assumed that they had joined together; they were working, as one, as the barrier to the outside world. Raymond was linked to mother against me, someone who might accuse Stanley of being mentally ill. Mother looked, moved, and talked in step with Raymond but mostly with gesture and expression, and not words. Raymond did most of the objecting, most of the challenging, and I chose to engage with him in the effort to disarm the family. Part of what I did was because I experienced him as menacing; indeed, physically menacing. He is big, his sleeves were rolled up, and he crossed his arms in a defiant manner. My fear of his aggression aroused my own wish to challenge him and made me feel all that much more certain that he had been preselected for the role he had assumed with me. However, in some ways I also saw myself in him. There was reason to want to befriend Raymond and I tried, knowing also that neither he nor I must be allowed to lose face. We connected enough to allow me access to the family, but not enough to return him to the next meeting.

The second and last time Mrs. Jeffrey came in she appeared in an attractive wig and with what looked like a going-out dress. Her face was open and receptive and I felt welcomed. She made me feel liked and I liked her and her family. We had each accomplished our purpose in meeting. We had found a solution to a family task, the liberation of her last son, without sacrificing any person or other vital pattern of relationship in the family. I had been able to enter the life of this family during a brief moment in their history and helped change the channel through which one member would continue his development.

The Theory and the Session

A family with its structural organization incompletely developed presents a serious personal challenge. It is not uncommon that with an underorganized family the process of the relationship with the therapist will be discontinuous. Continuity is an issue in any treatment but more so with an underorganized family. The longer the treatment the more difficult it is to maintain sight of the goals and one's roles in the multiple relationships in the process of therapy with the family and its members.

The inherent structural limitations of the family structure are a distinct dimension in understanding and solving a problem. Conflicting demands among the components of a family system define a level of therapeutic issue. These are the conflicts that grow out of the contradictory needs of individuals or sets of people in a household. On the other hand, inadequacy of development in an individual personality and in the patterns of relationship among people add a dimension that is a problem in itself and that makes it difficult to pinpoint the structural locus of the other family problems. The lack of organization confuses issues and offers fewer avenues in the family for solutions.

The underorganization of a family may make the family appear needy and powerless. The family may seem to lack the tools to even begin coping with the issues it faces. For the therapist, the reaction can be helplessness and fatalism. "They can't handle it and neither can I." On the other hand, high self-confidence and/or great determination in the face of the family's apparent weakness can inspire the urge to take over. The "they can't do it without me" and the "I'll take care of it" impulse can get a therapist through some impossible obstacles, but it can also rob the family of strength in treatment and ultimately defeat the therapist. The paradox is that with the underorganized family, the therapist may feel both inflated and useless and accordingly spark similar emotions in the family.

To overcome, the therapist must look for firm areas in the family's structural organization on which to build. The therapist must get into the family to find them, but without losing his or her own ability to maneuver. By the very nature of the structural deficiency in such families, their strength may be overly developed in certain areas of functioning but in rigid patterns that will not bend to changing circumstances in a particular family function nor be transferable to other family operations as needed. The therapist may be encouraged by their ability in one aspect of their life and then discouraged when this talent appears inaccessible to solve another problem. Moreover, potential may also be a sometime thing that can surge up but unpredictably and repeatedly throw the therapist off balance as he or she tried to depend on the family's efforts.

And then there is the problem of to whom to get close in the family—with whom to identify, empathize, and work. With each goal or task, the therapist must link up with some person or combination of people in a sequence of actions that proceed to the desired goal. The determination of the therapist needs to be tailored to the most economical and effective path through family relationships to the solutions of their problems.

In an underorganized family the number of people who look like ready allies for the effort to a solution can be none. Conversely a person or particular combination of people in the family may appear very promising, may go with the therapist to a point, and then seems to evaporate; then it may reappear as a functional ally later down the road only to vanish from sight again. The family structure can also be so rigid and fragmented that it is impossible to join with one person or combination of people without losing another, a frustrating dilemma that hinders connecting closely with anyone with any consistency and thus prevents solving anything. The therapist must maintain images of operational structures among the family members which he or she can tap as required regardless of their discontinuity and rigidity. Personal disappointments will not achieve this. Clarity about structural options and personal commitments to the family will.

An underorganized family's rigidity, discontinuity, or lack of definition can make treacherous territory to explore. It can be impossible to enter, the family keeping the therapist out of all or some part of its life. If the therapist stays out, he or she may be able to maintain clearly defined personal and professional identities at the risk of not knowing the family and being ineffective. If the clinician enters this unchartered territory, the family can also bind the therapist by its rigid patterns or absorb him or her into its confusion. The clinician cannot know a family without personal involvement, but his or her immersion is particularly perilous in the more diffused or rigidly underorganized family. This family which is most in need of the therapist's consistent involvement, also has the greatest potential for confounding him or her. The issue is particularly relevant with families who require many hours of personal contact over a long period of treatment. Interviews in the homes are particularly treacherous, because the therapist is a guest subject to the household rules and therefore acting with diminished control over the environment of the transactions. Any therapeutic effort without personal commitment and involvement can be worse than useless, but the strain on the therapist's personal boundaries with an underorganized family will be considerable.

In an encounter with an underorganized family we can feel good if we believe ourselves more competent at living than they but can feel powerless once we have tried to solve their problems. We can feel needed and linked when we work with various family members; but we can feel betrayed when the relationship dissipates and leads to no solution. If we allow ourselves the needed personal entanglement we may lose perspective of the family and of our relationship to its members.

In working with such families we see patterns of many brief therapeutic encounters with treatment apparently being aborted after a few interviews. We also see the pattern of longstanding relationships with a clinician or particular agency that lasts for years and sometimes through generations that lead nowhere.

An underorganized family, as any family in therapy, requires our emotional involvement if we are to understand and to affect them. Therapy requires a personal commitment and a readiness to extend ourselves and our influence but this extension of self will involve risk of personal and professional disappointment and confusion. To the extent that we are willing and able to involve ourselves and experience the travails of the relationship we will better grasp how the people organize their lives with each other and with others. However, this involvement will require a personal and professional frame of reference to give meaning to the experience. It will require discipline and ability to exert control over the transactions to be able to study them and to change the patterns that call for change. A therapist will need to bring to the therapeutic involvement with a family the flexibility, consistency, and variety of personal options that the family may lack in attacking its problem. An underorganized family demands all the diagnostic and therapeutic skills of the therapist plus more.

Conclusion

The detailed description of a few moments with a family is my effort to communicate about personal accessibility to oneself and the family in therapy within the framework of our professional training. The example was with a poor and underorganized family. Many poor families that appear in clinics suffer some significant degree of underorganization. Some form and degree of un-derorganization exists in all families. I have told my story through a poor family to include the poor with all others and to offer them as an entry point for therapists to all other families. Life has a common base of experience for all and through it we are each available to one another.

References

Aponte, H. The Family-School Interview: An Eco-Structural Approach *Family Process,* 1976 *15* (3) 303—310.

Aponte, H. Underorganization in the Poor Family. In *Family Therapy: Theory and Practice.* New York: Gardner Press, 1976, Chapter 25.

Minuchin, S., Montalvo, B., Gurney, B.G. Jr., Rosman, B., and Schumer, F. *Families of the Slums: An Exploration of their Structure and Treatment,* New York: Basic Books, 1967.

Minuchin, S. *Families and Family Therapy,* Cambridge, Mass.: Harvard Universtiy Press, 1974.

Whitaker, C. The Hindrance of Theory in Clinical Work. *In Family Therapy: Theory and practice.* New York: Gardner Press, 1976, Chapter 8.

7

The
Divorce Labyrinth

David V. Keith, M.D.
and
Carl A. Whitaker, M.D.

This is a two-part report of a family therapy that was gratifying to the therapists and the patients. The first part is formed out of the therapists' shared recollections, taped and reprocessed. We hope to create the effect of time-lapse photography, where it is possible to see a tree grow, a flower bloom or all the day's clouds pass by in 5 minutes. The second part of the chapter is a 1-year follow-up interview with the family written by Gus Napier, Ph.D.

The course of the therapy led through endless corridors, exposing the multigenerational components of marriage and divorce that we have been studying. We learned more about cotherapy, working with children in family therapy and schizophrenia as a family process.

Carl Whitaker was the primary therapist. David Keith, a Senior Child Fellow at the time, joined as cotherapist in the fourth interview.

Overture

When Molly Tilman called Carl to make an appointment, she and Ed had been separated for 15 months after 12 years of marriage. She was having trouble with the kids and felt that Ed was not carrying his share of the load.

Carl interviewed the Tilmans, Molly, Ed, and their 5½-year-old twin boys alone for three visits. Molly, 36, was a professional psychotherapist. Ed, 37, was a research biochemist. Molly was the one who wanted out of the marriage, the one who initiated the divorce. The twins were living with her. Ed took care of them regularly, but their arrangement was an informal one. Ed was living with Linda, a 28-year-old biochemist. Molly was dating a man who lived in another city.

Both parents were complaining of distortions that had developed around their separation. Ed felt out of recent touch with the boys and with Molly. He was complaining about the loss of his family. He wanted to get the remnants together. Molly felt that she was losing control of the kids and at this late date was not being supported emotionally or financially by Ed. Andy was emerging as a covert scapegoat. He was having troubles in school, had started wetting the bed, and, as an added note designed to catch the psychiatrist's attention, had exhibited cruelty to animals on his father's farm. Tom was softer and an easily frightened child; the parents were worried about his passivity and clinging qualities.

Beginning Process

Carl and Molly developed an almost instant bilateral positive transference at the first interview. Molly had a noticeable schizophrenic component in her personality. This component locked into Whitaker's schizophrenic receptor sites almost immediately. The presence of this strong bilateral transference was signaled by the rich fantasies and somatic sensations that it stimulated. This type of therapeutic contact can be destroyed by interpretation and attempts to understand it may render it less effective. The therapeutic potential of such a relationship is enhanced when there is a cotherapist present, especially when the voltage in the bilateral transference is high. By the second interview, Carl realized that he would need a cotherapist, but he equivocated about it, which accounts for late entry. He had established a profound intimacy with Molly and did not want it exposed or interfered with. On the other hand, he was scared and felt impotent about being able to handle the family in the face of the close lock-in with Molly. Dave Keith entered the therapy in the fourth interview. He felt unusually shy and cautious about how to involve himself with the case. It occurred to him that his awkwardness was related to the fact that Carl was deep into a therapeutic psychosis with Molly. The problem is similar to the one a teen-ager has when he goes along on a date with his best friend and his friend's girl.

One indication for cotherapy is the special lock-in that occurred between Carl and Molly. Carl picked a child psychiatry fellow for a cotherapist, with the idea that he might do some separate play therapy with the children. The act of getting a cotherapist condensed two impulses: (1) to get help for himself and (2) to get rid of the children so that they would not disrupt the therapeutic contact with Molly. When less experienced family therapists encounter a lock-in of this sort, they are likely to interpret it as an indication for individual therapy. It is a way of preventing the family from spoiling the fun of the special one-to-one relationship.

It is not unusual for Whitaker to begin a case alone and then to bring in a cotherapist later. Dave always sees families with a cotherapist; for him it is not an option. Carl, on the other hand, has a generational distance with some families that makes a cotherapist less necessary. Additionally, he has several cherished old phantom cotherapists from earlier days in practice. Family therapists gain an early awareness of the palpable presence of ghosts and how to include them.

The cotherapy arrangement in this case is a variant of our usual form. Carl had a head start with the family. In fact, Molly's transference predated the first interview by 7 years. Carl was like a single mother, alone with the kids. A husband was essential. He brought Dave in for *himself*, but just like in a second marriage, the new stepfather is the reality the *children* want to deny. The mother and stepfather have an intimate relationship, but the stepfather remains an outsider and competitor for the kids.

Molly split her ambivalence between us. Carl got the tenderness and lovingness. Dave tended to be the target for anger, irritability and inadequacy.

In an expert cotherapy team, the partners take turns moving in and out of the family reciprocally. In this one, Dave stayed out while Carl would go into the family system and then return to him. In his stepfather role Dave was not so sure he made it with this family.

Outline of the Treatment

The family entered therapy in late August, 1974. Their divorce was legally finalized in December of 1974. Dr. Whitaker was away from Madison and his practice for January and February of 1975, at which time Dr. Keith saw the family alone on four occasions. After Whitaker's return there were weekly meetings during the spring of 1975 and into the early summer, at which time the appointments became spread out. Dr. Keith went into private practice in October of 1975, and withdrew from the case. Dr. Whitaker continued with the family alone and they gradually withdrew from therapy in the spring of 1976.

Play Therapy

As the first cotherapy interview came to an end, Carl said, "Why don't you plan to see the kids in the playroom next week?" That did not seem right. For one thing the therapeutic regression was so far along with the whole group that it was hard to tell which kids Whitaker meant. The twins were much too preoccupied with their parents' struggle to get much out of play therapy. The time to take the kids to the playroom out of the family therapy arrangement is when there is only one parent available for therapy and the generation gap is absent. One arrangement is for the child therapist to work in the playroom while the family therapist sits on the other side of the one-way mirror with the parent.

We decided to keep the kids in and continue with the family group. We have had a deep fascination with the process of doing psychotherapy with children in the family. Children have a nonverbal, intuitive style that blends primary and secondary process, which in family therapy can add up to disruption. Some therapists do not like the disruption the children provide; we thrive on it. We assume that the disruption is part of the way the system works and that the kids are disruptive when things are tense. That is when they need to be worked with most and it is a horrible time to exclude them. Do all family therapists need play therapy experience in order to learn about the special stresses of children?

These twin boys, especially Andy, were into a grandiose trip. They had replaced the absent father and become a double husband to Molly. We have almost developed a technique for working with omnipotent children in family therapy. It involves overpowering the children and turning them back into little kids again. Usually only a couple of visits pass by before their sense of omnipotence is extended to include the therapist. That is, they begin to challenge us and, at that point, we start anticipating a fight. The fight may start as a tease, then gradually become more real. While we start off strategically, the confrontation has never stayed technical for either one of us. Tussling with the children might be compared to a handball game. No matter how many times we play, the excitement that it sparks is always real.

Molly was terrified by the children's grandiosity. It was not clear how Ed felt about it. We could not tell whether he was more frightened than Molly or whether he was pressing for them to take on Molly for him, *a la* David and Goliath. Carl had brought a cotherapist in to work with the children, but he was jealous and took them over. He not only had Molly, but he also wanted the kids for himself. A lot of play battling focused on Whitaker. Again, Dave, the stepfather, had to work hard to get involved. Perhaps grandfathers seem a little safer. The play with them was rough. After a while, they got the idea that maybe they could take one of us, especially if they ganged up on us. There is more fun in playing with the kids when there is a cotherapy team. The roughhouse often creates a lot of anxiety in the parents and the cotherapist can be helpful in managing it. We do not let the kids win. We always hit a little harder than they do. If they kick, we kick back a little harder. If they bite, we bite back or push their own arm into their mouths. We talk silly and expand their sadistic fantasies of tearing heads off, poking eyes, or knocking brains out.

The fights with Tom and Andy would go on for entire interviews.

Sometimes the boys got hurt and then they went off to their parents for comfort. Other times they tried to engage their parents in the same way that they had us. In the early part of the therapy the parents would be awkard and it was not successful. But later on they learned something about fighting with the kids and defeating them. Sometimes the children were humiliated and would hide under the couch or leave the room. Later on it got so that they were not really afraid of the fight. In fact, they would use it as a way to relax in the beginning of an interview. As the physical fighting began to wind down, they started into fantasy play with each other and alone. They drew pictures and brought dreams to the therapy hour. This play therapy with the children occupied much of the first 4 months of therapy.

During these 4 months there was a pattern in the sequence of events in the therapy hours. One of the adults would begin by talking about an episode that occurred in their lives or would report on a dream fragment. That might take 10 minutes and then things would start cooking with the kids. Near the end of the first 4 months, the sequence changed so that a session often started off with the focus on the kids, who would then relax while the parents went to work during the rest of the hour. Molly began to feel differently with her kids. It was a relief to see someone else work with them, to enjoy them, and also to be able to control them. She had been afraid that if she brought the kids in, they would destroy the office. Actually, she had been afraid they would destroy her. Our control provided her with some periods of happy distance from the kids. She began to see them as little 6-year-old boys instead of wild monsters. Early on in therapy, Molly had experienced a number of minipsychotic panics. At the end of the 4 months as the kids were winding down, she was less dominated by the "facultative schizophrenia." The part in her that would fragment in close interpersonal settings became better intergrated.

Divorces are a *real* problem for children. Adults are able to romanticize a divorce or to make it into a creative adventure. Children feel much more sharply the interpersonal failure and the way in which it is a psychological amputation. The children need to know as much about the divorce as possible, and it is best that they find out in the total family situation that therapy provides. Their dreams and fantasies are way ahead of the reality in terms of the horror that they permit. Bringing the children in blocks the parents' attempt to pretend that they (the parents) are still adolescents and exposes the "we" they would prefer to deny on the way to divorce. Secondarily, the children provide a medium to mix secondary and primary processes in a way that turns us on and gives us access to a special part of the parents and the marriage.

Near the end of the therapy, Molly and Andy came in alone one day. Molly was feeling very discouraged, as though she could not handle him. He had been dominating her at home and went on doing so in Carl's office. She complained to Carl that she was afraid of him and was unable to handle him. Carl told her that she better start fighting with Andy now lest he get the idea that he could defeat her and then grow up with the idea that nobody could stop him. She started to fight with him physically, and he escaped under the couch.Whitaker coached her in what to do. He told her to pull him out from under the couch, then told her how to fight him and how to overpower him. This she did, and felt renewed afterwards. This was the way in which she had physically defeated her own psychosis. Craziness no longer dominated her; it became a form of energy that she could harness. The change was an obvious relief to her and to the boys.

The Marriage

Ed and Molly had established a distance between themselves when they came in to therapy. Ed was struggling to get things back together in a half-hearted way. Molly did not trust him. Their fights focused on time and money. They circled like dream pugilists connected at the waist by a 10 foot beam that would not permit them to get any closer or any further apart. Molly was the most integrated during the therapeutic work. Ed was raveled and needy. He was a big man who looked mean as hell but oozed a need to breast feed. With brief exceptions he never quite made it into therapeutic contact with us. This role reversal contrasted with their initial marriage contract, where Molly was helpless and disorganized and Ed provided a reality orientation. The reversal is standard in working with divorcing marriages. The metaphor stays the same while the roles are exchanged.

Early on we had them bring in their current bed partners. It is always help-ful to get these amateur therapists in when divorce is pending. While we are not always successful in accomplishing it, we usually try. Linda, Ed's girlfriend, came in first and then later, Molly's boyfriend made two or three visits. On several occasions, all three sets of lovers were there with the children. When Molly's boyfriend came in the mood was cordial, but Ed would paw the earth and snort as though there was not room enough for another bull in the herd. Molly's boyfriend quickly left the therapy and their relationship. The palpable integrity of the biological unit surfaced in these expanded interviews, while the outside love affairs looked more tentative.

In contrast to Molly's boyfriend, Linda became a regular member of the therapy group. She and Molly had a profound relationship through it all. Molly was supportive of Ed and Linda's love affair, and she was careful not to disrupt it as if she feared that she would become responsible for Ed again. Linda had a strong transference to Molly, in which Molly became Linda's mother. There was a secondary transference to Ed and Molly's marriage; Ed and Molly would become parents to Linda. When Ed and Molly would rejoin in an interview, with either hostility or tenderness, Linda would shrink back, politely, as though she had interrupted her parents. She never showed any evidence of jealousy or anger with Molly.

The court divorce proceedings came and went. There was an interview on the day after the final proceedings. Molly did not attend either the hearing or our interview. Ed was deeply shaken by the divorce. He talked as though he had been through a frightening ritual of the Inquisition and divested of his personhood. When Molly came back, she was matter of fact and efficient about the divorce proceedings. She only wanted to be certain that the financial details were straight and responsibility to the children well defined. We were assuming that the biological unit would be reconstituted because of a load of ambivalence on both sides, and thus thought the divorce would not last.

Our goal in working with the threat of divorce in a marriage is to make the move for individual growth possible without necessitating the end of the marriage. We think that legal divorce leaves spouses with too many damaging residuals.

Comments on the Therapists' Involvement

In experiential psychotherapy, the therapists work on two levels. The first level has to do with the administration of the case and establishing the ground rules. The primary administrative move in this treatment involved getting in as many of the cast as possible as early as seemed reasonable. The next administrative move was Carl's decision to bring in a cotherapist. The second level of therapist work has to do with the therapists' styles based on individual functioning and our own coupling as cotherapists. The question "What are the techniques?" does not seem answerable. It is like asking Picasso how he ended up painting the *Guernica* as he did. Our methodology is peculiarly nonstrategic. We share our own impulses, anxieties, and associations and do not attempt to structure an hour. Underneath our effort to make therapy a creative enterprise for the patients and ourselves is the concern that we may have nothing to offer. We think in terms of "Was it too rich? Was it too lean? Did these people ask for something we didn't hear?" We assume that a therapist should always push to expand the family anxiety and we try to stay ahead of destructive crises in that way. The therapy becomes the life event; the crisis occurs in the office, giving a playlike quality to what happens outside. Another way of saying it is that the therapists' anxiety is not related to "What do I need to *do?*" but "Can I be alive enough to help them grow?"

Midway through the work with this case, Dave related a dream that reflected the kind of anxiety evoked by working in experiential psychotherapy. "Carl and I arrived in a gymnasium where there was a large crowd sitting on bleachers. We were to teach them about family therapy. We arrived late because Carl had forgotten something and insisted on going back for it. We took seats in front with our backs to the audience and waited for someone to introduce us. No one did, so Carl stood up and began to talk about family therapy. His talk was painfully irrelevant and the crowd became quite restless and angry. He sat down and the crowd turned to me to find out what Carl was trying to say. I had lock-jaw, my mind was a blank."

When two therapists combine to make a cotherapy team, we think that there are three therapists. The relationship between the two therapists is the third therapist. Although we do not understand it, we have always been impressed by the way a style of relating in the family can develop in a cotherapy team. It did not occur to us until long after the therapy had ended how the Whitaker—Keith relationship recapitulated the marriage of Molly's parents.

Molly's mother was a schizophrenic who had been in a mental hospital for 24 years before she moved into an old folks' home. Molly had been heavily exposed to her mother's psychosis during her developing years. Her parents remained married although obviously quite separate. Molly's father (who died when her twins were 9 months old) had been a real person, but Molly was aware of his remoteness. He was also a square and Molly could not get to him. Her dad would call to announce a visit, describe his need to be closer and then be unavailable during the visit.

Obviously, Carl was the mother while Dave was the father. Mother had been too intense, too closely involved. Father was concerned but stayed distant. He wanted more from his family but was too cautious and perhaps too concerned with administration to get it. Molly was locked into Carl in a way that was intense and confusing, but growth promoting. Her relationship with Dave was much more distant and frequently she directed angry and impatient feelings at him.

Molly did not tolerate our cotherapy relationship very well. Dave felt very clearly her attempt to take his place. She assumed that she was sexier. On several occasions, she took the cotherapist's chair in the room and paired with Carl, once in a dispute between Carl and Dave.

Another characteristic of a cotherapy team is that each cotherapist permits the other to have a private metaphor with the family that need not include both cotherapists. The extent to which this is possible is a measure of the cotherapists' comfort with one another. Sometimes a family system simply cannot permit equal intimacy with each therapist. Carl had his private metaphors in spades. Dave had his moments with the family, but there was one occasion when Carl unconsciously kept Dave out. Molly was trying to get a statement from us that the feelings we had for her were stronger and deeper than for other patients. Dave reacted angrily to this testing and responded in a double-binding way, saying, with a note of irony, "Of course we care. We are professionals and professionals are trained to care." Whitaker cut him off, gently. Dave felt embarrassed and caught in his countertransference. Later on he wished he had told Carl to quit being so jealous. It was not that Keith had blundered; this system simply did not permit that much intimacy for him with the family. The mother was not certain that the stepfather loved the kids as much as she did.

The Affair

We think of affairs as a form of amateur psychotherapy. When there is trouble in a marriage, the partners get together to decide who should go off and have an affair in an attempt to heat up the dying marriage. If the couple is moralistic, they will oftentimes send one member out for psychotherapy. Ed had started living with Linda after separating from Molly. Linda became a regular member of the treatment group after the first six interviews. Like Molly, she was a nicely featured woman with a boyish style. She was more inhibited than Molly and had a strange, distant, premenarche quality. She was also divorced. Her first marriage had gone dead with no regrets, leaving her nonsubjective and matter of fact. She described a family of origin remarkably similar to Molly's. Her mother sounded schizy and fragmented. The mother had had a number of "nervous breakdowns" and was addicted to prescription drugs. Her father, a physician, sounded friendly and square with a covert diabolical component disguised as innocence.

Although Linda became a regular part of the therapy group, she stayed out of the therapeutic contact with us. She did not expose much of her own subjectivity. We had the sense that she was avoiding becoming a patient and we were not certain what to do about it. She had a very strong transference to Molly, who became a mother-in-law to their live-in affair. Molly had a natural indulgent mother quality and would fall into a psychotherapy interviewing style with Linda very easily.

Dr. Keith was annoyed with Molly for trying to be so helpful to Linda and with Linda for accepting so much therapy from Molly. Perhaps he was jealous. On the other hand, Carl ignored Linda almost provocatively. He acted as though she was Ed's personal therapist, and made little attempt to engage her in therapeutic work.

While Linda and Molly were by no means carbon copies, they came from families which were very similar. The women discovered their developmental similarities in secret outside the therapy hours. It strengthened their relationship. The parallels dawned on them again as they talked in therapy one day about their mothers. Molly and Linda noted with amusement how they would sometimes pair to mother Ed. The children steered clear of Linda. They orbited mainly around Ed and Molly. The two women, however, were the best weekend parent set for the boys. Linda was in therapy mainly to keep Ed from falling back into the marriage and away from her. However, she was supported in this by Molly. When Linda and Ed would talk about difficulties they were having, Molly would see in those difficulties the things that had gone wrong between Ed and herself. Ed's inaccessibility to us was created in part by the triangle.

We have observed an interesting phenomenon when the girlfriends, boyfriends, or rebound spouses come into therapy sessions with divorced or divorcing families. The fundamental intimacy or bonding of the marriage tends to be clearer and all parties bend themselves in strange postures to stay out of a regression back to the marriage or to the family group. There was a moment when it looked as though Ed and Molly might remarry. Linda was overwhelmed by the bond between them and started to withdraw. In several interviews she became a wide-eyed little girl with Molly and Ed as the parents. However, Ed and Molly avoided closing the distance between themselves.

Late in the summer of 1975, Linda's mother, who had been ill for a long time, went into renal failure. Her father called, saying that mother was comatose and would die soon. Linda asked if she should come to visit. He said that she did not have to. Linda was deeply perplexed and asked us what she should do. This was the first time that she had ever presented us with a personal demand from her own heart. One of us suggested that she do whatever seemed most importan' to *her*. Linda left the hour and went directly to the airport without stopping for any additional clothing and caught the first plane to Washington, D. C., to visit her mother. Her mother recognized her when she arrived, but lapsed into a coma from which she never recovered the next day. Linda later felt that it had been a very important decision and a valuable trip.

Linda's dilemma came up on the last day that Dave met with the family group. He had a new job that was going to impinge on his availability for work as a cotherapist. Dave found it difficult to bring up the fact that he was leaving, especially in light of Linda's pain and postponed announcing his withdrawal until the last few minutes of the hour. After they left, Carl said, "We ought to write a paper entitled 'Why I Don't Believe in Transference'." When Dave did not know what he was talking about, Carl said that Linda looked hurt when Dave announced that he was leaving. Carl thought that this was evidence of her feelings about Dave, who had completely missed her disappointed look. Later Dave wrote her a note to say that he felt saddened by her distress and regretted withdrawing at a time when she most needed us.

Subclinical Schizophrenia

At the core, at its bright center that cannot be looked at directly, this is a treatment of schizophrenia in the family. In this treatment case, the schizophrenic process had not coalesced in one person but was active in the marriage, in the parenting style, and in the relationship between grandmother and the rest of the family. Experientially, schizophrenia is treated by diffusing it into the family system. The treatment needs a biologic or marital system in order to make it work. It can be diffused horizontally in the parent generation, it can be diffused backward into the grandparents and forward into the children. Early on in the beginning of cotherapy, Whitaker pointed out Molly's "facultative schizophrenia." Carl attempted to explain it in terms of the quality of her anxiety. He said he thought of it as an interpersonal process that develops between a psychotic parent and a child. It is the way that the child adapts to the psychotic parent. There is an anxiety-provoking fragmentation that reappears in close interpersonal relationships. This fragmentation can be deeply disturbing to the person.

While Carl was off on a visiting professorship in Seattle, Dave had a glimpse of what he had meant by Molly's "schizophrenia." Ed and Linda had cancelled out of an interview and Molly showed up alone with the boys. Dave noted a lot of anxiety and confusion in himself which he attributed mainly to Whitaker's absence. He had a strange fantasy that somehow Molly had arranged it so that she could be alone with him, that is, without Ed and Linda around to monitor. This simply was not true; Ed and Linda had called earlier in the afternoon to cancel. Dave scrapped with the kids a little bit, although it was not as wholehearted as he is able to do with his own patients. Molly said that sometimes it seemed to her that the two boys were trained leopards on leashes and that men she dated were often scared off by their aggressiveness and wildness. It was during this hour that Dave experienced some very vivid fantasies in relation to her. One of them being that she wanted Dave to take her in his arms, but he thought that if he did she would be only a stick. He did not describe any of the fantasies during the interview. He stayed professional and as a result, impersonal. Dave thought that he had missed a chance to make contact with her at that point.

Whitaker wondered if we should tell her that she was a "schizophrenic" and that was what we were up to treating. Ultimately he did tell her. We joked about the possibility that later we might have to tell her that she was not a schizophrenic, "just another hysteric."

Part of what our playful nonstructured style is all about is (1) to allow the schizophrenic process in the family to surface so that its energy can be used to produce change in the family, and (2) to desensitize the family to the kind of irrationality that flows through the heart of the family system from generation to generation, so that the irrationality can be enjoyed instead of ignored.

Work with divorcing couples oftentimes does not involve therapeutic change. It is, rather, a process whereby the divorcing couple *decourts* and in separating, regains the portions of themselves that they have invested in one another. Decourting was one part of the therapy with this family, but all members experienced some therapeutic change, facilitated in great part by (1) the work with the children which we described earlier and (2) the work with the grandmother, Molly's mother.

The Queen in the Woodwork

Grandmother entered the therapy somewhere around the sixth month. The process that led up to her first visit was not clear but Molly had pointed toward it for a long time.

Molly's mother was a schizophrenic who had lived first in a mental hospital and at the time of therapy was living in an old folks' home. Molly's family had been heavily exposed to the mother's psychosis throughout Molly's growing years. Molly had worked to save her mother in the early years. Seven years prior to this family therapy, she had made a final attempt to contact her mother and failed. At the time she entered therapy, Molly said that one-half hour with her mother left her panicky and disorganized. Her last social visit to her mother was 8 months before the beginning of this therapy. She wanted her mother to know and to appreciate her children, but when she took the kids to see her, grandmother would insist that they were not her grandchildren, that she was too young to have grandchildren, and besides, she did not think that Molly should ever marry.

We had expected Molly's mother to be a wizened, dead woman, probably flat and burned out. Instead, when she arrived, Molly's mother was a sight to behold and clearly alive. She was dressed all in white, including white stockings and a white hat. She had very white skin and pure white hair. She wore her hair down hanging to the middle of her back. She looked like an apparition, like an actor from a play who had stopped by for lunch without changing costume. Whitaker connected with her almost as quickly as he had with Molly. "So tell me what Molly was like when she was a little girl," said Whitaker. Grandmother began to talk about Molly. They got around to Molly's father. "What happened to him?" said Whitaker. "I understand that he died several years ago." "Oh, he's not dead," said Grandma, "he's just in another state." "You think he might be on State Street?" said Carl. "There's many states of being to be observed." "No," Grandma said. She was not sure where he was, but she assumed that he would be back. "That brings up another question that I've always wondered about," said Carl. "Do you think Christ really died on the cross?" "No, he's not really dead either," said Grandma without batting an eye. "I've suspected that all along," said Carl. "I think that it was a trick the nuns played during the Middle Ages when they were copying the Bible." Grandmother agreed that there were a lot of women, and especially religious ones, who could not be trusted. That conversation went on for a long time, at least 30 minutes. Whitaker and Grandmother had a great chat together. Dave tried to get in on the act but both of them ignored him. Molly was speechless. At the end of the hour, we invited grandmother to come back. She said that she would. Molly was quite pleased with the experience with her mother, although she still did not know what to make of it. Molly was different, she had managed to inherit a large piece of herself and the change was clear. Several weeks passed and Molly decided to bring her mother again. Grandmother came, but this time she refused to talk. She sat silently during the whole hour in spite of Carl's attempts to get her to talk. A third visit was scheduled and when Molly came to pick her up, grandmother refused to come. Carl sent along a teddy bear with Molly at the end of the hour, telling her to give it to her mother next time she saw her. Molly went to visit her mother, and mother refused the teddy bear, sending it back to Whitaker saying, "Tell him I don't do those things any more." She was talking about a prepayment to a mistress, or perhaps she saw it as an engagement present. Carl then wrote the following letter to her:

Dear Pamela,

I'm sorry you didn't want to cuddle my teddy bear. He needed some extra cuddling and he seemed to like you when you were here for your last visit. We both miss you and wish you would visit again. By the way, I have a papa bear, a mama bear and a little baby bear and I really need a Goldilocks. Could you make me a Goldilocks and bring it up when you come next time?

Affectionately,
Carl

Two months later, Molly went down to see her mother. Her mother was showing her some junk jewelry which she had recently purchased. Suddenly, Molly remembered two bracelets which had jingled on her mother's wrist when Molly was just a little girl. She asked if Grandma still had them. Grandmother dug into her things and found them. Molly asked if she could have them and Grandmother said yes. Molly put them on. Just as Molly was about to leave, Grandmother said, "Oh, what am I going to wear on my wrist now? You know, I've never had a wristwatch." "Well, how come?" said Molly. "No one ever gave me one," said Grandmother. "Well, why don't you have this one," said Molly, giving her her own. Molly left in tears as contrasted with the old days when she would leave in a disjointed schizy split. It was after that that Molly's schizophrenia-like symptoms diminished. The effect was similar to the lifting of the delusions of grandeur which the children had. The kids and Molly had had enough of the intrapsychic psychosis and primary process flowed more freely between them. There was greater comfort with craziness and it added an excitement to Molly's personal style.

It is impressive how much turmoil stirred in the lives of these three adults during the time that we saw them. Each of them entered a vocational as well as personal crisis. Ed went through a brief "therapeutic psychosis." Ed came in alone one day in the spring of 1975. He was confused and in a panic. He didn't know what to do; he didn't know how to think of himself.

Dave had a dream at about that time in which he was standing at the end of a runway at an airport. An airplane approached for a landing. It was a jet fighter with one pilot. The plane was just going to touch down when suddenly the nose went up and veered to the left. The plane touched down sidewards on one wheel; it flipped over, went tumbling down the runway, and stopped. Dave thought, "My God, that man is dead." The cabin opened, Ken jumped out, he waved at Dave, picked up the airplane, crumpled it into a ball and threw it away.

This "therapeutic psychosis" did not have a great observable impact on Ed's life. The experience was most important as a way he had of resolving some of his ambivalence about the divorce. A way of regaining some of his investment of himself in Molly and of using the despair of the divorce to push his own growth.

It was after Molly received the bracelets from her mother that the termination phase of therapy began. It went on between Carl and Molly. Dave was not involved in the treatment during this phase. Ed and Linda had also dropped out. Families end casually. Family therapists seldom talk about ending. Families usually close the gestalt on their own, away from therapy. This case took a little longer to end. The termination involved a series of revisits every 3 or 4 weeks for about six times. These were warm and pleasant interviews between Carl and Molly. They represented a reintegration of herself on a more peerlike level.

Epilogue

The practice of psychotherapy is filled with coincidences. One Monday, Carl and Dave set a Thursday date to start organizing this case review. On Tuesday, Ed and Linda called Carl for an appointment because of a problem in their relationship. Carl gave them the Thursday time which he and Dave had scheduled. Ed and Linda were going through a crisis in their relationship. They had taken the day off prior to the appointment and it sounded as though they had resolved whatever it was very nicely and we congratulated them. It was like a pleasant visit to grandma's.

Ed and Linda were recently married. They bought a house about six blocks away from Molly. They have a communal arrangement between the two houses. Molly has her house where the kids live most of the time. They come to spend some periods of time with Ed and Linda. It is clear to the kids who their real parents are and who is sleeping with whom. They have experimented with all kinds of unique arrangements between themselves and seem to be getting along fine.

It is difficult to know how to think about outcome in psychotherapy. How can therapists know whether or not their work is useful to their patients? We took some things away from this treatment, so the family probably did too. Some of the things we did and felt good about include: (1) We modeled a parenting style that included disciplining and playing with the kids. The children lost their omnipotence and the system as a whole learned how to keep them in their own generation. (2) We modeled right-brain living. We had fun with the schizy grandmother and played with the slivers of pathology in each of the family members and in ourselves. We saw them learn a nonrational freedom during the course of therapy. (3) We modeled living with the freedom to love and to be separate. (4) We modeled disorganized pairing.

The parent-child relationship serves as a model for the therapist-patient relationship. Like parents, we find ourselves wondering about our kids and how they are going to do. We also have some residual concerns.

We are both married. We think of ourselves as not pushing for or against marriage, but we may have put Ed and Molly in a place where they could only resolve their ambivalence about marriage by fighting us and staying divorced. We hope that we gave Tom and Andy some increased freedom to enjoy themselves and to grow. We did less for Ed and Linda than we might have. In this regard, they both were quite grown up at the follow-up visit noted above. They gave us the impression that they both had been into a regression which we had not estimated very well during the time of therapy. Perhaps we could have been of more use to them.

It is clear that the people in this family have a lot of growing left to do. The style of life that they have established will be stressful, but for now, they don't have to think of themselves as needing more psychotherapy.

The characterization of all persons mentioned in the chapter are based upon the subjective observations of the therapists and in some instances are in sharp contrast to the thoughts and feelings of the family members.

8

Follow-Up
To Divorce Labyrinth

Augustus Y. Napier, Ph.D.

Increasingly, the family therapist is a technician. He or she is busy advising, interpreting, and prodding the family to change its relationship structure, its conflictual communication patterns, its reinforcement contingencies, its level of individuation, perhaps even its budgetary habits. The therapist's major contribution is what might be called "expertise in living," a consultant's purchase on the skills of surviving within this most difficult of human systems. Often the sum of the therapist's effort constitutes a kind of pressure on the family to behave differently.

The therapy described by Whitaker and Keith is of a *very* different sort. Rather than being expert intellectual "nags," these therapists supply a complex of emotional ingredients which have been largely absent from the family's previous experience. They become parents; they assist in giving birth to a new quality of emotional life. And while they furnish, in this account, intriguing clues regarding the therapeutic process, they fail to describe it explicitly, perhaps because some levels of this powerful interchange are not subject to rational analysis.

In an attempt to look at this family's progress in therapy, I drew upon three sources of information: 1) an evening spent with the family discussing the therapy, 2) a transcript of the family's meeting with Carl's family therapy seminar following the termination of therapy, and 3) a lengthy dictation by Molly on her perspective on the therapeutic experience.

In my meeting with the family, I found a complex system comprised of two households living comfortably and affably within two blocks of one another. The boundaries of the two households were solidly established, yet there was close teaming between all adults around the children's needs and interests. While the children clearly "lived with" Molly, they were an intimate part of Ed and Linda's life and moved freely between the two homes. Molly and Linda had a relaxed, "sisterly" friendship; and while there were undertones of sadness in Ed and Molly's relationship, as well as a carefully-gauged, polite distance, there were also notes of consideration and friendly interest. I found it especially impressive that this "extended family" could get together to share the holidays, and that, independent of psychotherapy, they could call "crisis conferences" in order to metacommunicate about their relationships.

The following excerpts are taken from the family's discussion with Carl's family therapy seminar following the termination of therapy. They indicate some of the changes that have taken place:

Molly: "It's really a miracle to me the distance we went from August of 1974 when I really felt murderous—I mean I really didn't know what to do I felt so murderous—to December when we all spent Christman together. I'm sure the fact that we were in therapy had a lot to do with it."

Linda: "The way things are right now is that we sort of have an extended family. Ed and I live two blocks away from Molly and her kids and the kids sort of come and go. They seem to be comfortable with having family in two houses instead of one, and I get support from having Molly there, as though she were a sister or somebody to rely on in emergencies and, you know, have holidays with. We do that kind of thing; it's comfortable. There are times when we draw closer and there are times when we're not so close, but it's a kind of supportive system."

Molly: "It was surprising to me how long it took the children to work out the divorce in their own minds so that they accepted it. For a long time they would say, 'Remember when Daddy used to live with us?' And, 'Why doesn't Daddy come back—you two don't fight any more?' I think it was just last spring or summer that they really integrated it and liked things the way they were."

Molly: "I felt like the old anger always got in the way of Ed and I being able to communicate about even the simplest things. It was only after we got divorced and then the therapy that we could communicate with a lot more ease."

Ed: "There have been several occasions recently when I've talked with Molly and it's been like talking to a friend that I'm not so entangled with. Just some anxiety or depression at the moment that it was helpful to share with Molly, and that it would be more difficult to share with Linda because we are so involved."

Molly: "And I thought, gee whiz, you know, we had to go through all this, we had to get divorced and get other people involved before Ed and I could take Andy and Tom out for a hike and have a nice time. And I really believe that it's true—our relationship requires the presence of other people, even though they aren't always physically there."

Molly: "One of the products of therapy is that the three of us, when we reach those points of tension, are able to do our own therapy. The first time it happened was when you were going to buy the house two blocks away from me. At first I thought, 'Oh great!' Then I started to have real anxiety about it—'What am I doing moving these two right into my own neighborhood, in my own territory and what's going to happen?' So we all had lunch and we each expressed our anxiety and we each cried and we all felt better."

While this family seems to have moved from a high degree of interpersonal conflict to interpersonal "rapport," a remarkably successful negotiation of the divorce process, I think it would be mistaken to look only at these visible, interpersonal relationships. In a long statement prepared by Molly, we see another perspective on the therapy, notably the profound *intra*-personal changes that were taking place. A closer look at this statement also provides us with information about Carl and Molly's relationship, which was quite intense. Shifts in this relationship formed a model which radiated into the other family members' lives and into their respective families of origin.

There was a great deal of preparation before therapy began. For years Molly had been developing her fantasy of being in therapy with Carl Whitaker, accumulating a massive transference as she re-worked this idea internally. She first became intrigued by Whitaker when she was a graduate student and read *The Roots of Psychotherapy*. Later she listened alertly to reports of those who had been in therapy with him and was drawn to the notion that he was "tough": "I think one of my half-conscious formulations must have been that if you really had guts you went into therapy with Carl Whitaker. I also heard stories that he 'made' people bring in their parents, and I fantasied bringing in my mother and thinking it would be impossible and then imagined being thrown out of therapy because I couldn't bring her in."

Carl had also spent years treating schizophrenic patients individually, an experience that was very rewarding for him and allowed him an early "turn on" to the subtler aspects of Molly's "facultative schizophrenia" and, I suspect more importantly, to her mother's more overt craziness. Carl's secure relationship with Dave Keith also allowed him the freedom of a profound involvement with the family; assistance from and periodic retreat into the professional "marriage" is particularly critical when the family contains either a latent or overt psychotic process.

The initial question for the patient is whether he or she can trust the therapist. Molly had expected forcefulness in Carl, though she worried that he would be invasive and destructive like her mother. Several critical events allowed Molly (and other members as well) to move into therapy with more security.

Soon after Molly had scheduled the first interview, she had a terrifically angry explosion at Ed, frightening everyone in the family. When she related this incident in therapy, Carl said casually, "Well, there are orgasms and there are orgasms." Molly was "jolted" and intrigued by the remark. Carl's casual tone seemed to imply a lack of fear of her anger, and he found something vaguely "positive" in her outburst. Where she saw murder, Carl saw sex. It was the first of Carl's "one-liners," sudden, offhand remarks that everyone in the group found spun them around with such power.

Molly's suspiciousness of Carl continued, however, for several months. She was afraid he would not accept her decision to divorce; she feared losing her autonomy and coming to obey Carl's every wish. Molly also wondered about Carl's adequacy, and in an early dream she pulled three masks off his face until she arrived at the face of a little boy.

Then came a turning point: "Sometime in the fall of 1974, around October, I related a very frightening dream I had which entailed a group of robbers systematically moving down my street robbing every house. I knew they were coming and I left Andy and Tom in the house and went next door to the neighbors, hoping the robbers wouldn't realize the boys were sleeping there and would bypass the house. After some scenes and struggles, I escaped down the highway with a man I was currently in a relationship with and ran into a gas station to tell the highway patrolman about the robbers, only to discover that the highway patrolmen were the robbers. Carl's reaction to the dream was that I was the mother bird luring the danger away from my nest to protect my babies. This interpretation affected me deeply; it moved me and surprised me. Carl somehow managed to give me a very positive feeling about myself in an area in which I felt the most vulnerable and suspect—my ability to mother my children and my own craziness interfering with it. I had only seen that in the dream I left my children and ran off with a man plus all that other crazy stuff going on. After that remark, I accepted Carl as my therapist and the program for my part of the therapy for the next few months was outlined."

Molly had preconceptualized her therapy on an intuitive level, and had chosen a powerful figure to help her carry out her "plan." Once she had answered her doubts about the therapist's "humaneness" she was able to allow those yearned-for changes to begin.

Another decisive element in the beginning of therapy was Carl and Dave's forceful take-over of the children. Molly: "I remember feeling tremendous relief when Carl wasn't disorganized or panicked by their chaotic behavior. I seem to remember endless sessions where they ran in and jumped on him and wrestled with him while I just sat there and watched."

What Molly "just watched" was probably the only example of confident "parenting" that she had ever witnessed at close range; in addition to freeing her temporarily from her role as parent and allowing her to regress in the service of the family ego, Carl's play with the children also modeled the process of therapy: the tough, caring, "in-charge" parent being available to the entire family.

Of all the qualities which the symbolic parent (therapist) offers the family, perhaps the most basic is the validation of not only the family group but of the individual persons. All three adults found it quite important, for example, that Carl and Dave accepted Ed and Molly's decision to divorce and did not pressure them to stay married. And each of the three was deeply touched when the therapists, at different moments and in different ways, found something positive in aspects of their person that they had despised. Ed: "I felt that it became all right for me to be crazy, or angry, or just upset. I had always downgraded and hidden those parts of myself."

It is one thing for a family to find a symbolic set of parents and to participate in a bilateral psychological "adoption" process during which they seek in the therapists some of the qualities of the "good parent" that were absent in their own actual parents, and during which the therapists symbolically reparent aspects of themselves which they identify in the family; it is another thing to deal with the agonies of being disloyal to the family of origin. One of the advantages in this therapeutic approach is that the patient is not forced to choose between the original parent and the therapist, but is helped to maximize gains in the existing family relationship and at the same time "borrow" qualities from the therapist. The therapist actually *gains* power by not trying to "steal" the patient. It is only through being available to the larger system that the therapist acquires at least the minimal trust of that system, and is thus able to insert himself/herself into the family's set of loyalties. By being Molly's mother's therapist, Carl was able to mingle with Molly's *introject* of this mother on a very profound level. He probably did not help the mother, but he was able to infiltrate Molly's internalized image of this mother in a way that would not have been possible if he had ignored the actual person of the mother.

There were several identifiable stages in Molly's deepening involvement in therapy:

1) Validation of the actual parent. Molly had been sure that her mother would not come for an interview, and she was "all worked up" to bring her bodily if necessary when her mother meekly capitulated. Molly: "All I remember doing during that session was sitting there and crying while Carl and Dave talked with my mother. I felt it was a great achievement and something that I had always imagined would be entirely impossible to do."

Molly's mother had appeared dressed in sepulchral white, an impressive if somewhat bizarre figure. Carl and Dave had not only talked to her, but Carl "had a marvelous time" with this long-institutionalized woman. I can remember Carl's telling me about this exciting case where he was having a good time with the schizophrenic mother, and I have no doubt that his enjoyment of these interviews was profoundly significant for Molly, a validation of the mother at whose hands she had suffered so much disappointment and of whom she had probably been very ashamed. For several sessions, then, a positive relationship between Carl and Molly's mother.

2) Symbolic mourning. Molly's attention then shifted to her terribly ambivalent relationship with her lover. She had hopes that this relationship would work out, but events forced her to realize that it would not. She entered a period of deep despair and depression, "which was almost a relief in that I didn't feel it necessary to keep up a brave and cheerful front any more." Molly also felt hurt by her sister's refusal to come for a joint session, and she felt abandoned when Ed and Linda did not appear for a session. She saw rejection and abandonment on all sides, plainly reexperiencing the early loss of her mother. Carl suggested that she bring her mother for more sessions, and while she was puzzled by the request, she complied.

3) Reunion. Molly brought her mother three or four times during the summer of 1975, and these sessions were particularly meaningful since her mother interacted with her children for the first time. She recounts: "By August, I felt more at home in the world, more relaxed with myself and more hopeful that

perhaps I could be and was an adequate mother. I was absolutely amazed at the relationship that had developed between myself and my mother, taking her out to lunch with the kids, etc."

Before therapy Molly's mother had quite literally refused to admit the existence of Molly's children, and this denial was undoubtedly part of Molly's terrible self-doubt about being an adequate mother. Within the context of therapy, the family experienced a "normal" three-generation set, Molly feeling reunited with her mother and accepted as her mother's child and as a parent herself. This was possible partly because of Carl's "marriage" to the unstable mother, permitting Molly to assume a normal generational position.

4) Bilateral individuation. September, 1975. Molly was driving over to get her mother for a session, feeling good about herself, and wondering if she needed her mother to come anymore. When she arrived, her mother refused to budge. Molly fought back: "I asserted myself, expressed my anger and in general acted freely and did not conform to my usual sweet daughter role. I drove away thinking that my mother would die because of what I said and that it would be the last time I saw her. She didn't, however, and I began to have a new freedom in relating to her." Having established a long-sought closeness with her mother, Molly proceeded to enter a rebellious adolescence. Her mother made her individuation easier by fighting hard for Molly's loyalty, railing against "that doctor" who had brainwashed her and hypnotized her. With coaching from the therapists, Molly kept up both the visits and the fight for her autonomy.

5) Release. During the fall of 1975 and the winter of 1976, Molly's relationship with her mother underwent a change. Her mother stopped fighting for her loyalty, as though releasing her. Molly not only felt free to be a separate person, but to enjoy the "breast feeding" regression in therapy; she also began to have very tender feelings toward her mother. As Molly entered the core phase of therapy, the generational roles were reversed, and Molly, who was receiving "parenting" from the therapists, became her mother's mother. In this way she probably felt less guilt about taking from the therapists.

6) Expansion of individuation into other relationships. Molly had often felt weak and ineffective in her relationship with her children. In January of 1976, which was the time when her fights with her mother had begun to ease, Molly felt very anxious about the boys' upcoming birthday and found herself feeling helpless with them in the interview. Carl said blandly, "You're being too nice to them." She made a feeble attempt to deal with one of the boys in the interview, but his testing continued through most of the following week. "Saturday morning when I was trying to get them ready to take them over to Ed's, Tom totally exasperated me by passive resistance. He was dancing around with his toy gun and not getting ready. Suddenly, I grabbed his gun, threw it on the floor, and smashed it under my foot. This impressed him, but it made me feel very guilty. I felt that I had gone crazy and quickly confessed to Carl that perhaps I should let Ed and Linda raise the boys. He said that it was a muscle that I hadn't exercised and that I would get stronger." Molly began to fight harder for control of the

children, and during this time she received considerable support from Linda as well as from Carl and Dave.

7) Therapeutic symbiosis. During February of 1976, Molly began to use some art materials (water colors, pen and ink) which she had bought several months earlier on impulse. She felt a great release and a surge of free expression as she became totally absorbed in making these drawings and designs. "I don't remember ever before creating anything without any fear of judgment, self-criticism, inhibition or censorship. I brought a whole bundle of these drawings in for Carl to see and at that time began to realize their psychological significance."

She also recounts dreams during this period involving babies and children, dreams which she interprets as dealing with the birth of the self. "In one of my dreams, I was in my basement with several people, and there was a woman in the next room with a new-born infant. Carl was there and he wanted me to come in and touch it. I went in to look—it was pink and seemed to have transparent skin. I was repulsed and frightened and didn't want to touch it. Carl interpreted this dream as meaning that he was encouraging the birth of my 'schizophrenic self' and I was frightened."

This is the core phase of psychotherapy, in which the patient luxuriates in a profound symbiosis with the therapists, and in this condition of feeling taken care of and cuddled finds new trust in herself. Having broken through the binds in many of her "real-world" relationships, she is free to relate to herself in a more unitary manner, expanding her sense of her own power and dissolving barriers that have impeded her own creativity.

8) Return to the parent. In June of 1976, an incident occurred which was extremely significant for Molly. Her mother was talking about some bracelets she had bought recently, and Molly was reminded of some bracelets her mother wore when Molly was a child. She asked if her mother still had the bracelets. "They always had a kind of magical quality to me. I remember the sound of the bracelets tinkling as my mother moved around the house when I was a child, and that tinkle was my mother's sound. Well, I was so surprised when mother said, 'Those? Yes.' And she got them out of the drawer and put them on my arm. 'You can have them,' she said. I asked her where she had bought them, and she told me it was the local department store." Molly looked at the bracelets on her arm beside her Timex watch, thinking the watch did not look right beside the "magical bracelets." She took off the watch and gave it to her mother. "My mother said, 'Oh.' It was like she was accepting a little bit of reality—you know, to have a watch and know what time it is. She didn't know how to set it or wind it and I showed her how and she thought I was quite clever to be able to do it."

Only when Molly established considerable independence from her mother was this tender moment possible. Molly's mother gave her a token of the childhood years which she had usually refused to acknowledge and in effect made them real for Molly. In return, Molly offered a bit of symbolic parenting to her mother. Through this ritual mother and daughter seemed to be exchanging symbols of the past (the bracelets) and the present (the watch), and in doing so went beyond time-bound experience, establishing more firmly an evolving person-to-person relationship. The patient's involvement in therapy had not fractured the parent-child relationship, but had expanded its potential.

In her account of the therapy, Molly devotes surprisingly little attention to her relationship with Ed, saying only, "My problems with Ed just seemed to straighten themselves out. Aside from the binds we were in at the beginning of therapy, I don't remember anything dramatic." The decision to divorce seemed firm from the start; therapy became a way of making the agony bearable. Even the children seemed convinced that divorce was essential, as we see in an episode recounted by Ed and Linda:

Linda: "Carl made some joking reference to ... he was saying to me and Ed that we had better not start sleeping with each other because if we split up then Molly would have to take Ed back. And the kids, who usually, you know, rough-housed during the therapy session, hid under the sofa and they were crying—I'd never seen them so upset."
Ed: "And one of them said, 'I don't want to say; I don't want to talk about it.'"
Linda: "They *wouldn't* talk about it."
Ed: "Oh my God, Daddy's going to come home again...."

Though everyone seemed convinced that divorce was inevitable, in some respects this couple seemed to elect to keep their relationship, but to make it tolerable through the inclusion of others. One has the sense that though Ed and Linda's relationship is more "fun" than Ed and Molly's ever was, the major affective investment is between Ed and Molly—and will remain so. As in the situation where mother and adult son fight because of their anxiety about their Oedipal involvement, and are able to have a more loving relationship when son finally marries, this larger system allows the protagonists to expand their experience in a way that is more difficult for them in a dyadic relationship. Ed and Molly can love one another now that they are less dependent on one another, while the existence of this "old marriage" allows both Ed and Molly to be freer interpersonally with their new partners.

At one point the decision to divorce did seem to weaken. Molly's relationship with her lover had collapsed, and she and Ed moved closer together. But Linda protested anxiously, and soon Molly met someone else. Molly's relationship with the lover occupied much of her conscious struggle during therapy, and he seemed to have represented "the bad mother" in her life. Breaking with him was a ritual liberation from the intimidation of this kind of relationship, and it was made possible largely through an internalization of the "good mother"—Whitaker and Keith.

I have chosen to focus on Molly's account of her experience in therapy because her involvement seemed more intense and because her growth in therapy seemed to catalyze others into action. Some further commentary from Ed and Linda's perspective should be useful, however. One of the dramatic changes in Ed's orientation came when he shifted out of his counter-schiz position, as revealed in this dialog:

Molly: "At the beginning of therapy I was constantly afraid that I would lose control. I had had those fears early in my relationship with Ed, and he always reassured me and said that I would be all right. He was a good therapist. Carl's thumbnail diagnosis was that Ed married me so that he could go crazy and I married him so I could go sane—which was true."

(Questioner from seminar): Ed, did you fear Molly's craziness?

Ed: "Not the way she did. My mother went crazy, and to her everlasting credit, it has really helped her. She had a heart attack and she retired. Things just got a lot better between us. A lot of it comes from me now too, comes from the way I relate to her cause she's really mellowed and I've never had such personal talks with her before. And I think I got that from therapy, too. Being able to go crazy a little bit myself and get into it or you know, feel like it's going to be all right."

Keith: "Wasn't there a time when you went through a crisis in therapy yourself, when Linda's brother-in-law was killed?"

Ed: "Yes. And I remember when Carl would talk afterwards about the time I went crazy. I don't remember the details, just the feeling."

Molly: "I remember Carl's saying how great it was that you took yourself apart and put yourself together again."

It seems clear that Ed's "psuedo-therapist" relationship with Molly was one way of masking his own disturbance. Therapy allowed him to "go crazy," if only momentarily, and to see that part of himself as valuable. Being more in touch with his own craziness also allowed him to develop more rapport with his own mother, who had apparently been quite disturbed. With Molly's model prompting him, Ed broke a long-established distance from his parents and began to move into closer relationship.

While she initially had more difficulty becoming part of the therapeutic process, Linda's peak moment in therapy came at the time when her mother was dying:

Linda: "One of the most significant sessions for me was when my mother was dying and my father was doing that number where he said, 'Oh, dear, there's nothing you can do; she's in a coma.' And I didn't know whether to obey my father or not. We all came to therapy, and I didn't know whether to go or not. Carl wouldn't advise me either way. But then he said, 'You and your father are in a Mexican standoff, aren't you?' And, you know, great, one of those insights. I thought, 'Yeah.' I went right out afterwards and just got in an airplane without taking any clothing, or anything...."

All of the adults in the family seemed profoundly grateful for these moments of *insight*. The discoveries did not seem the result of bone-grinding intellectual machination, but were spontaneous gifts of the therapist's intuitive process. They also came peculiarly wrapped, the meaning often hidden deep inside, to be teased out at a later date. And they were delivered with a sort of liberating, impelling force.

All were grateful at finding their own craziness validated and enjoyed by the therapists.

All felt reassured when the therapists took firm charge of the arena of therapy, especially of the children.

They were grateful that the therapists did not tell them how to live.

Though they mentioned Carl's name more often in their statements, they all felt important positive contributions from Dave Keith, and from his and Carl's ability to team.

All felt that the most important part of therapy was that Dave and Carl cared about them. Ed seemed to speak for everyone when he said, "It was the first time anybody really cared about me, I think."

9

The Family That
Had All The Answers

Peggy Papp, M.S.W.

In presenting the following case it is important to describe the context in which the family had been seen, as this is an essential element of the treatment. This family was part of the brief therapy project at the Nathan W. Ackerman Family Institute, a project that was formed 2 years ago by ten self-selected family therapists* to experiment with various brief therapy techniques for treating families of symptomatic children. The experimentation focused on three major areas: the use of a peer consultation group as an integral part of the therapy; the use of the therapeutic double-bind as a method of dealing with the resistance; and the use of planned strategies based on systemic predictions of change.

Our theoretical framework was built on an understanding of the family as a self-regulatory system and on a definition of the symptom as an attempt to regulate a dysfunctional part of that system. Interventions were aimed at changing the cycle of family interaction in which the symptom was imbedded. Since this systems model is common to most family therapists, I shall not elaborate on it further here, except to say that our work has been influenced most by those therapists who have developed and written about brief planned intervention: Jay Haley; Milton Erickson; Watzlawick, Weakland, and Fisch; Salvador Minuchin and Mara Selvini Palazzoli. Our concept of dealing with resistance through redefining the entire family system is based on the work of the Palazzoli team

---

*Olga Silverstein, Richard Evans, Gillian Walker, Joel Bergman, Betty Lundquist, Paul DeBell, Lynn Hoffman, John Clarkin, Anita Morawetz, Peggy Papp.

and their research with schizophrenic families at the Centro Per Lo Studio Della Famiglia in Milan.

Since child-focused families are known to be notoriously resistant to change and since eighty percent of our families were casualties from other types of therapy failures, much of our preoccupation was centered on methods for counteracting this resistance. In our experience, this was an essential step in preparing the groundwork for the strategies.

Inherent in a family coming for therapy is a self-contradictory situation for the therapist which might be described as follows: The family conveys to the therapist that they want to change the symptom of the child; the therapist conveys to the family in order to do this they will have to change their system; the family conveys to the therapist (in subtle and covert ways) they cannot do this because if they could they wouldn't have needed the symptom in the first place. We dealt with this in the following manner:

1. We defined the symptom as serving an essential function in the system.

2. We defined the system which the symptom served.

3. We agreed with the family that the system could not and should not be changed (giving very specific reasons for this) and therefore the symptom could not change.

4. This was totally unacceptable to the family since they had come there to change the symptom.

5. The therapist reversed the double-bind and faced the family with their own contradictions.

Therapy took the form of a duel with resistance, the therapeutic double-bind used as the rapier.

The ten therapists were divided into two working groups of five. Each interview was observed from behind the one-way mirror by the remaining four in each group. The observation group was used as the third member of the therapeutic system which consisted of the therapist, the family and the consultation group. The group was described to the family as an added dividend made up of experts in the field. Periodically messages were conveyed to the family from the group via the therapist. This invisible voice from the outside added tremendous impact to the intervention. Since it was under the control of the therapist it could be molded to serve whatever purpose was appropriate to underline each intervention. It was variously used as a Greek chorus commenting on the proceedings and making systemic predictions of change; as a senior consultant supporting the therapist and lending unanimous weight to his decisions: as an authoritative parent correcting him and pointing out his mistakes; as a public opinion poll sometimes divided along sex lines to highlight the male-female issues; as a dissenting voice forming a triangle and forcing the family to take sides; as a soothsayer sending curious messages to confuse or amuse the family. The end result was a two against one coalition in favor of the therapist.

Tasks were prescribed when the resistance had been neutralized and the family itself was requesting a change in their system. The tasks were accompanied by systemic predictions of the negative consequences of change which were delivered to the family at regular intervals. This served as a constant counterbalance to resistance and continually defined the interconnectedness of family relationships 'with the symptom.

In order to give the reader as clear an understanding as possible of these concepts in action, I shall present the following case session by session commenting as I go along on the interventions. Although the original contract was for 12 sessions, we terminated after 8 based on the disappearance of the symptom.

The "W" family was an attractive, middle-class family consisting of a mother and father in their early forties and two children, John, the identified patient, age 12, and Debbie, his sister, age 15. The precipitating event was John's being arrested for stealing a transistor radio from a neighborhood store. John had been a behavior problem since the first grade when he burned the house down playing with matches. He was described as being hyperactive, disruptive in class, working below his capacity, having poor peer relationships and learning difficulties. At home he was described as "having a bad temper" which was demonstrated by his abusing the dog, kicking holes in the wall, banging doors down, smoking pot and "taking pleasure in annoying his parents."

The mother had dragged the reluctant family to the clinic, meeting resistance particularly from her husband who had at first refused to come. His face looked worn and haggard as he stated, "I must admit I'm pessimistic about therapy." And with some reason. Six years ago when the trouble began, they had gone to a family agency for help. John was seen by a psychologist and the parents by a social worker for two years. The parents reported "This was not helpful and there was no change whatsoever." They then took John to a clinic for hyperactivity. The tests for organisity were negative and the clinic referred the family to a behavior modification institute. They went only twice as they felt the approach was "absolutely ridiculous." For the past two years, John had been seen by a private psychiatrist who the family stated "has good credentials." They felt this was a "complete waste of time. We were totally shut out and left to cope with the problem at home." In desperation they put him in a private school with ungraded classes. This made things worse and he was put back into public school. Disillusioned and discouraged, the father felt they should try and work out their problems themselves giving the children "more time and patience."

First Session

During the first session the father tended to minimize John's problems, stating it was something he would probably grow out of and thought the bigger problem was the intense sibling rivalry between John and Debbie. "We have two normal healthy children, I just don't understand why they fight like they do." Mother, looking like a small frail bird, declared in a childlike voice, "We are a very close, loving family," while John and Debbie stared grimly into space. Debbie sat next to mother, a younger version of her, with long dark hair. John sat next to father, a sad expression on his handsome face. They reminded me of my own children and I was glad I was using an approach which would prevent me from becoming overly involved with them. It was a physically beautiful family acting like a TV ad and desperately attempting to appear normal.

During this session I followed my general practice of evolving a systemic view of the family by focusing on the symptom and the family's reaction to it. The symptom is a nodal point around which the most vital family interactions take place. By asking what, where, when and how questions regarding each family member's reaction to it, the therapist remains relevant to the family and at the same time can evolve a total view of the family structure.

At the end of the first session, I felt I did not have enough information to make an intervention and so I closed the session by sympathizing with their disillusionment with therapy, told them I would probably not be of much help to them either and that people tend to set too much store in therapy. If any change did occur from their coming here it would probably be a minor one—but maybe that would be better than nothing.

Since this was a family who had been innoculated against therapy and developed an immunity to it, this was done to lower expectations.

Second Session

The second session was spent in gathering more information and in this session the family presented a clear picture of their functioning. For example, I asked the mother if it was her husband who did all the disciplining and she stated, "Yes, unfortunately, because the children will respect him in the end and I'm afraid they won't respect me. I'm a ball to be with and I'm a barrel of laughs and a lot of fun. I tend to make him the bad guy. I get very angry and I start yelling and screaming at the kids and then he sees I'm angry and he punishes them. He does all the disciplining and I don't do any at all. I have no backbone when it comes to that."

The father continued to normalize everything by saying, "She leans on me, I don't think that's so terrible. I lean on her for a lot of things. It's reciprocal."

The mother continued, "All my friends say to me, 'Your children are your children, they're not your friends.' Everyone thinks my relationship with my daughter is too friendly. My daughter and I happen to be very close. I'd rather be with her than with my friends. I treat her sometimes like a friend instead of a daughter and maybe I should treat her more like a daughter but I enjoy her too much." To which the husband responded, "I resented doing the disciplining a while back. My daughter was beginning to hate me a little bit—I wasn't worried about it that much because there's love between us and that's not going to go away. I don't worry about it that much. My wife used to worry that my daughter was going to hate me. It's very funny. My wife will say 'No' to her about something and my daughter will yell at me and get mad at me. She gets mad at me instead of her mother. I think we all know what's going on, that's why I'm not worrying about it."

I sat there thinking "They have obliterated my job as therapist. They have told me what the problem is, what they should do about it and why they cannot do it. I'm set up for defeat." I decided my first move must be to extricate myself by constructing a counter double-bind. This is difficult to do in the middle of a session while simultaneously listening and responding to the family. I excused myself at this point for a group consultation which gave me a chance to pull my ideas together with the help of my colleagues.

Group discussion focused around the following points:

If I told the parents that the *quid pro quo* in their marriage was harmful to the children and if I suggested mother be more firm and father be less of a disciplinarian they would probably agree with me then proceed to tell me all the reasons this couldn't be done, ending up denying it had anything to do with the problems in the children anyway. With a family that is less resistant the therapist can give direct suggestions with some assurance they will be followed; but my evaluation of this family led me to believe they would sabotage any direct advice.

The first questions we ask ourself in arriving at an intervention are "What is the cycle of family interaction which escalates the problem and what function does the symptom serve in that cycle?" My definition of that cycle, at this point, was that the more John misbehaved, the more helpless mother became; the more helpless mother became, the harsher father became; the harsher father became, the more John misbehaved; and the more John misbehaved, the more helpless mother became and so on. John was thus preserving the balance of power in the marriage through his misbehavior. Father could be strong and mother could be weak. Debbie contributed to this by fighting mother's unfought battles with father. I do not believe, as do some family therapists, that it is always necessary to change the marital relationship in order to alleviate the symptom in the child. However, in this case because of the rigidity of the roles, I felt the children could not be freed without a shift in the marital arrangement. Neither child could get close to the father as long as he remained the family policeman. And neither child could differentiate him or herself from mother until she acted like a mother. But if they changed their parental roles it would affect their marital roles, and I anticipated a great deal of resistence to this.

We therefore decided to circumvent this by prescribing the entire family system, defining each person's behavior as serving a function in it, predicting the consequence of change and advising against it.

Returning to the session I told the family that the group was concerned that I was exploring their family roles in such a way as to imply they should change them and the group felt this would be wrong. "They feel that it's very important for you, Mrs. W., to continue to act helpless and incompetent because that gives, your husband a real opportunity to protect you and to be strong and show that he cares. This is very important as it would upset the balance in your marriage if you should change this. And we feel it's important for you to continue to be the bad guy, Mr. W., because if you didn't Debbie and John would begin to fight with their mother and that would be very upsetting for everybody." (Debbie denies this.)

"And John, they feel that you have been provoking mother to get her to try and take over more and become the strong woman you know she is, but we feel that's not such a good idea because then Dad would be out of a job and he can't take that. He can take being the bad guy and if you all got out of these roles it would be upsetting to everybody in the family."

There was a stunned silence. The parents turned and stared at one another for a long moment as they tried to comprehend the multiple messages. The mother was the first to break the silence after a long pause. "First of all, I'm not incompetent." The therapist quickly interjected, "I said *act* incompetent." The mother continued, "As far as our marriage is concerned, we don't have to prove anything to each other."

The father began to question this, "That's not entirely true. There's something to the role playing. Yes, there's something to it. Maybe that's the culture we were brought up in and maybe that's the way we want the roles. I'm sure that's the way my wife wants the roles. Because, I don't know if you remember, but years ago you mentioned that your father was the boss and you wanted a boss relationship with me. I don't particularly want a 100% boss relationship. I can take being the bad guy, that is, I don't like being the bad guy, I'm not that happy being the bad guy, but I can take it if I have to—but I don't like it, it hurts me sometimes—my daughter's view of me does bother me."

The father was already reversing his position but if I supported this too quickly, he would more than likely revert to his former position. I kept pushing the bad guy role and defining it as protecting the relationship between Debbie and her mother. I cautioned him, "If you stop being the bad guy, there will be some kind of friction between Debbie and her mother because at this age when a girl is 15, trying to be on her own, establishing her own identity and moving away from home, there is always some kind of conflict that arises between a mother and a daughter. But as long as you're the bad guy, you see————"

The mother interrupted, "We don't have any of that." The therapist agreed, "That's what I mean." Mother continued, "Whereas I know other girls have it with their mothers and lots of times——" The session was interrupted by a knock at the door and the group informed me the next family was here and we must vacate the room.

I ended the session by saying, "Look, I'll tell you, the group could be wrong. Sometimes I disagree with the group. I disagree with them slightly right now." (It had been prearranged that I would take a more lenient position regarding change with the group remaining cautious, hoping the family would eventually side with me against the group.) "I understand what they are saying about change and how upsetting it would be to all of you, however, I'm not so sure. I'm not sure but what you couldn't change a little bit without things being that upsetting, but anyway I'd like you to think about it a couple weeks."

This left them to ponder the two positions.

During the next two weeks I tried to speculate on the effect of the session and prepare for the next one. I anticipated there would be a slight change in the parental roles, that mother would react against the group calling her incompetent and she would make an effort to become firmer; and that the father, obviously disturbed by my pushing his bad guy label at him, would begin to reevaluate his role with his children. However, each parent would probably stop the other from straying too far outside their roles as each obviously had an emotional investment in the other spouse staying the same. The father had stated clearly in one of the sessions, "I don't want a tough broad who has all the answers." If mother became more assertive, he probably would not be able to deal with her, would feel he was being deprived of his central role in the family and would more than likely become depressed. Mother had definitely stated she wanted to be dominated by a boss like her father which relieved her of the responsibility of being a mother and permitted her to maintain her little girl position in relation to her husband and her sibling position in relation to her children. I anticipated they would come back and reconfirm their love for one another and emphasize the beauty of their union.

My next intervention should be aimed more directly at focusing attention on the marriage. I searched for a way to break through their defeating mechanisms but could think of nothing until I began thinking in terms of a way to *use* them rather than *break through* them. I then came up with the idea of deliberately allowing them to defeat me in a session. I would stage a failure and use it to dramatize the way in which the marital roles affected the parental roles and made change impossible. My plan would be as follows: I would attempt to establish a better relationship between Debbie and her father which would be bound to fail as the other part of the system in the room would not allow it. As long as the no fighting rule stood between Debbie and her mother and between mother and father, Debbie and father would have to fight to preserve both the mother-daughter relationship and the husband-wife relationship. The group would intervene through a prearranged signal to comment on my failure and advise me to discontinue this course of action, giving as the reason that it might upset the marriage. I would preceed to get a better relationship going between John and his mother by trying to get her to be firmer with him. This would also be bound to fail for the same reasons, and I would come to the conclusion that problems in the children were a small price to pay for preserving their marriage. This would, of course, be an unacceptable solution compelling the parents to re-evaluate their relationship.

As a springboard for focusing on the relationship between Debbie and her father, a video excerpt from the previous session was played back to the family. In this excerpt, Debbie had intimated she'd like a better relationship with her father. He had diverted her attempt first by criticizing her, then by defending himself, then by bringing his wife in to justify his position. The therapist commented on Debbie's inability to get her message across and asked her to try again. This ended up in a round robin of accusations, defensiveness and denials. I scratched my ankle (the signal for the group to call me out of the room) and came back to report, "The group disagrees with what I'm trying to do in getting a better relationship going between the two of you and they think Debbie should fight more with her father because if she is to establish her sense of identity she has to fight with one of her parents and it's better she fight with father instead of mother." The following dialogue took place.

Father: That would devastate me over a long period of time.
Therapist: Well you said it's okay for you to be the bad guy.
Father: It's okay here and there for me to be the bad guy but not over a sustained period of time.
Therapist: But you're protecting your wife—
Father: I would love a better relationship with my daughter—
Debbie: I don't think what they say is true because a lot of my friends fight a little bit with their father and a little bit with their mother, but they're not enemies with one of their parents.
Therapist: You have to fight doubly hard with your father because it would be too upsetting to your mother for you to fight with her.
Father: Is that true?
Debbie: I don't know, it's—maybe—
Therapist: I don't know either. (To mother), Would you agree with that?
Father: I do agree with that, I'll tell you why, I think they have something there. How many times has Debbie been angry with me over something and I had nothing to do with it; something between you and her and Debbie would get angry with me and I would say why are you angry at me? and you would say because I can't get angry at her.
Debbie: That's true.
Therapist: The group feels there's a good reason for that.
Mother: Where does it say in the book that every teenager has to fight with one of his parents?
Father: They have to rebel.
Mother: Every teenager in the world has those feelings? That's hard for me to believe.
Father: They're establishing their independence, they have to learn to be adults and break away from childhood.
Mother: I had just the opposite. I was very close to my father, and I feel very upset about their relationship (indicating Debbie and father) mainly because of my background. I was very close to my father, I still am and my father did so much for

me. I thank him for my relationship, I think it helped my marriage, my father made
me love men.

Therapist: Would you like to see that kind of relationship between Debbie and her father?

Mother: Yes I would because—

Therapist: Well you see what the group feels is that the price you would have to pay for
that is that Debbie would have to fight with you.

Mother: Why does the group make me so weak? I didn't realize I appeared to be so weak.
I'm really not. I'm a very strong person.

Therapist: Let me tell you I disagree partly with the group as I see you as a much stronger
person with a lot more resources than they do.

Mother: I think so.

Therapist: So we have our disagreements. But anyway I wanted to give you the feedback
and test it out with you, as you are the one who really knows.

Mother: I've had a lot of tragic things happen and I have never cracked up over any of
them, so I guess I could handle it.

Therapist: You think you'd be able to tolerate Debbie disagreeing with you?

Mother: We disagree. She's always asking me to buy her something and I say, No.

Debbie: But I take it, I take the answer.

Mother: We almost had a fight the other day.

Mother then proceeded to completely contradict herself by telling a story in
which Debbie wanted something, mother didn't want her to have it, could not
say no and turned her over to father. It ended with father punishing her and
Debbie being angry at father.

Therapist: (to father) But you can take it.

Father: I can take it—you know the old story about laughing on the outside and crying
on the inside. There's a lot to that. I can take it but there're a lot of things I take
that I'd rather not take.

At this point I was conflicted over whether or not to investigate father's
"crying on the inside" or keep defining it as the price he paid for his noble role in
the family. I was tempted to explore it, as much of my previous training had been
in exploring feelings. It almost seemed sacreligious to miss what seemed to be a
ripe opportunity. I heard voices saying "Why didn't you pick up on his feelings."
On the other hand in this case it could prove to be a red herring which would
end up in "yes, but," "however," and "because." Although something might be
gained from it, I decided more could be gained by sticking to my systemic
strategy and I replied "but I really admire you for protecting your wife and
daughter and holding the family together."

Father: (Laughing) Yeah, but I'm crumbling on the inside.

I also ignored this implying he could take it and went on with my overall
plan which was to focus on the relationship between mother and John. This
ended in a sibling quarrel between the two of them in which mother stated, "If
you treat me lousy, I'll treat you lousy."

Again the group interrupted through a prearranged signal and the therapist returned with the following message. "Let me give you some feedback from the group. The group seems to be in disagreement with me today more than usual and that's all right but I don't know what to do about it. Usually they are very helpful, but I must tell you that they have disagreed with me consistantly today and so what I am going to do is just tell you about it. They feel I am wrong again in trying to get you, mother, to be strong and firm with John because that means father would have to be soft and since you seem to have such a nice balance going now and your roles are clear, they're afraid it would upset the balance in your marriage to change your relationship with the children. Their feeling is, your marriage is more important than anything else and if the children have a few problems, that's a small price to pay for maintaining the stability in your marriage."

Long pause.

Mother: I don't think anything can affect our marriage.
Therapist: My feeling is that your marriage is strong enough and you have enough resources going that you could risk something. You see, there will be changes in your marriage if you behave differently with the children. But my feeling is you'll be able to tolerate that and have a different experience.
Father: I agree with my wife, our marriage is extremely strong.
John: Then why did you say my problems were interfering with your marriage?

This was the first time either of the children had dared to mention this. The parents quickly minimized and denied it. The father explained to John, it naturally had an effect on them, but it couldn't interfere with the marriage. I decided to seize this opportunity to try and tease out some of the disagreement between them. I asked the mother and father to sit together and the children to go on the other side of the mirror so they wouldn't be tempted to interrupt while their parents discussed what would happen to their marriage if they changed the relationship with the children.

This exchange ended up with father asking "Is it possible for us to try changing roles for a week?" This is what I had been aiming for, but I must be careful not to move too quickly. I maintained a reserved attitude and said cautiously, "Well that makes me a little bit nervous. Let's decide to do it very slowly, decide to do it for one day—"

Father: Where she would take care of all the problems with the kids for one day and I stay out of it.
Therapist: Mmm, Mmm ... You mean you would be soft and friendly with them, and you, mother, would be firm?
Mother: I don't know if I can. That's my problem
Father: Well we'll find out. (Turning to therapist) What you're saying is that this is very ticklish and dangerous ground.
Therapist: It's tricky, however, I disagree with the group that you should go on the way you're going, because I think you have more strength and resources than that, and

I don't think it's always best to be so careful about preserving a marriage at the expense of your children having problems. I'm for risking something.

We made an appointment for two weeks hence.

This intervention had produced the desired result within the session. The father asked to change roles. The suggestion came from him rather than the therapist. The family had been put in the position of convincing the therapist to risk change and the therapist in the position of initially resisting their request, finally relenting after serious thought as though rewarding them with the privilege.

Fourth Session

I was unprepared for the aftermath of this session which resulted in an extraordinary and unexpected change in the mother. She came on like a house on fire with her family scattered in all directions like scared jack rabbits. (A therapist can seldom predict consequences as colorful as those that actually occur.) She suddenly rebelled against her whole life set-up and the therapist got a picture of what that was. Her husband did not come to this session and the mother delivered the message, he had to work. The therapist wondered if the last session had scared him, and the mother laughingly said, "No. But I must say I've changed in the last two weeks. And I don't think anybody liked it. I don't know if the session had any effect on me at all, but all of a sudden I started telling everybody off. One night my husband didn't like the dinner I gave him, and I said, 'That's tough. If you don't like it make your own dinner. I work the same hours you do, if you don't like the dinner, make your own.'"

Therapist: That was something new, you never said that before?
Mother: I guess not. Every time I come home, I have to empty the dishwasher, I have to feed the dog, I have to clean up, I have to do the pots and pans; I have to set the table, I have to get the dinner, I have to do the laundry and everybody else just walks away. Debbie helps me clean up a little bit, just a little bit.

I said to my husband, "Why do I have to come home and do all this? Just because I'm a woman I gotta do all this? You can't help?"
Therapist: You mean you've been doing this all these years? Without complaining?
Mother: I guess I complained sometimes, but all of a sudden I got very angry, just because I'm the woman of the house doesn't mean—

I work harder than anybody, really, and there's no reason why everybody can't help and I told my husband, "Just because you're a man doesn't mean you can't do some of this work." He said he knows it but I should ask him. I said "Why do I have to ask you?"

It ended up with her husband apologizing.

Therapist: Well, listen, I told your husband he probably wouldn't like it if you got stronger.

Mother: They didn't like it either (indicating the children). I had a thing with John this week.

Therapist: Yeah, remember John, my saying last week if your parents changed roles I didn't think anyone would like it. So what happened? What was she like?

John: A pain in the neck.

Debbie: I didn't stay home. I stayed with a friend for three nights.

Mother: I didn't even miss you.

It seems in the process of changing roles, the mother had suddenly realized just what her role was and all the anger and resentment she had been hiding under her good girl role emerged. Most of this, now directed toward her husband, had probably been misdirected toward John all these years. This was the evidence I had been looking for as to his place in his parents marriage. Now that it was out in the open, it could be dealt with—but the husband wasn't there. I was frustrated. The time was ripe for focusing on the issues between the parents. As a substitute, we talked about the mother's relationship with both the children. Mother made light of Debbie's leaving home for three days, saying she trusted her in contrast to her great distrust of John. She proceeded to list all the reasons why she didn't trust him, based on past behavior.

John accused his mother of loving Debbie more, and of the two of them having a buddy-buddy relationship from which he was excluded. As the session began to degenerate into accusation and counter-accusation, I became ill at ease. I struggled to find a way of using the material that was emerging but felt I lacked a clear direction. I do not feel it is helpful or constructive for families to just "get all their feelings out" or "communicate openly and honestly" for long periods of time.   John's expressing his anger and hurt over the alliance between mother and Debbie does nothing to change that alliance. Mother, openly expressing her distrust of John, does nothing to change either her distrust or John's behavior. For me, the main value in open expression of feelings is to provide the therapist with working material. Once I have this I feel extremely uncomfortable in letting this type of communication go on. My frustration over the husband's absence interfered with my ability to shift gears and focus in a different direction.

I excused myself to have a consultation with the group. We decided to turn the sibling rivalry into a good behavior contest and use it as an incentive for change, to define John's behavior as a loving act toward his sister to keep her in the role of the good one and also to keep mother and Debbie close since mother couldn't be close to anyone who wasn't good. This was to be a message to mother that Debbie's good girl role was being maintained in relation to John's bad behavior. Regarding mother's distrust of John, it was decided I should tell John to give up trying to get his mother to trust him since we couldn't see any way he could do this as he couldn't change the past. This would be a message to mother that she was expecting the impossible of John.

The first intervention fell flat so far as the desired effect on mother was concerned as she used it against John saying, "You see, you're making Debbie and me even closer through your bad behavior."

Later in trying to figure out where this had gone wrong, I realized I had merely made an interpretation. It was not enough to define John's behavior as preserving the relationship between Debbie and her mother. I should have prescribed it, telling John he must persist otherwise they could not maintain their closeness. The mother then couldn't side with me against John if I told him to keep misbehaving.

When John was told to give up trying to get his mother to trust him, he insisted he would find a way. He cited the fact he was "going straight now" and doing better in school. The therapist pointed out that despite this fact, his mother still didn't trust him, to which he replied, "That's her problem. Even if no one in the family trusts me I'll trust myself."

He was congratulated for his independent stand. At the end of the session, I sent a note home with mother in a sealed envelope addressed to father. It said, "Dear Mr. W, I wish to apologize for having set a fire under your wife. I hope she's not too strong for you to handle. I'm concerned about this and will be discussing it with you."

This statement challenged him to deal with his wife, at the same time the therapist was taking responsibility for her changed behavior. It also assumed he would be coming to the next session, which he did.

Fifth Session

In this session, the family reported that John's behavior had improved and Debbie's had deteriorated. On John's weekly report from the school, he had received all Satisfactorys except for two. (This in contrast to all Unsatisfactorys when the family first came.) Mother and Debbie had had a fight and father described his wife as being a "terror." At this the mother launched into a tirade regarding her husband's health and her exasperation with him for not taking care of it.

After two heart attacks, he was smoking three packs of cigarettes a day, not watching his diet and getting no exercise. Rather than helping her with the household tasks he collapsed in front of the TV set every night. John also expressed his worry over his father's health and this was seized on as an opportunity to strengthen the bond between father and son. John was put in charge of an exercise plan for his father in which he agreed to supervise their exercising together for fifteen minutes every night.

Whenever possible I give a task to strengthen a bond. An action outside a session creates a new experience more effectively than a mere verbal discussion.

During this entire session, Debbie behaved in a disruptive and disrespectful manner. She kicked John's chair, acted bored and restless, yawned and stared out the window. During my consultation break, while the family was left alone the following exchange took place which epitomized the changes in the family.

Mother: (to Debbie) I think your behavior is terrible and I can't stand it. If you keep on acting like this I'm not going to let you go to that party.
John: (Chuckling with glee) I think she's doing it on purpose.
Father: What she does tonight is strictly your decision not mine.
Debbie: You told me—
Father: Yes, I was inclined to let you go tonight. In fact, I was the one who was trying to make it so you could go, but right now I don't care whether you go or not. It's mommie's decision.

The focus was off John, Debbie was the "bad one," John was the "good one," father was the "permissive one" turning the role of "tough guy" over to mother.

The manner in which I respond to change is crucial in this approach. If I am to maintain my systemic view of the family, I must interpret change systemically. Since I had advised the family to remain the same, based on my evaluation of the consequences of change, it is more appropriate to worry rather than rejoice over this occurence and use it as another opportunity to define all the family relationships as being interconnected. This requires a great deal of discipline on my part as my natural tendency is to become pleased in the face of change and express it exuberantly. If the family feels I am emotionally involved in its changing, they are apt to add it to their secret armamentarium. On the other hand, if they feel I am trying to hold them back their attitude can be "Why should I stay the same for her," rather than "Why should I change for her?"

In order not to seem unsympathetic to personal accomplishment, (such as John getting good grades) we decided to divide the rejoicing and worrying between me and the group. Since I had the personal contact, it was decided I would do the personal congratulating and later be reprimanded by the group for not taking into account the consequences of that achievement on the rest of the family. The group was consistently made the antagonist of change pitted against the therapist as protagonist.

I returned to the session with the following message:

Therapist: First let me tell you the group is unhappy about my congratulating John on his progress because they started worrying about Debbie and the effect that might have on her. Remember we had talked last week about how if you stopped misbehaving then Debbie's behavior wouldn't look as good and by your protecting your sister, she always comes off looking great and now she's not looking so great. You see if you start behaving—
John: So then don't let her look great. I'll look great and that's what I want.
Therapist: But what will happen to her?
John: She'll look like a bum.

Therapist: Don't you care if she looks like a bum?

John: No! Well, yeah, but . . . .

Debbie: I disagree with him because his behavior has nothing to do with the way they feel about me because if it does, they shouldn't have two children.

John: Yeah, I care about her. You don't care about me do you? (No answer from Debbie.)

Therapist: If you care about her you should—Well, never mind, I'll leave that up to you.

The group thought it was a good idea for father and John to exercise together and they wondered if the family thought John and father would ever be as close as Debbie and mother. (John and father thought they were.)

Regarding father's not taking care of himself, the group sent the following message:

Therapist: You know my group gets a little frisky now and then and I'm going to tell you what they said although you don't have to take it seriously. They thought mother should take out a huge amount of insurance and start looking around for another husband. (There was much laughter and mother seemed delighted with the suggestion.)

Mother: I like that, I'm serious, I'm going to call the insurance man. I'm not kidding!

Father: Fair enough.

Mother: At least I'd be taken care of.

Father: And I'd pay the premium?

Mother: Of course.

Before the next session I tried to anticipate the reaction to the major role shift. The main impetus for change had come from the mother's asserting herself. What would be the repercussions of her shifting her dissatisfaction and preoccupation from John to her husband? Since it was more than likely John had developed his symptomatic behavior as a deterrent for this, what would the penalty be? I speculated father would probably become depressed and might withdraw as his pattern was to avoid open conflict with mother. One of the ways he handled his depression was to become angry at the children. More than likely he would revert to this. If he engaged in open warfare with mother, she would probably become frightened, feel guilty about causing a heart attack and pull back herself.

The other possibility (usually not considered) was that the improvement might continue and the family might stabilize around the change. We have been caught many times without a strategy as we have failed to contemplate this possibility. I decided if the improvement continued in John, I would worry about father now that mother had turned her worry toward her husband. If it did not I would interpret it as John's way of taking the flak away from father again.

Sixth Session

The family opened this session with the announcement that "John has been making tremendous amounts of progress as far as behavior is concerned." For the last two weeks he had received all Satisfactorys on his report card. After an acknowledgement of John's achievement, I became concerned over the effect this would have on the marriage, and addressing myself to father said, "If your wife stops worrying about John I'm concerned she will start to worry about you and I don't know if you could take that. You looked worried at the last session."

Father: Yeah, I was.

Therapist: And I was thinking probably John can take it better than you.

Father: I've no doubt about that. No doubt about that. He probably could take—Maybe he's had more experience than I.

Therapist: I'm really wondering if I did right by getting into those issues of your marriage and causing some kind of change. You said your wife has been different. And what kind of problem is that going to cause you?

Father: Well, she's always had that concern about me. It's true she's probably given up to a certain extent. I feel bad about it because I don't seem to have the will power or the strength to do anything about it. I felt more embarrassed than anything else. I knew I was wrong and I had no defense. Why I do things that are bad for me I don't know.

Therapist: So if she starts worrying about you how are you going to handle it?

Father: She's been worrying about me for years.

Therapist: But, I mean if she really makes an issue of it, like last week.

Father: It could cause a lot of problems. She knows it, that's why she does it in a certain amount of moderation. She bears down on me and then eases up on me. Because I don't think I could live with it everyday and don't think she could either. Who could live with somebody constantly on their back?

Therapist: Uh, huh ... Well, you see, John can.

John: I have to live with it. I can't help it.

Therapist: And let me say that I think it's better the preoccupation goes to John because I think John can handle it better than you would be able to handle it and as long as it's on John, it won't upset anything in your marriage.

Father: I guess like most people, we have come to a certain accommodation with each other. I guess she's given up on certain things with me and I've given up on certain things with her also. We give up then we try again. We don't harp at each other constantly which wouldn't accomplish anything other than to make things worse. We ease up on John too sometimes. I don't think any kid could live with someone constantly pounding him.

John: (Wryly) Well, I'm living ain't I?

Father: Yeah, because we don't constantly pound you into the ground.

Therapist: (Keeps reiterating the point) But you see if John keeps on behaving better, then I do think your wife will direct more of her worries and concerns toward you.

Father: What are you suggesting?

Therapist: I don't know. I'm really in a bind. I—For a second there I was about to say to John, "You'd better start misbehaving again to save your parent's marriage," but then I decided that sounded silly so I won't say it.

Father: (To John) You know what she's saying?

John: Yeah, I know.

Father: In other words, if we don't pick on you, we're liable to pick on each other. (Laughing.) So, it's a good thing we have you. Well, I don't know, what do you do about a situation like that?

(Now that father is wondering about the situation, it is best for the therapist not to have any answers, but to let him arrive at his own conclusion.)

Therapist: (Sighing to mother) I don't know. Do you have any ideas?

Mother: Well, I'll tell you one thing. He's been sitting saying I'm not capable of this, and I'm not capable of that, and that's a crock of bullshit!

Father: What am I saying you're not capable of?

Mother: You were sitting saying, "Well, you've got to be the bad guy because my wife's not capable—" When the time comes when I have something to do, Goddammit, I do it. There are a lot of times in our family when things could be settled very pleasantly, but right away—you know, I'm beginning to agree with the kids—you are very unpleasant lots of the time! You come home grouchy, and you say, "Don't bother me, don't discuss it". There are a lot of situations that could be settled pleasantly, if you didn't blow up right away.

Now that the parental conflict has flared into the open, I asked John to change seats with father so he would not be in the middle. John was delighted with this, saying with a big grin, "I like the way she's talking."

Father takes off his coat for the fight.

Therapist: (To John) You like that?

Father: You like her giving me hell?

John: Yeah, you should get it once in a while!

Therapist: Rather than you, you mean?

John: Yeah!

For a short period of time, mother continues to assert herself, bringing up the issue of her husband's asking her to make calls for him and stating vehemently, "From now on you go call yourself!"

The husband manages to smooth things over, calm mother down and ends up with "We have our problems, but we can settle them. I'm satisfied with our marriage the way it is." The wife concurs. The couple has pulled together once more against change. The therapist decides to go along with the resistance saying, "Maybe, you should keep it that way."

The group supports the therapist sending back a message of praise, "The group wishes to express their admiration for the manner in which you protect one another. They are really touched by this show of affection."

The wife reaches over and holds her husband's hand and lovingly taps his foot. He is unresponsive and doubtful.

Father: I don't know, I don't know.

Therapist: What do you mean?

Father: The thing that bothers me a lot about what you said that my only involvement with my children is in a disciplining role—or that's what my main involvement is. (He has reverted to worrying about the children to avoid confronting his wife.)

Therapist: But it's an intense involvement—

Father: I'd like to be involved in other ways.

Therapist: How would you like to be involved?

Father: More on the friendly side, on the loving side, (stroking his heart) rather than on the disciplining side.

What you've just said makes me start thinking, maybe that's my main involvement, is the discipline department and I wouldn't want that to be the main involvement which maybe that is what it is without my realizing it. (The therapist, deep in thought, reminds him when they tried to change it, it affected the marriage.)

Father: (Shifting nervously in his chair) You can't change roles too abruptly without its disrupting something along the line.

We then have a discussion as to whether or not it's time for change and the therapist leaves John with the suggestion that when he notices friction developing between his parents he should misbehave and then take the spotlight onto himself again.

John reacts to this sourly with, "I'm not going to misbehave!" Father gently supports him with, "No, he can't start misbehaving. It's not in him." The therapist counters this with, "Well, I think you could if it was a matter of saving your parent's marriage." To which John vehemently replied, "Let them divorce!"

Seventh Session

This last intervention boomeranged. The intent was for John to continue to resist my suggestion that he sacrifice himself for his parent's marriage as he had done in the session by saying, "Let them divorce!" The message was actually directed towards the parents as a way of underlining the way in which John was used to avoid their marital conflicts.

The parents opened this session by complaining that John had reverted to his old behavior, was a hellion at home and a defeatist at school. The mother stated she was angry at me for my suggestion that John should misbehave in order to save his parents' marriage because everything had been going beautifully up to that time and she felt I had ruined everything.

I was completely taken back by this turn of events and sat thinking, "What the hell do I do now?" It was difficult to know if John's change in behavior was actually due to my suggestion, so I first decided to check this out with him. He affirmed this. But father didn't believe it and reprimanded him for kidding around. John insisted it was true saying, "I don't want your marriage to break up." I tried desperately to think of a way to use this positively and decided to rely on an old rule which I have found to be helpful, which is when you don't know what to do, simply follow their logic and run it into the ground. Turning to John I said, "Well then, you must have been worried your parents would separate for a long time because you have been misbehaving for many years."

John denied that this was the reason, and I looked puzzled. Mother then stated that although John had been difficult to live with, her husband had been even more so. "He just can't leave John alone. He had to pick on him for everything. He drove me crazy." Mother no longer supported father's harshness.

The father admitted this and gave as the reason for his irritation the school report in which the teacher said John had reverted to his defeatist attitude. "It's his attitude about himself and his work that infuriates me."

At this point, I had the choice of exploring what was obviously the father's projection in terms of his feelings about himself and his own work (I had known about this for some time) or to deal with it as an interactional issue in the family. I recalled how many times in the past I had labored to help a parent to arrive at an insightful conclusion, "Oh yes, now I see. I'm overreacting to my son's failure because I feel like a failure myself." And then to my consternation witnessed the parent continue to behave in exactly the same way despite this great wisdom. Although I had long since discarded this path as being ineffective, every now and then I forget a person's emotional behavior is not based on logic and therefore will seldom respond to logic. It seems like all you should have to do is point out to people what they are doing wrong and why they are doing it and they should be able to stop doing what they are doing. Unfortunately, this seldom works, the issue being not so much what one brings from the past but what one does with it in the present. I decided to explore defeatism as an interactional issue.

I wondered who had the greater defeatist attitude, John or father and which gave mother the bigger problem. Mother conceded it was father, but there was nothing she could do about it. She also felt defeated. Defeat was defined as a family problem.

In the group discussion before closing, we decided to label the family regression as a reaction to their changing too quickly. They were instructed not to try and change any relationship for the time being as it would be too upsetting. Whenever we reach what seems like a stalemate and cannot come up with an inspired intervention, we counteract the therapist and the family's feeling of defeat by labeling it as a reaction to change. One can always be sure there will be enough truth in this to have validity.

The family broke the next appointment giving as their reason the rush of the Christmas holidays, making it impossible for them to leave their business. I always accept the family's reason for a broken appointment as being legitimate and never challenge them on it as this would only make them defensive. Because of the holidays they were not seen for over a month. I anticipated that the holidays would provoke a great deal of anxiety in the family which would result in increased stress in all relationships with increased acting out on John's part.

Eighth Session

I was totally unprepared for the direction the family had taken. In working with preplanned strategies the therapist must be prepared to quickly shelve a carefully worked out plan and move in a totally different direction as the situation calls for it.

Father opened the session by saying,"It's been a perfect month, we have nothing to talk about." After the therapist collected herself, she said, "I used to say, 'Gee that's great, goodbye and good luck,' but now that I know what happens to families when they change too quickly, I'm going to say, 'I'm worried. What happened?'"

Both parents insisted they had nothing to complain about. John had been "great." A teacher had called to say how extraordinary he was doing. He was accomplishing work in school which his mother didn't feel he was capable of. She no longer felt he was going to get into serious trouble. I apologized for advising John to give up getting his mother to trust him because evidently he had succeeded. Debbie was the only person in the family who did not agree that everything had gone well. She complained about her brother. The therapist stated it must be very difficult for her to hear John praised so much. She denied this, of course.

I reviewed with the family the problems that had brought them here and the progress they had made. They admitted there were some minor problems still but these were "normal, like in any family." The one problem that had not changed was the sibling rivalry.

I suggested that we stop the therapy for the time being and keep the four sessions left in reserve for a future time. I took a break to check with the group to see if they had a different opinion. They agreed with me that therapy should be terminated, reminding me before I dismissed them to rehearse how they could get back to their former positions. It was decided I would interpret Debbie's dissatisfaction as her having higher expectations of change than any other member of the family. Since father still tended to get overly involved with the children, as a parting shot it was agreed I would tell mother how lucky she was to have a husband who really took over the kids and that she should take advantage of all that free time by going out and having a good time.

The parents responded with much laughter to this suggestion with father saying, "Do you hear a little—" and mother joining him with "yeah, we always hear a little—." The therapist asked innocently, "A little what?" The father said, "A little, ah, what do you call it, ah, nudge, a dig?"

This was the first indication the family gave of having recognized the double messages. We have no way of measuring this as we go along. However, whatever their perception it did not seem to reduce the effectiveness of the interventions.

The therapist responded with, "Well, the group just wanted to make sure that mother had a good time." Mother laughingly stated, "I'd like to, that's what I'm doing tonight—but I'm going with him. It's his birthday."

When the therapist interpreted to Debbie her high expectations, she admitted father had changed and things were much better between the two of them.

I asked the family to call me if a new difficulty arose. At this writing it has been nearly a year and I have not heard from them.

Reflections

This approach is relatively new to me, my experimentation with it being of several short years duration. Because of its swiftness and power, it often leaves me exhilarated, thinking I have discovered a magic key. However, when it doesn't work this well with other families or other situations (obviously the results are not consistent), I am left perplexed and disappointed. It is like finding a key to a door and then losing it again. Unable to go back to the more conventional way of working, yet unable to make the key work consistently, I find myself in a state of constant searching. The disadvantage in working this way is that each case requires an enormous amount of time, thought and energy. The interventions must be based on a clear knowledge of the family system and precisely aimed at the cycle of interaction in which the symptom is embedded. Otherwise they are ineffective. All families are not as easy to decipher as this one nor are they as susceptible to the interventions.

Whenever I present this work (seminars, workshops, classes), I am consistently asked the same questions. Since these same questions have probably arisen in the reader's mind, I will attempt to answer the most common of them briefly.

1. Question: Don't you feel this approach is manipulative?
   Answer: Yes, like all forms of therapy from Freudian analysis to behavior modification, it attempts to manipulate the behavior of people. The only difference is that in this method the emphasis is on manipulating the transactional game rather than just one individual within the game.
2. Question: Do you ever feel dishonest when you work this way?
   Answer: Dishonest, no; apprehensive, yes. There is a certain performance element in rehearsing and giving double messages

which caused me some discomfort in the beginning. However, this disappeared as I began to realize with each paradoxical message I was stating the underlying truth in the family. It sounds absurd because it is a systemic truth rather than an individual truth. When I tell parents the problems in their children are a small price to pay for preserving the marriage, I am defining their system as they are actually living it. The only deceit is in advising them not to change as a way of getting them to change. I call this using "psychology" on a family. In a profession based on psychology, we are strangely reluctant to make use of that art.

3. Question: Since this method does require a certain performance skill on the part of the therapist, can anyone do it? Or do you have to have a particular kind of personality?

   Answer: I believe anyone can cultivate the ability to sound sincere while delivering ambiguous messages. The main requirement is the ability to perceive the ambiguity in all human relationships and to appreciate the absurd and contradictory way in which this manifests itself in human systems. As stated in the *Pragmatics of Human Communication* "What has been found to drive people crazy must ultimately be useful in driving them sane." It is this conviction that enables the therapist to feel legitimate.

4. Question: Do you ever feel you are being disrespectful to the family?

   Answer: No, on the contrary, I always feel I am being most respectful. The very heart of this approach depends on a non-judgmental, noncritical totally accepting attitude. It respects each person's unique method of surviving within the political system of the family without blaming anyone. It is based on connoting all behavior as benignly motivated to keep the system going.

5. Question: Do you use this approach with every family?

   Answer: No. It isn't always necessary or even appropriate. It should be used with discretion depending on the receptivity of the family and their particular situation. Sometimes the conventional techniques of clarification, confrontation, communication and just plain old-fashioned support are sufficient to move a system. I reserve this method for situations when I feel the above will not work.

6. Question: Do you miss the kind of relationship you develop with a family when you work with them over a long period of time?

   Answer: Yes, I sometimes miss that old-friend-of-the-family feeling which comes from a lengthy acquaintance. I also miss the image of myself as a warm, wise sympathetic benefactor without whom the family could not function (a major reason for most of us choosing the profession in the first place). What I gain instead is a secret joy in observing the rapid changes albeit without direct credit or appreciation from the family. Above all, I miss all those Christmas and Chanukah presents I used to get!

Bibliography

Dunlap, K., The Technique of Negative Practice. *American Journal of Psychology, 55,* 270—273 (1942).

Frankl, Viktor E., Paradoxical Intention: a Logotherapeutic Technique. *American Journal of Psychotherapy, 14,* 520—535 (1960).

Haley, Jay, *Strategies of Psychotherapy,* New York: Grune & Stratton, 1963.

———, *Problem Solving Therapy,* Jossey-Bass, 1976.

———, ed. *Advanced Techniques of Hypnosis and Therapy: Selected Papers Milton H. Erickson, M.D.* New York: Grune & Stratton, 1967.

———, *Uncommon Therapy: The Psychiatric Techniques of Milton Erickson, M.D.* New York: W. W. Norton & Co., 1973.

Hoffman, Lynn, Breaking the Homeostatic Cycle. *Family Therapy,* ed., Philip Guerin. Gardner Press, 1976.

Minuchin, S., *Families and Family Therapy.* Harvard U. Press, 1974.

Newton, J. R., Therapeutic paradoxes, paradoxical intentions, and negative practice. *American Journal of Psychotherapy, 22,* 68—81 (1968).

Papp, P., Brief Therapy with Couples Groups. *Family Therapy,* ed., Philip Guerin. Gardner Press, 1976.

Selvini-Pelazzoli, *Self Starvation.* London: Chaucer Press, 1974.

———, The Treatment of Children Through the Brief Therapy of their Parents. *Family Process,* 13—4, 1974.

Watzlawick, Beavin, Jackson, *Pragmatics of Human Communication.* New York: Norton, 1967.

Watzlawick, P., Weakland, J. H., and Fisch, R., *Change: Principles of Problem Formation and Problem Resolution.* New York: W. W. Horton & Co., 1974.

Weakland, J. H., Fisch, R., Watzlawick, P., and Bodin A., Brief Therapy: Focused Problem Resolution. *Family Process,* 13, 141—168 (1974).

10

In-Laws and Out-Laws: A Marital Case of Kinship Confusion [1]

James L. Framo, Ph.D.

After 5 years of working together in cotherapy in our evening practice, my wife and I should have arrived at the point where we could predict after the first few sessions which couples were going to make it in marital therapy. In all honesty, however, our predictions have turned out to be pretty lousy. Couples who looked hopeless in the beginning often ended up with a new, vital marriage with the same partner, and others we were sure were going to put their marriage together got nowhere in therapy or later divorced. Considering that behavioral scientists have isolated only about 50 out of the million or so dimensions of marriage, maybe we do not have to turn in our credentials.

In any event, we were most pessimistic initially that Fred and Lynn's marriage had much of a chance of lasting in any meaningful way. Lynn had a whiney, highpitched, irritating voice with which she righteously harangued her husband, and Fred had that maddening, smiling passivity that drives people up

[1]Mary D. Framo, M.S.S., my wife, was cotherapist with me in the treatment of this couple. Views of this case were exchanged back and forth during the therapy and Mary also contributed her impressions to this writeup. Both separate and concurrent opinions are specified in this paper.

walls. Although on one level we liked them, we both had fantasies of choking them; evidently they stimulated some aspect of *our* shared introjects. Lynn was highly motivated for therapy *for* her husband; she was not only defensively impervious to any point of view but her own but was incapable of looking at her part in any transaction. It was more difficult to get Fred to commit himself to therapy because he had had a bad experience with a psychiatrist where each had engaged in a contest as to who could keep silent longer. Besides, Fred was weakly motivated to stay married, whereas Lynn desperately wanted to keep her husband. I do not know whether it was these challenges or the tangled relationship between Lynn and Fred's family that intrigued me conceptually that made me decide to continue with them. Furthermore, I planned to put them in a couples' group, where a lot of help would be available in handling them (for a description of my method of conducting couples' groups, see Framo, 1973).

Fred and Lynn's problems were rather interesting. Both in their 30s, physically attractive, and moneyed, they were married 3 years and had a 2-year-old girl and a baby boy. Fred, very successful with his own business, had recently left his wife and children and moved into his parents' house because "I wasn't sure I wanted to be married." After a few days he had decided he did not want to break up his family, and when he returned home he agreed to come for therapy. When asked how she saw their problems, Lynn poured forth the following story, insinuating that once the therapists heard it they would look at Fred in astonishment and start therapizing him forthwith. Lynn said that they married in another city, where her own family was, and moved here, where his family was. Although Fred's sister Elaine vehemently opposed him marrying Lynn, she and Fred's mother, Ann, actively tried to ingratiate themselves with Lynn by buying her gifts, inviting her daily to go shopping with them, and dropping in to see her every day. Lynn said that initially she was flattered and pleased to have another family to take the place of her own; she had not recognized that her acceptance was based on being adopted and absorbed into the old system. Lynn said, however, "All that togetherness got to be more than I could handle. We had no life of our own because his family members were always under our feet." But Lynn said she was less bothered by the overcloseness than she was by the unusual displays of affection between Fred and his mother and sister. She said that Fred kissed his mother and sister "full on the lips, and they sat on his lap often and he patted their rear ends and caressed their legs. It's positively disgusting the way they slobber over him; everybody notices it and comments on it and when I mention their behavior to his mother and sister they say, 'But we *love* him; we're a close, affectionate family.'" Lynn went on to say with intense feeling, "He knows I can't stand it; it eats me up alive. I told him to stop it for my sake. I want to fight for my husband and get him away from them." Lynn said she could not understand why Elaine's husband (Elaine had recently married) did not seem to be bothered by the near-incestuous relationship between his wife and brother-in-law. Lynn began withdrawing from his family, yet she manifested increasing preoccupation with them, becoming furious whenever Fred visited his family.

She was giving contradictory messages, however; she felt spurned and hurt when Fred's sister did not invite her to be maid of honor at her wedding. Fred felt he was being forced to choose between his original family and his wife and he was resentful over having to sneak around to see his mother and sister. I did not realize Fred even had a father until Lynn said, "Fred's Dad is a nothing, a zero, completely dominated by his wife." The incident which precipitated the open rift occurred when Lynn approached her mother-in-law for help in handling her problems with Fred, and her mother-in-law asked to speak to Fred alone, at which point she advised her son to get a divorce. Lynn had not realized that not only is blood thicker than water but that it is wise in this world to know who your friends and family really are. Fred's private conference with his mother made him leave Lynn, but after he told us some history of his family we understood why he again left his parents' home to return to his wife.

Fred said that while he was growing up he hardly knew his parents. Since his parents had a business in which they worked together 18 hours a day, he and his sister, who was 5 years younger than he, spent a great deal of time together and were "very, very, very close." With the utterance of each "very" I got an image of one intertwined body of fused parts. He said, "She came to me for everything, I tucked her in bed and read her stories and gave her baths and listened to her; I guess I was like a father to her." Fred's mother was 18 years older than Fred and his father was 15 years older than his mother, age gaps which promoted the realness of being an oedipal victor. As a matter of fact, Fred's mother became openly involved with another man and when Fred was 15 years old she asked him if she should leave his father. Fred said he was flabbergasted at being placed in this position, and finally asked mother to stay because of the younger sister. Mother's boyfriend became like a member of the family and Fred said he felt closer to that man than he did to his own father. He was bewildered by his father's indifference about the situation and infuriated at him for doing nothing about mother's affair, but he said nothing. Although the other man died some years ago, to this day nobody has ever said anything about this affair, which went on for years; Fred said it was like an elephant in the living room with everyone pretending it was not there. He and his father became so alienated in subsequent years that when one entered the room the other would leave. In more recent years, Fred said, he and father had made some sort of peace with each other and they were now partners in the business, although one got the impression listening to Fred that his father, in effect, worked for him. Early in the therapy Fred said, longingly, "My father and I get along now, but I don't really know him and I'd like to have a relationship with him before he dies." This kind of statement is always my cue to state that our therapy includes bringing in the family of origin of each partner for a session, usually toward the end of therapy, after they have changed and are ready to deal with their parents and siblings when they bring them in. (This method of involving adults in sessions with their family of origin is explicated in Framo, 1976). Although most people fervidly rule out such sessions for themselves, invariably they encourage the spouse to bring in his or her original family, reasoning that all the stuff the partner had been dumping on them would revert back to the original targets. In Lynn's case it was different: She strongly opposed Fred's bringing in his family. This position made us recognize that she had an investment in his family which went beyond her surface complaints. Her family background provided the clues for understanding her secret agenda of wanting to be the daughter in his family, something which could never be.

Lynn's parents divorced when she was 2 years old and she was raised by her mother, grandparents, and mother's three sisters. She spoke glowingly of her relationship with her mother, saying they were very close and mother was "a perfect mother." Lynn was extremely bitter toward her father, saying that he had nothing to do with her when she was small, and that when she was a teenager he would only see her every few years when he went to her city for a convention. Their relationship was characterized primarily by conflict followed by long periods of hurt withdrawal on both sides. She knew little about the causes for the divorce because her mother did not want to talk about it; for years her father had been trying to tell "his side of the story but I refused to listen to it because he'd tell a bunch of lies about my mother. I owe her a great deal and I owe him nothing." I initially got the impression that Lynn had had almost no contact with her father through the years, and it was only when pressed for more details that she reluctantly indicated that he sent her gifts, telephoned and wrote her frequently, and at one point took her to Europe with him and one of his daughters from his second marriage. Then Lynn added, acidly, "He never came to my wedding or invited me to his, and he never introduced me as his daughter to his second wife, who threatened to leave him if he had much to do with me." Lynn's mother remarried when Lynn was 13, and after that man was killed in an accident her mother married for a third time, this present marriage being described as "disastrous." When we suggested that at some point we would have a session with her and her parents she said, as anticipated, "No way. If you insist on that you'll never see me again. My father still hates my mother after all these years and feels I have sided with her, which I have because I have good reason to." Then, crying, she said, "Do you think I give a damn about that man who's supposed to be my father?" I indicated that if she could ever bring herself to deal with her parents, and if I could give a father back to her, she would be less hooked into her husband's family and she and Fred might have a chance to have a real marriage. Her uncharacteristic silence for several minutes following that intervention gave us our first hope that maybe change was possible in this situation. Insofar as Lynn rejected her own yearning for a father, she attributed to her husband an attachment to his family which she endlessly complained about but envied. Fred was also the target of her displaced fury. The fact that Fred's primary loyalty was indeed to his original family does not negate the validity of her dynamic efforts. For me, the best way of resolving this problem was to take Lynn's problems back to where they began, to bring her and her father together and to strengthen that relationship. At this point in the therapy, however, she was nowhere near ready to do this.

When Fred and Lynn joined a couples' group with two other couples Lynn proceeded to impress them with the juicy details of Fred's sexy relationship with his mother and sister. She went on and on about Fred's family, expecting the other two couples to be sufficiently shocked to tell Fred he should renounce his original family. However, the other two couples had been in a group for some time and were too sophisticated to take Lynn's words at face value; as a matter of fact, one group member picked up quickly how obsessed she seemed to be about his family. No matter where a discussion started in the group she referred the topic back to his family. Mary and I and the group made valiant attempts to get Lynn off his family and onto herself. It did not work; we would get a flood of self-justifying words. I then used an intervention that had been quite effective in the past with people who were openly critical of their in-laws: I told Lynn that by carping about his family she was doing herself a disservice and sabotaging her own goals. So long as she criticized his family, he, of course, had to defend them and never had to get in touch with his own anger toward them *because she was expressing it for him.* I had not reckoned with Lynn's formidable defense; that confrontation brought a change in her behavior for only 2 weeks, and when Fred still could not acknowledge any negative feelings about his family, she went back to her broken record. I began to feel helpless. I was supposed to be the expert; besides, all those assistant therapists in the group could not budge them either.

Now to be sure we knew that the sexual overtones in the behavior between Fred and his mother and sister would have given a psychoanalyst a field day; the oedipal interpretations were so obvious you could get them for half price. But we wanted to deal with this material on our terms and with our timing, not his wife's. Moreover, since this "sexual behavior" was so egosyntonic for him we had to discover another route to changing the order of Fred's priorities. Luckily, Fred's family provided an incident that for the first time made Fred deal with them in a different way. They did something which really got him mad at them; these are the serendipitous things that sometimes help the therapy to go. Fred was much better off financially than his sister and brother-in-law, and his parents, feeling their two children should have equal material advantages, would buy things for Elaine and charge them to the business where Fred and Dad were "partners." On the occasion of this particular incident, while Fred and Lynn were out of town, his parents went into Fred's house and removed some valuable items to give to his sister. Fred said that not only did they violate the privacy of his home, but they lied to him, saying they took the items for themselves rather than his sister. (It should be mentioned that in recent months, since Elaine and Lynn had had a falling out, there had been no contact between Fred and his sister. Fred's parents acted as the communicators between their two children.) On seeing Fred's anger to his family Lynn was triumphant, but we all had to sit on her to get her to keep her two cents out of it. When Fred hinted that he could get back at his family by cutting off their funds we began to get some sense of the power he had in that original family, in contrast to the relative impotence he manifested in dealing with his wife. At this stage of therapy the most Fred could do relative to his original family was to ask his parents not to come in his house when he was not there. He was not yet ready to deal with his family about the real issues.

Because the sexual relationship is extremely sensitive to other difficulties in a marriage, it was no surprise to discover that this couple had sexual problems. In one session Fred said that one reason he left Lynn was because of his dissatisfaction with their sex life. This statement made Lynn very angry; she said she was the one who had to approach him for sex and, besides, how dare he bring this up in the group without first discussing it with her at home? This interchange confirmed further Fred's reluctance to confront Lynn, except in the sanctuary of the group; Lynn, too, often said she had to come to group to find out what Fred was thinking. I have seen this phenomenon many times and have come to believe that one of the reasons people go to conjoint marital therapy is to provide a safe setting to tell their mates what they really feel or think. Husbands and wives, I have learned, are often afraid of each other. When they can level with each other, on all levels, on their own, they are probably ready to terminate therapy, or perhaps the marriage. In any event, Fred related that in the past he had always been attracted by "showgirl, trashy broads," and one of the reasons he was uncertain about being married was that he was not sure he wanted to give up a swinging bachelor life. Lynn, he said, was more refined, like his sister and, moreover, she had a habit of compulsively washing her genital area before and after sex, which turned him off. The material that Fred had given was rich. I wondered to myself whether Fred split the erotic introjects of mother and sister into the familiar whore-nun dichotomy that men fantasize about women, and I thought he was bound to have difficulty relating sexually to a wife who chastely washed away dirty sex. I could not resist the temptation to communicate a piece of this thinking to him by wondering aloud whether he did not feel unfaithful to his mother and sister when he married Lynn. Following that observation Fred started giggling and then went into paroxysms of laughter he could not stop. His uncontrollable laughter contagiously spread to the rest of the group, suggesting that a universal theme had been triggered off.

In addition to exploring the deeper cross-currents in the marriage, I also dealt with the more external manifestations of the disturbed relationship. From time to time I used such techniques as *quid pro quo* negotiations, paradoxical instructions, task assignments, clarifying of communication, and the feedback technique (where one partner must listen and repeat back the other's message until the content and emotional meaning are heard correctly). Fred and Lynn had to repeat the messages many times before the partner agreed that it was right. Fred's withdrawal and inability to share opinions or feelings was based in part on his feeling of being overwhelmed by her barrages and his inability to match her clever use of words. Audiotape playback of Lynn's monolog sometimes helped her realize how she must sound to others and why people often closed their ears to her; Fred also came to see how silence can be more devastating than screaming. Closely connected with their style of communication were their fight styles (Bach & Wyden, 1969) and their difficulty in reconciling the natural ambivalence of love and hate that exists in all intimate relationships (Charny, 1969). Compared to her howitzers, Fred felt he had a pop gun; besides, her belt line was so high and she was so sensitive to criticism that Fred had to be most circumspect in dealing with issues with her. On the other hand, Fred's dirty fighting technique of avoidance of fights and being Mr. Nice Guy did not change until he observed the angry interchange in other couples and came to learn that intimacy without conflict is impossible.

As the sessions progressed Fred became more assertive and unwilling to tolerate Lynn's onslaughts. His anger grew to match hers, culminating in a fist fight between them at home followed by Fred again leaving her to live with his parents. I was discouraged anew by this turn of events, although the fist fight in their case was at least an indication that Fred was relying less on camouflaged and silent hostilities. Mary was more hopeful about them than I, and the group's impressions were mixed. I myself learned from this experience that sometimes physical violence can paradoxically communicate that important matters are at stake; it can show deep concern and can represent a desperate bid to be taken seriously. Fred kept telling Lynn that she was too needy and demanding; he was alluding to what Martin (1976) has described as the "lovesick" wife. Lynn got very upset at this, saying, "I want to give him so much and he wants to give me so little." Group members kept telling her that she sounded like she wanted to possess him 100%, and that the hungrier she was, the more he moved away from her; they felt Fred could give more if she stopped pushing. With respect to her obsession with his family, she was repeatedly given feedback that it was his family, not hers.

Among the reasons I've come to believe that couples group therapy is the treatment of choice for premarital, marital, and separation and divorce problems is that the other couples provide not only models of how marital struggles can be worked out but also models of what to avoid. An event took place in the group that had the serendipitous effect of stimulating their movement in the therapy. Another couple in the group was planning to divorce, and the turmoil this couple was going through really shook up Fred and Lynn. For the first time they faced the real possibility of divorce, with its attendant pain. At this time another therapeutic dimension of couples groups emerged: Certain events in a group can create a contagion of affect which reawakens in full force early, forgotten feelings. This phenomenon seems to have the same effect as Paul's (1976) cross-confrontation technique in reviving old suppressed or repressed feelings. The transactions of the other couple put Lynn in touch with her unremembered anguish surrounding the divorce of her parents, and Fred connected with the shock and anger about his parents' near divorce of many years ago. Both of them, like everyone else whose parents had had bad marriages, consciously wanted better marriages than their parents. Furthermore, basically, neither partner wanted to lose the other. I myself became convinced again of the old adage about psychotherapy—that people do not change unless they *have* to, when they feel it in the gut, and when the consequences of not changing are unacceptable. Shortly after their fist fight, Fred moved back with his wife again and they arranged to go away together to a resort area for a few days where they planned to "talk over our problems." Fred said he wanted to tell Lynn how difficult it was for him to balance all his roles of son, father, brother, and husband, and Lynn had wanted to tell him she could more see how she was driving him away. "Instead of talking, however," Fred said, "we swam, had some great meals, slept late, made love, and then we didn't need to talk." (Remember the old advice of family doctors to "take a vacation"?) They were both, by now, strongly motivated to work on self, and the enormous resistance to bringing in original families had faded. Now I was ready to bring to bear that most powerful of therapy techniques, family of origin sessions.

I have become convinced, as have Bowen (Anonymous 1972, and Bowen 1974), Boszormenyi-Nagy and Spark (1973), Haas (1968), and Whitaker (1976), that working things out directly, face-to-face, with the family of origin, rather than via the transference with a therapist, can have a powerful effect on the original problems for which people come to therapy. Verily, my experience with this method has persuaded me that one session with the family of origin, conducted in a specific kind of way, is usually far more potent and effective than numerous regular therapy sessions. It needs to be kept in mind that this method does not just consist of bringing in family of origin; clients need to be prepared to really deal with and confront their original family members in special kinds of ways (see Framo, 1976).[2] The clients' inordinate unwillingness and outright refusal to involve their parents and brothers and sisters in the treatment process testifies to the great power of this approach. Considerable experience is needed with the method before a marital or family therapist learns how to deal with the resistances. One of the reasons I integrate couples' group therapy with family of origin work is that in attempting to overcome the nearly instinctive aversion to bringing in original family I will use whatever help I can get. I push in this direction forcefully because of my convictions about what these sessions can do. An atmosphere develops in the groups whereby everybody is expected to bring in their original families. Bringing them in has become almost like a final exam before graduation, and the group members exercise considerable pressure on others to do it, even while they are frightened to do it themselves. When the

[2] In recent years I have had a number of requests from family therapists to have sessions with their families of origin. Although the preparation for these sessions has to be foreshortened, since these therapists are not regular clients in ongoing couple or family therapy, even these brief encounters, according to those who have had them, have proved worthwhile and productive. No other publication of mine has prompted so many letters from professional therapists in terms of how the family of origin paper has affected not only their professional practice but their personal lives as well. There is, I believe, a universal longing to try at least to come to terms with parents before they die.

reluctant members see the leaps in progress made by those who have their sessions, they become more willing to consider it.

While Lynn was now intellectually prepared to consider bringing in her parents, when we got right down to it she was terrified of having her parents come in together. She said that her father would not sit in the same room with her mother. In addition, she was not sure her father would even come in with her alone. I told her I had confidence in her and that when she herself really wanted him in she would find a way. Late one night I got a call from Lynn and she said, "Waddayaknow, my dad said he'd be glad to come in. I'm surprised." Further preparation of Lynn for the session consisted of going over her family history again, this time in more detail. She was again resistive to the suggestion from all of us that she listen to her dad's side of the story, saying that she could not do that to her mother. I said that listening to him did not make her a disloyal traitor to her mother. Her fixed view of her father seemed so immutable that I wondered whether the session would accomplish much. Mixed in with her resentment and defensiveness, however, were the detectable signs of great foreboding that are prodromal for family of origin sessions. I have speculated that perhaps one basis for this intense fear is that people must feel they were loved by their parents, and there always exists the risk that they will discover otherwise, so they are afraid to expose themselves to this last chance to find out the truth. The group was supportive of Lynn around her anxiety about the session, and they helped her delineate the issues she would take up with her father. Lynn knew that she would be on her own in the session with Dad, that even Fred would not be present.

Mr. T., Lynn's father, was a prominent research scientist in a nearby city, and when we met him we were struck with his obvious interest in Lynn and her welfare, contrary to her statements about his disinterest in her. In the early part of the session Lynn could not contain herself and told her father how she had felt rejected by him all her life, that he had abandoned her as a child, and that through the years had little to do with her. She said the rejection got confirmed when he did not come to her wedding and did not invite her to his when he married again. Her father was taken back by this onslaught, and keeping in mind our belief that incoming parents need support, we cautioned Lynn to slow down and listen. Obviously relieved that finally Lynn agreed to listen to his version of past events, he told the following story. He said that his marriage to Lynn's mother failed because his wife put her own family before him (sound familiar?). He said that they lived with his mother-in-law, and when his marriage relationship worsened his wife and mother-in-law teamed up to get a court order evicting him from the house. Furthermore, they had the money to hire "tough" lawyers who managed to legally block all his efforts to see Lynn. Mr. T. cried as he remembered, not only the humiliation of the experience, but the torment over being cut off from access to his little girl. Lynn was astonished at this story. She went through a period of great confusion, trying to reconcile her lifelong animosity toward her father with this new information that made the bitterness untenable and inappropriate. She had never seen her father cry before and she did not know how to deal with it, except to cry herself with a perplexity that seemed to say, "Damn it, I'm not supposed to care for you. You're my pet hate." They went on to talk about the misunderstandings and miscommunications that had occurred through the years, but Lynn kept going back to that stunning realization: "You mean you didn't see me when I was little because you were legally *prevented* from doing so? My God, do you know what this means to me?" A number of other issues were discussed during the session but the foregoing interchange overshadowed everything else. However, another issue came up that was important. Mr. T.'s present wife could not tolerate any mention of his previous wife or child, and whenever Lynn visited him she could not stay at their house and instead had to stay with Mr. T.'s sister. Mr. T. decided at this session that he was no longer going to allow his present wife to determine the kind of relationship he was going to have with Lynn and that she would be welcome in his home any time. Before he left the session he asked me for the name of a marital therapist in his home town because he wanted to work on his problems with his present wife.

Following the session with her Dad, Lynn had to face her mother with the truth; and for the first time she got angry at her mother, not only for what her mother and grandmother did to keep her father from her, but for concealing the facts all these years. The rigid dichotomy of father-devil and mother-saint began to dissolve, and this external shift was reflected in an inner rearrangement which in turn created some new behaviors in Lynn. Her voice lost much of its stridency, she began talking with her father for the first time about what was going on between her and Fred and his family, and everyone in the group noticed her lessening preoccupation with Fred's family. Since people fear not only change in themselves, but also a change in their intimate other, it was not surprising that Fred subtly began trying to nudge Lynn back to some of her old ways. It became obvious that Lynn's behavior had served a defensive function for him *vis-a-vis* his family, and when this time she did not cooperate he was forced to face his own conflicts about them. Fred, furthermore, had progressed so much in therapy that only a few interpretative comments were needed to block these efforts to use Lynn. There was now no escaping the need for Fred to deal with his family. He handled his anxiety about the session by doing a lot of preliminary work with each parent alone prior to the session. Although he did not want to be met with any surprises in the session, the one person he did not speak to was his sister Elaine. He had not seen her for a long time because of the hard feelings between his sister and his wife, and also because, as he put it, "Elaine's so damn spoiled I really didn't want to see her myself." Since his parents were the go-betweens, his mother informed Elaine about the session. Some members of the group developed hypotheses about what would happen during Fred's family conference (e.g., whether the family would discuss the other man in Mom's life), and Lynn said she was really looking forward to listening to the tape of the session.

Both of Fred's parents and his sister Elaine were present for the session. Elaine and Fred were polite to each other, with the kind of controlled wariness that old lovers display when they have not seen each other for a long time; they had to be careful not to let the other know they still cared. Dad, looking like the grandfather of Fred, said almost nothing, and Mom, a handsome, well-dressed woman, did most of the talking. It quickly became apparent that Fred called the shots in this family, however; whenever he started to speak everyone deferred to him. This was a Fred we had never seen before. Mom, early in the session, brought up the subject of her relationship with the other man. (Fred, it will be recalled, had prepared his mother to do so.) She attempted to justify it by saying that she came from a family where money was extremely important. She had married Fred's father, a much older man, because he had money, but shortly after they married he lost his business and in order to regain his wife's love he worked 18 hours a day in a new business. She said, "My husband came from humble beginnings and would have been satisfied with less, but I spent the money faster than he could make it. So I don't blame him in a way. Still, he was paying more attention to the business than to me and finally I told him, 'You either stop being married to the business or I'm getting a divorce.'" It was apparently at that point that she asked Fred, at the age of 15, whether she should divorce, and also at that time she got involved with this other man who had money. The tension in the room began to rise at this point, and Fred confronted his father with how angry he had been for tolerating having this other man living in their house. Fred's father, paralyzed with feeling at that point, could not speak. Recognizing his inability to deal with this loaded area, we moved on to the relationship between Elaine and Fred. Elaine said that all she remembered about her childhood was being alone, except for Fred. She cried when she remembered the day Fred told her he was getting married. She was quite open about her jealousy, but we were startled when Fred said he had the same feelings of shock when she got married. At that point in the session Elaine switched from tears to intense anger, saying that Lynn was responsible for the alienation that existed in their family. Other issues were discussed, such as the open display of affection between Fred and sister and mother, the resentment over Fred "ruling" them, and Fred's trying again, unsuccessfully, to reach his father. When the session ended we knew there would have to be another one, the next time including Lynn and Elaine's husband. In addition to the unfinished business from this session, there was the issue of the parents trying to push Fred into taking Elaine's husband, Barry, into his business. We also knew that the two natural enemies, Elaine and Lynn, had to work out some rapprochement in order for their respective marriages to survive.

Following Fred's family of origin session, Fred's mother got in touch with Lynn and the two of them became friendly again. Lynn was very pleased by this development but several members of the group cautioned her that perhaps her mother-in-law was using her in a tactical maneuver to gain favor with Fred. Besides, this alliance was an unstable one since Elaine was now on the outside of the triangle and could not stay out. Lynn had changed considerably by this time and had more objectivity about the situation. Fred felt that while his session with his family had accomplished much he was concerned about the rift between him and his sister, as well as his inability to get through to his Dad. When he mentioned that he hardly knew Elaine's husband I suggested he have lunch with Barry to get to know him. The following week, coincidentally, Barry invited him to lunch and Fred reported that when they got together he realized for the first time Barry's resentment of him.

In preparation for the session to include Fred, his parents and sister, Lynn, and Barry, Lynn was warned to play it cool. She had a lot of feeling about being scapegoated, but did manage to be less reactive. In this session several important things happened. Barry told Fred in no uncertain terms that Fred was arrogant, that he treated his parents badly, and he said, "Everybody in this family is supposed to cater to you." He went on to say that Fred's worship of money indicated a distorted sense of values about life. Fred's Dad, speaking up for the first time, noted that Fred had some of his mother's preoccupation with money. Fred said that before he would take Barry into the business Barry would have to prove himself. Barry said, "Don't do me any favors." Mom kept deploring in the background the possible breakup of the family. Barry knew the history of the relationship between his wife and Fred, yet denied any feelings of jealousy. I then told him the story of a Sid Caesar skit I had once seen where Sid Caesar comes into a room and catches Carl Reiner kissing his wife. They all agree to handle this matter in a civilized manner and discuss it rationally, but a few minutes later Sid Caesar gets furious with Carl Reiner over the way the martinis were mixed. Barry got the point even if he could not respond to it. The highlight of this session, however, was that Fred and his father were finally able to have a dialog about the important things that happened between them through the years. We had to exert some effort to keep mother out of that interchange. What really touched father was when Fred said he had longed for more closeness with him. Fred, like Lynn, was surprised that parents can feel rejected too. They broke through to each other when Fred told Dad that he had never wanted to be passive like him and that he also paradoxically wanted to beat him out and be more successful. While Fred felt he had turned out to be a better businessman, it was a hollow victory because he realized that he did not want to lose a father in the process. He also said he had come to admire many fine qualities in his Dad, qualities that he himself did not have. The entire family then witnessed an event they had never thought they would see—a withdrawn, isolated father deeply sobbing about all the disappointments in his life. They were even more stunned when he pulled himself together and began, at long last, to take charge of all the squabbles in the family. He even mediated some agreements between Fred and Barry, and Elaine and Lynn.

Only a few more sessions were needed with Fred and Lynn following Fred's second family of origin session. Fred said that some pervasive, nameless dread that had always been present in his family of origin (a dread that other clients had reported in previous family of origin sessions) had disappeared. He felt he could love Lynn and his own family without feeling untrue to either. Fred said that he and Dad had continued to talk personally, ever since the family session. He was enormously pleased to have a relationship with his father, at long last. Lynn recounted an event that had enormous significance to her. On her birthday, her parents were together with her for the first time since she was a little girl, and she took a picture of the two of them together. Her father's bitterness toward Lynn's mother had vanished after he felt Lynn had forgiven him. Lynn also reported that she and Elaine had gone shopping together for their children (Elaine was pregnant); Lynn's involvement with Fred's family appeared to be on a realistic basis. On their way to the last session Fred and Lynn had an argument, which I saw as the usual termination regression. When I called them 6 months later they said they were doing "just great and felt truly married for the first time."I thought to myself, considering where they started, not bad for 25 sessions.

Summary Evaluation

Although in some respects the marital problems that Fred and Lynn brought to therapy were of the garden variety, I selected this case to write about in order to illustrate the powerful effects that extended families have on a marital situation. We all know of the past dynamic forces that families of origin exert in shaping people and marriages (best exemplified in Dicks' work at Tavistock, 1967), but less widely realized are the *current* influences of both families and both sets of in-laws on the husband and wife. If you are treating a couple and you do not specifically ask what is going on in their relationships with parents, brothers, sisters, aunts, uncles, and in-laws, they usually do not tell you. Individual therapists focus on their patients and tend to ignore the marital partners or the children. Family therapists and marriage counselors all too frequently ignore the families of origin, both from the standpoint of understanding the marital struggle or utilizing extended family as a therapeutic resource. It is possible that Fred and Lynn's marriage relationship would have improved just from marital or couples' group therapy. (I do believe, however, that they would have had a destructive divorce without treatment.) Most of the marital cases I have seen, nevertheless, made their breakthroughs following the family of origin sessions. Through most of the therapy Lynn was not willing to bring in her father, and we had to clear away some other aspects of the troubled relationship before she could deal with that dimension. Once the more superficial aspects of their difficulties were handled, and under the threat of losing her loved-hated husband, her antipathy to dealing with her father was surmounted. When she got her father back, the force of her need to work out her intrapsychic conflicts *through* Fred nearly dissipated.

One aspect of Fred's role in his original family was that of the parentified one; his being an apparent winner resulted in a thin triumph, which exacted a high price. His exalted position in that family created a sense of confidence that enabled him to be successful in the outside world, but, like many prominent and socially successful people, he was severely damaged in dealing with intimate relationships. His emotional radar signaling system chose a mate who would fight the battle with his family that he could not; Lynn expressed his anger *for* him. His family of origin sessions had many aspects, but the critical event, like that of Lynn's, was getting the father he felt he never had. Both Lynn and Fred shared the introject of the longed-for father.

The couples' group format provides many more therapeutic benefits than just serving as leverage to bring about family of origin sessions. In the group sessions the partners learn by identification, get support and understanding, and profit from the confrontations from the other group members. Since marital interactions are often driven by strong, often overwhelming emotions, the group helps in tempering these, leading to more reality thinking. One part of my method of conducting couples group sessions consists of every member of the group of three couples, in turn, giving feedback to the couple that had just been focused upon. By alternating in the "patient" and "observer" roles the individuals often treat themselves through others, and they also gain a sense of adequacy and competence. Spouses, moreover, get to see how other people respond to their partners, and this helps loosen the fixed, distorted views that all people have about their mates. In Lynn's and Fred's case, the group did not see either partner as crazy and unreasonable as each saw the other.

Lynn's and Fred's therapy was an instance when the treatment worked the way it is supposed to, according to my conceptual outlook (Framo, 1965, 1972). It should go without saying that not all my cases do. Too often case reports in the literature make the treatment sound smooth and easy, as if therapy progressed evenly and barriers were easily overcome. Someday a book should be written on treatment failures, because I think we can learn a lot from them. I was glad to participate in this volume, which is a first in requesting contributors to describe the process of treatment as it really happens, like marriage, with its ups and downs, backsliding, treatment errors, despair, hope, times when nothing seems to be happening, and times when those occasional bursts of movement occur that make it all worthwhile. I happen to believe that it is extremely difficult to change oneself or other people, and one is damn lucky when it happens.

References

Anonymous. Toward the differentiation of a self in one's own family. In J.L. Framo (Ed.) *Family interaction: A dialogue between family researchers and family therapists.* New York: Springer, 1972

Bach, G.R., & Wyden, P. *The intimate enemy.* New York: Morrow, 1969.

Boszormenyi-Negy, I., & Spark, G.M. *Invisible loyalties.* New York: Harper & Row Medical Dept., 1973.

Bowen, M. Toward the differentiation of self in one's family of origin. In F.D. Andres & J.P. Lorio (Eds.), *Georgetown Family Symposia* (Vol. 1) (1971–1972). Washington D.C.: Georgetown Univ. Medical Center, Dept. of Psychiatry, 1974.

Charny, I. Marital love and hate. *Family Process,* 1969, 8, (1).

Dicks, H.V. *Marital tensions.* New York: Basic Books, 1967.

Framo, J.L. Rationale and techniques of intensive family therapy. (Section on "Marriage problems in family therapy"). In Boszormenyi-Nagy, I., & Framo, J.L. (Eds.), *Intensive family therapy.* New York: Harper & Row Medical Dept., 1965.

Framo, J.L. Symptoms from a family transactional viewpoint. In Ackerman, N.W., Lieb, J., & Pearce, J.K. (Eds.), *Family therapy in transition.* Boston: Little Brown, 1970. (Also reprinted in: Sager, C.J., & Kaplan, H.S. (Eds.). *Progress in group and family therapy.* New York: Brunner/Mazel, 1972.)

Framo, J.L. Marriage therapy in a couple's group. In Bloch, D.A. (Ed.), *Techniques of family psychotherapy: A primer.* New York: Grune & Stratton, 1973.

Framo, J.L. Family of origin as a therapeutic resource for adults in marital and family therapy: You can and should go home again. *Family Process,* 1976, 15 (2),

Haas, W. The intergenerational encounter: A method in treatment. *Social Work,* 1968, 13 (3).

Martin, P. *A marital therapy manual.* New York: Brunner/Mazel, 1976.

Paul, N. Cross-confrontation. In Guerin, P.J. (Ed.), *Family therapy.* New York: Gardner Press, 1976.

Whitaker, C. A family is a four dimensional relationship. In Guerin, P.J. (Ed.), *Family therapy.* New York: Gardner Press, 1976.

11

On Becoming
A Mystery

Marianne Walters, M.S.W.

Preface

Mrs. M: Joan (her daughter) assaulted me last night while I was sleeping, and I went to the hospital and was examined; the earring was torn from my ear. They have stitched it together. I have earrings that go through on the inside so they just don't come out. Well, I didn't have much pain in my ear, but I do have a small contusion here (on her forehead) and my neck and my ribs.

Ther: Have there been any other emergencies like this?

Mrs. M: One other, that happened about two years ago; the attack was on my mother (the grandmo. of Joan).

(Seperate interview)

Grdmo: I was beaten in my sleep.

Ther: I don't understand that.

Grdmo: I was assaulted in my sleep. This was two years ago.

Ther: What do you mean assaulted?

Grdmo: I was beaten.

Ther: I am confused, I don't understand—did Joan beat you?

Grdmo: Yes.

Ther: But you are not saying that.

Grdmo: Yes I am.

Ther: You said you *were beaten.*

Grdmo: Yes.

Ther: You were beaten by whom?—I want Joan to hear this, apparently Joan didn't hear. Who hit you?

Grdmo: My granddaughter, Joan.

Ther: Joan beat you.

Grdmo: Yes.

Ther: And you were sleeping but you did not wake up?

Grdmo: No, when I tried to wake up . . . I thought I was dreaming at first, but then I tried to get myself together, I tried to move but I couldn't breathe, couldn't speak.

Ther: So what did you do?

Grdmo: And then I realized that something was over my mouth and eyes and the other part was going like this at my head and . . .

Ther: What did you do? Did you wake up?

Grdmo: I finally got up. I was in a daze, I couldn't get up right away because I was dizzy. Then I started yelling for my daughter. She was in the next room but she didn't hear me, so I got up and found my way to the door and I said, "Janie, Janie I've been beaten, I've been beaten . . ."

Ther: You never saw her?

Grdmo: Actually saw her?

Ther: Yes.

Grdmo: I only saw the end of a white thing going down the hall . . .

When a family comes for help in crisis—referred as an emergency—the experience for both therapist and family, as they begin to work with each other, is immediately intensified. For the therapist there is a sense of caution, a defensiveness born of anxiety in the face of extremity. For the family, there is the pressure for some immediate relief—there is shock and anger—and time is somehow constricted. Both therapist and family are responding to immediate, compelling events.

What do you do when a mother says, "My daughter attacked me last night"? There is a visceral response, a sense of danger—different from "my daughter is misbehaving in school" or "my daughter refuses to listen to me." You enter a situation where attention is rigidly focused on a threatening event, on specific behavior. You feel the need to "do" while at the same time you are constrained by the intensity produced by the crisis. The way you listen to, and hear information is altered; you do not need to seek the precipitating event . . . it is there, directing the therapist to understand it while trying not to be organized by it. A difficult task. You know not to be judgmental, but questions of guilt and innocence are almost irresistable.

The "M" family, referred to the Clinic by a nurse from a neighboring hospital, called early in the day. The family had come to the emergency room of the hospital where the mother was treated for a torn ear lobe and minor contusions. Her daughter had allegedly assaulted her during the night, tearing an earring from her ear during the attack. The maternal grandmother was present at the hospital. The nurse described all three as confused and agitated. The intake worker at the Clinic accepted the referral on the phone, spoke with the mother to obtain identifying data and requested that one of my students see the "Ms" on an emergency basis.

I decided to supervise from behind the one-way mirror.

The family, Mrs. M., Joan (15) and Mrs. R., the maternal grandmother, was a picture of depression and controlled fury. Even behind the one-way mirror the tension was tangible. Mrs. M. recounted the story of the alleged assault in a low monotone. Everything about her was constricted as she described Joan as a belligerent, angry girl who had committed this act as a result of mounting "pressure" inside her.

Mrs. M. has lived in this city for about ten months, moving here to seek employment. She, her daughter and mother live with another couple and their four children in a crowded inner-city house. Mrs. M. shares a room with her daughter. She is an accountant, obviously a capable and intelligent woman, articulate and attractive. She presents rigid, moralistic belief systems, especially about parenting. Joan is pretty, fashionable and very bright. She attends a parochial school. Mrs. R., the maternal grandmother, is like the "rock of Gibraltar"—unbending, unyielding, judgmental. To see them at the beginning of the first interview, one would find it hard to believe that these three people were capable of sharing any pleasures.

To complicate matters, Mrs. M. has a debilitating medical history; she is a victim of juvenile diabetes, requiring multiple hospitalizations and extensive surgery within the past 15 years. She is threatened with the possibility of a leg amputation. During some of her mother's hospitalizations, Joan needed to be temporarily placed in foster or group homes. Other times, her grandmother stayed with Joan. In either case, Mrs. M. was frequently a patient in her own home, requiring her daughter's care. Thus, Joan's activity among kids her own age was greatly curtailed, and her responsibility for the care of her mother dominated her childhood. Mrs. M. was divorced when Joan was four and has had no contact with her husband since then. Her work life has been erratic due to her illness. Mrs. R., the grandmother, has a heart condition, having suffered several mild strokes. She carries a bag of pills "at the ready." When we saw them, mother's unemployment compensation had run out and she was receiving minimal disability insurance.

All of this made for a grim picture and there was an overwhelming sense of depression and desperation in the room. For the first twenty minutes of the initial interview Joan sat with her head down, between her mother and grandmother, while each recounted examples of Joan's angry, acting-out, uncontrollable behavior. Joan is doing poorly in school. She lies and refuses to obey her mother's rules. She is involved with older boys of whom her mother disapproves. She once threatened her mother with a knife. She is irresponsible and gets into fights in the neighborhood. This, in addition to the latest episode of assault.

The account of the alleged assaults was mystifying, accusation coupled with excuses: she attacked me last night, but she must have been sleep walking; she lies, but is under such pressure she doesn't know what she is doing. For every statement a disclaimer; for every affirmation a negation. The mystification process seemed to come full circle when Joan spoke up to deny both attacks:

Mrs. M: The time the attack was on my mother, to be truthful with you, I don't really think Joan even knows about it.
Joan: I *didn't* do it.
Ther: Joan, can you tell me about it?
Joan: I was asleep just like she was . . .
Mrs. M: Did you know about it?
Joan: No I didn't; (to her mother) you didn't even tell me what was wrong with you this morning.
Ther: (to grandmother) Mrs. R., did you have any idea what was going on this morning?
Grdmo: This morning, I did not. But having gone through the experience I do know what *had* to have happened.
Ther: I wasn't there last night, so I don't have the vaguest idea of what happened but whatever it was, it scared the hell out of everybody.
Mrs. M: That's true.
Ther: It scared you, and you in the end (to Joan).
Joan: Me, I didn't even know about it 'til now.
Ther: But you know about it now.
Mrs. M: It's true, she didn't know about it this morning. I did not tell her about it and laid on my side, so she did not see the ear split or anything. I spoke to her from that position, that's all. Because I had to have time to think.

Behind the one-way mirror, where I sat with several colleagues and trainees, people debated whether Joan had really attacked her mother. It seemed bizarre that Mrs. M. had not confronted her daughter in relation to the assault; had, in fact, covered it up. Some felt that perhaps the torn ear lobe had been self-inflicted. I could see a bunch of "child savers" in the making. My own sense of things at this point, was that the family urgently needed an intervention which would change the mood between them, relieve the anger that constricted their range of responses to each other. Until now they had rarely spoken directly to one another, and when they did it was only to accuse, defend or deny. I knew that "a search for the truth" would be a dead end. The student therapist was bogged down in history and information, which she was having difficulty translating into material the family could work with *here*. I joined the interview to help extricate her and provide a direction for the therapy.

In seeking ways to change the mood of a family, the therapist must take leadership and offer people the opportunity of entering into a different experience with each other. Even if the change in mood is a temporary one it expands behavioral options for both therapist and family. Timing is important. If the therapist waits too long to make an initial intervention she can get lost in the power of a family atmosphere determined by events prior to the therapy hour. In beginning with a family I want to create the atmospheric conditions under which we will work together. For instance, the reduction of anxiety or moving from anger to disagreement are useful not only in themselves, but also in establishing a hierarchy and leadership in the therapeutic system.

I joined the M family with this in mind. I wanted to change the mood and establish leadership. My direction was to highlight the conflict between mother and daughter as opposed to the loss of control and internalized craziness that was presented. I wanted to test generational boundaries. I planned to introduce quickly—as part of creating a change in mood—the idea that Mrs. M. had some options in relation to her daughter, despite the impasse she felt they were in. Presenting placement as a choice would highlight their need to disengage. I expected Mrs. M. would object to this as a viable option, and we would then be talking about what to *do* rather than what had happened the night before.

JOINING THE FAMILY:
CHANGING THE MOOD, AND REFRAMING THE PROBLEM.

Ther: (Enters room, explains her presence and introduces herself to each member of the family; sits between Joan and mother; speaks to Joan, raises her head; turns to mother and puts her hand on her arm). I've been listening to you two; you're in a bind, both of you, in a bind, and so terribly angry with each other.

Mrs. M: I love my daughter, I really do but she ...

Ther: I know you do and she loves you. (To mother) Let me ask you something, you've talked about such serious issues and I'm sure you're very worried about what has happened, and Joan is upset about what is going on. (Joan shakes her head.) Oh, yes you are. (To mother) Are you thinking you need to place Joan, that you need to put her in another living situation? Have you thought about that? Does that strike home?

Mrs. M: Not to ...

Joan: To me it does!

Ther: Say it then, Joan.

Joan: Me?

Ther: Yes, you wanted to say something.

Joan: I said to me it does—to be put in a foster home or something ...

Mrs. M: (Talking directly to Joan for the first time) Is that your desire or is that what is striking you?

Joan: (Strongly) That is what I want to do.

Mrs. M: Is that what you think *I* am saying?

Joan: (Angrily) I don't know what you are saying.

Mrs. M: Is that the reason you thought I brought you here, Joan?

Joan: No, I don't know why you brought me here, you told me I had an appointment.

Mrs. M: Now that you're here, is that why you think I brought you here?

Joan: No ...

Ther: (To mother) Do you have any thoughts about different possibilities? Some kind of situation that will *separate* you two at this point?

Mrs. M: Yes, but medical, not foster parents or ...

Ther: What do you mean by medical?

Mrs. M: Medical—psychiatric, or psychotherapy, or whatever is needed to separate us.

Joan: Didn't she just get done saying she didn't think I was crazy? So why am I going to go to some psycho-somebody?

Ther: I am a psycho-somebody! (Everybody laughs and relaxes). Mrs. J. is a psycho-somebody. (Referring to student therapist).

Mrs. M: That doesn't mean crazy, Joan. It doesn't mean crazy, it means problems.

Ther: And you've come to a place to get help.

Joan: I don't want any help, I don't need any help.

Ther: Oh yes you do, come on, yes you do, *you do.* You do and I'll tell you why you do, why the *two* of you do.

Mrs. M: Yes.

Ther: Because you're knocking each other out in one way or another. I don't know what happened last night, and I don't know what happened before. What I see though, is *two* people who are in agony with one another. Who are really in agony, and who are not able to get along with each other, and you *do* need some help with that, Joan.

Joan: Well, couldn't there be some way that I could get out of the house and live with somebody else and just come and visit my mother?

Ther: I don't know hon, we can think about that; that is what I was asking Mom about, if that was something she had in mind at this point. (To mother) I don't know when you're saying separation, if you are talking in terms of your relationship or if you're talking about a placement kind of thing.

Mrs. M: No, I wasn't, I was talking about our relationship.

Ther: Okay, good, you are absolutely right on! That is *exactly* what the two of you need. You need some help in getting some distance from each other. Because you are on top of each other; *literally.*

Mrs. M: Yes. I see what you mean.

OFFERING A NEW PERSPECTIVE OF CURRENT CONFLICT

Ther: See, one of the things you described that I thought was very eloquent was having a daughter who needed to take care of you at different points in your life because you were ill. At those times you required different things of her; both that she obey you as a child, but also that she take on some kinds of almost really adult responsibility.

Mrs. M: That's right.

Ther: So, this kid of 10 or 12 was getting a kind of mixed message about whether she was a kid or adult. I think you're reaping some of the "rewards" of that period of time.

Mrs. M: (Thoughtfully) Maybe ... I see ...

Ther: And we can help with that, we can help with that. It's very hard when two people get "out of balance" that way to re-balance. You're on your feet and you want to say, be my kid again; now I don't need you to take care of me, I'm taking care of you; and then where is she going to go? How is she going to figure out what's expected of her, which direction to go in?

Mrs. M: That's true because she was cooking supper and fixing everything, and you know it was, Joan put this on for supper, and Joan go shopping ...

Grdmo: Excuse me, Joan had help.

Mrs. M: But not always mother.

Grdmo: But most of the time, huh Joan?

Joan: Um hmm

Grdmo: Wasn't I there to help?

Joan: Um hmm

Grdmo: Thank you.

Ther: I'm sure you were, but it is still a pretty confusing thing for a kid.

Grdmo: I understand, I just didn't want you to think...

Ther: To think that Joan was an exploited child?

Grdmo: No, to go down like Joan had the entire burden, because she had help.

Ther: I believe you, I believe you.

RELABELING BEHAVIOR

Ther: (To mother) The time with the knife, where did she hit you with the knife?

Mrs. M: No, no, no...

Ther: (Surprised) Oh, she never cut you up?

Mrs. M: No, she never cut me at all, the distance was from about that wall to here. She was standing by the kitchen door, and when I came down the steps, she just stood there...

Ther: She could have, but she didn't...

Mrs. M: Right.

Ther: Okay, fine! That's good.

Mrs. M: Yes, yes, it is...

Ther: You're not the first mother whose kid has taken a knife to them.

Mrs. M: I believe you, I know...

Ther: But, she didn't cut you up. *Very* good.

JOINING THE GRANDMOTHER

Mrs. M: Now we're trying to get settled.

Ther: Who, the two of you? You and Joan? This is your only child?

Mrs. M: We were all going to live together, my mother, my daughter, and myself.

Ther: Ummm...?

Mrs. M: That's what it was intended to be, but I don't think that can be...

Ther: Well, maybe it can be, but it's not an easy situation, is it (to grandmother)?

Grdmo: No!

Ther: I *know*; it's not, it's not (grandmother and therapist laugh; therapist goes to sit by her).

Grdmo: I've always had my own place. I just came here to help Janie out while she was getting settled.

Ther: Living with grown children is not an unmixed blessing. It's seldom what we'd choose.

Grdmo: I'll second that.

DEFINING STRUCTURE: SETTING A THERAPEUTIC THEME

Ther: (To mother and grandmother) I'll tell you what I think. Joan is sitting here now *exactly* how she lives with you two! Look, look. She sits just like she lives with you.

Mrs. M: (Surprised) You're right, you're absolutely right, she *is* right in the middle! She is pulled both ways.

Ther: Yes! And I think this is the kind of thing we can help you with.

Mrs. M: And she is forced by both people ... in different directions.

Ther: I am sure...

Mrs. M: I realize this, I do, but...

Grdmo: (Disagreeing) Let Joan answer that because ...
Ther: Oh wait a minute, your daughter is saying something.
Grdmo: I know, but ...
Ther: Hold it a minute; no, no, really you need to hold it just a minute.
Grdmo: Alright.
Ther: Because you know, your daughter is saying something she thinks is true, something she feels is important, and you absolutely will get a turn. Okay?

Mother goes on to recount ways in which Joan gets different messages from her and her mother, how they pull her in different directions. Grandmother disagrees, but mother insists. I define this interaction as evidence of the kind of thing that happens at home, and reaffirm that we can help with this, and will work in that direction. When the family leaves, mother and daughter are playful with each other; grandmother is left out.

My interventions in this initial interview, while shaped by personal style, were based on a theory of change, and a frame of reference about how to do therapy. I believe change occurs more readily in relation to current experiences rather than past events, and that it is the responsibility of the therapist to challenge the interaction within a family so as to induce altered experiences for people in the interview itself. I think change requires that the family be presented with concrete alternatives to the impasse or dilemma which brings them into therapy, and that they "try these on" in the interview. I don't believe change can occur until people begin to feel some competency. And I think the leadership of the therapist in bringing about change is dependent on her being intrusive, directive and in control of the process.

As soon as the opportunity presents itself, I move people from content to process, from information and rumination to interaction; and in doing so try to give the family a new perspective of the situation they are in. This business of giving the picture a new frame is as important for the therapist as for her clients. How often have all of us been faced with a family in crisis, and felt overwhelmed and helpless to do anything about it? Such feelings are not good for therapists. I want, in my initial contact with a family, to put the problem into a perspective for *both* of us, the family and myself, where I can begin to feel effective, and transmit this feeling, this sense of hope, to the family. I need to create a "workable reality," to select and reframe a piece of the action where some change can be initiated.

The preceding transcripts from the initial interview demonstrate some of these points. I joined with the family immediately, sitting between mother and daughter, making contact with each of them, noting their mood, while transcending it with my voice, behavior and attitude of knowing, being in charge. I put aside the content, (the alleged assault, past behaviors) and insist on reframing the problem as interactional. Then I select and use examples of family history (Joan needing to take on adult responsibilities at age 10, accept rigorous rules at 15) to give credence to the notion that they are not dealing with an individual's internalized craziness, but rather a process gone awry. I choose an example of past behavior (the knife incident) and relabel it to develop and support a sense of their having some control over what goes on between them. I highlight conflict as opposed to madness. I offer concrete options, indicate alternatives, and encourage discussion around these. And, finally, using a visual metaphor (their seating arrangement) I suggest a new perspective of their situation and an arena in which they can work.

Throughout I am intrusive, monitoring and giving direction to the unfolding scenario. I press a point of view and block interaction or content that interferes with it. I join, but impose my energy on the proceedings.

We decided that I would continue working with this family (with my student sitting in on interviews). Despite myself I began to wonder who was telling the truth—Joan or her mother? Had Joan really attacked her mother? Was mother making it up? Was there collusion between grandmother and mother? My professional voice kept telling me, the story is unimportant, it does not really matter, you need to work with the system. Knowing the truth would not make me any wiser about how to proceed. Even following the first interview, (in the waiting room) and certainly in later interviews, it was possible for grandmother and Joan, Joan and mother, or mother and grandmother to kid around with each other and have light-hearted, pleasant talks. Put the three together and the air crackled. I began to think what energy and courage it would take for any of these people to declare some differences let alone autonomy. And I began to get an inkling of how a kid might indeed become a mysterious night marauder in a desperate attempt to shake herself loose from the bonds of her family.

In the second interview, again with all three members of the family present, I was troubled to find myself moving into the position from which I had extricated my student; that is, a child advocate, I knew I was being inducted into the family system as I experienced myself beginning to view Joan as the "scapegoated child."

In this interview, Mrs. M. began to urgently insist that Joan needed to be hospitalized. The level of anxiety and anger became even more intense than in the preceding hour.

Mrs. M: Joan has to be controlled. Joan has to know responsibility and she is out of hand—when something gets out of hand...you have a dog that gets rabies, you gonna keep him because he is your pet, because you had him from a pup, so you'll take a chance? No—you may love that dog ever so much, but No. No, I am serious, I have had smaller animals and the cat, if it should get out and get rabies— the best thing for you to do...you mean to tell me it's wise to keep the cat in the house and let him give you rabies and scratch you to death and somebody else call the SPCA? Far be it from me, no, no. That's not practical thinking at all.

Ther: It's also an analogy I can't deal with.

I was not able to respond to the helplessness underlying the extreme position taken by the mother. The fury she expressed covered her fear; the rigid position she took disguised her anguish at not being able to control her daughter.

But, in that second interview I failed to deal with this, feeling myself drawn toward protecting Joan. When a therapist finds herself in such a position she can be pretty sure that it reflects the way the family is organizing her. They had been in this situation before. Joan described several experiences in previous therapy where her mother had terminated treatment because the therapist, as Joan put it, "began to take my side." The M's organize themselves for failure; and Joan is a willing victim, having learned that this is a role she can handle and with which she can manipulate others. It is a dysfunctional pattern, of course, but one in which all three are experts and with which they can defeat the best intentioned helper.

In retrospect, it was clear that I had missed signals from the grandmother in the initial interview that should have alerted me to the danger of too quickly supporting a boundary around Mrs. M. and Joan, and building positive interaction between them. Though I had tried to join grandmother, I was no match for her power in the family system when I later blocked her from entering transactions between Mrs. M. and Joan. There was no way I was going to be allowed to get away with this, and the family regrouped. The mutually dependent and disqualifying, deeply enmeshed and needy relationship between grandmother and mother was not to be so easily shaken loose. It was insufficient to focus on mother and daughter; a great deal of preparation would be necessary to enable grandmother to disengage and for mother to let her go.

I knew I needed help and at the end of the second interview told the family that while I was not prepared at this point to hospitalize Joan, because I did not see her as either crazy or out of control, I did realize the seriousness of mother's concern and wished to call in a consultant.

CONSULTATION: DR. SALVADOR MINUCHIN

(About 20 minutes into the interview, having reviewed conflicting stories from each member of the family).

Dr. M: Do you know why Mrs. Walters asked me to come here? Because she is confused. Because *you* say something, then *you* say something else, and so for somebody who has not been there, it is very confusing. Isn't it confusing to you?

Grdmo: Well, these uncontrollable moments . . . (To Joan) Alright, you're angry to a point and you grab a knife . . .

Dr. M: (To Joan) You grabbed a knife?

Joan: I did do that.

Dr. M: (Incredulous) You did what?

Joan: I pulled a knife on my mother.

Dr. M: When was that?

Joan: About three or four weeks ago.

Dr. M: You pulled a knife on your mother; what did you do? It was a kitchen knife or a . . .

Joan: It was a butcher knife.

Dr. M: A butcher knife. A big knife?

Joan: It had real jagged edges.

Dr. M: And what did you do with it?

Joan: I just stood there with it.

Dr. M: You just stood there with it. Well, that's not crazy, that's criminal. Did you hit her any place?

Joan: No, my mother was where I am right now, over there to the wall. (Indicating a sizable distance.) I didn't even go all the way up to her, I just wanted to scare her.

Dr. M: You wanted to *what?*

Joan: Scare her!

Dr. M: You wanted to scare her. And you are 15 you told me. So, I don't understand now. At this point I can't tell if you are crazy, or very childish or you're criminal.

Joan: So, what are you trying to say, I'm a split personality?

Dr. M: No, no. You have only one, I just don't know which one it is. In this incident with the knife she (mother) did not punish you?

Joan: No.

Dr. M: Then your mother thinks you are crazy. Because if she would think that you are childish she would punish you; if she would think that you were delinquent she would punish you. Then, your mother thinks you're crazy.

Joan: If she thinks I am crazy it won't be the first time. If you knew how many psychiatric hospitals I've been to, you wouldn't even worry about it. So, I figure it this way. If she thinks I am crazy I might as well do something to make her think I am crazy for.

Mrs. M: Dr. M., I wish you would define crazy.

Dr. M: Well, if somebody pulls a knife on you and you don't do anything to this person then you must think that this person is crazy. But I think you are doing something pretty bad to this young, childish, immature, little girl.

Mrs. M: Perhaps...

Dr. M: Because you are not treating her as if she is a little girl. I think if a child pulls a knife on her mother, the mother is doing something very wrong. If a child puts a knife to you, *you* (to mother) are doing something wrong. And I don't know what it is.

Mrs. M: I am being a mother to Joan and if that's bad then that's what I am doing to her.

Dr. M: No, no, much more—that's not enough, you must be doing something wrong, because she is acting as if she is not even 11—maybe 5 or 6 years old. Very infantile; thinking that she can do whatever she wants; very very young.

Mrs. M: She's becoming quite overbearing, that's true.

Dr. M: So what are you doing? You must be doing something wrong.

(Later, mother speaks for Joan).

Dr. M: No, no, no. I don't like what you are doing now.

Mrs. M: What is that?

Dr. M: You are talking through her mouth. You are putting words on her. If I am asking Joan what would you do, I want her to answer. What you say is not what she had said. You see, I know that when people like her do terrible things like that, I know that *you* are doing something wrong. And I am beginning to see the kinds of things that you are doing that keeps Joan who is 15 acting like she is 7 ... I look at you (Joan) and I think that you are really a very childish person; and if you are a very childish person—I am looking at you (mother) and saying what are you doing to keep her so childish? I don't think she is crazy but I am scared like hell for her.

(Grandmother intervenes to save mother, giving examples of Joan's obdurate behavior.)

Dr. M: (To Joan) You must be a monster.
Joan: I must be, I am serious.
Grdmo: No, but I wonder . . .
Dr. M: Your grandmother is afraid of you, your mother is afraid of you.
Joan: Can I say one thing? When my grandmother got beaten—when she liked me— but she was mad at my mother—she told me in the kitchen that she thought it was my mother who had beaten her; my mother said all the different things that my grandmother had said had happened.Like my mother would say, did they cover your mouth? And my grandmother said she described it perfectly, and so she thought it was her. And then when she got mad at me, she went and told my mother she just knew it was me.
Dr. M: So, what you are saying is . . .
Joan: It's *not* me.
Dr. M: No, no, no, what you are saying is that you are crazy because your mom and your grandmom . . .
Joan: They huddle, they huddle against me.
Dr. M: That is where you are crazy. (Mother responds to the use of the word.) No, no we are talking about something that is serious here. We are talking about who is keeping you (Joan) so confused.

(Later, a decision . . .)

Mrs. M: I am a parent, you come and you think the way you raised your child is the best way, right? So you hear things about yourself that you really don't want to hear or you find you haven't done all the right things.
Dr. M: No, you have made so many mistakes, it could fill a book.
Mrs. M: Yes, right. That's not the thing I want to hear.
Dr. M: Yes, but I need to tell it to you.
Mrs. M: If it's to help, it's to help. Now, what I want to know is what can be done constructively from this point on.
Dr. M: That is the issue, that is the issue. But it is very difficult.
Mrs. M: I will listen, there is no way in the world that I am trying to get rid of my daughter. It's just that, at this point Joan cannot control herself. For an example . . .
Dr. M: Can you change Mrs. M.?
Mrs. M: Can I change?
D. M: I just want to know if you can change.
Mrs. M: I will be perfectly willing.
Dr. M: You are asking me what can be done, I am saying you are doing things wrong. Okay. I am saying . . .
Mrs. M: But you haven't told me what.
Dr. M: I have told you but you cannot hear me because you are at this point, correctly so, very upset. The question is will that (hospitalization) be helpful?
Mrs. M: Wouldn't some sort of separation, at this point, be helpful?
Dr. M: We are talking about that—will that be helpful.
Joan: Well, why can't I go live somewhere with somebody else and come and see my mother.

Mrs. M: Would you like for me to answer that? Right, wrong, or indifferent Joan, I don't feel as though I want somebody else to raise *my* child. Now, if I am wrong I have to correct what is wrong and at the same time you have to receive help also. I'm not looking to give you to somebody else. And this is how I feel.

Dr. M: At this point, this is too chronic a situation. I would recommend that Joan should come to our in-patient unit for two weeks. I suggest that Joan first should go and see it so that she knows what it is. I am doing this *not* because Joan is crazy but because Mrs. M. is very scared.

The consultation expanded and reinforced a therapeutic theme. In defining the mother as a person who had made countless mistakes as a parent, and Joan as a stubborn, acting-out child, Dr. Minuchin had directly challenged the mystification process which maintained the dysfunctional aspects of the family system. This relabeling of their behavior with each other transformed obscure history into current, available behaviors. A mother who makes mistakes is different from a mother who cannot control her daughter; a teenager who is stubborn and acts in infantile ways, is different from one who makes crazy attacks on her mother.

Throughout the on-going therapy, I used this theme over and over in making the repetitive small moves necessary to help establish boundaries, support negotiation, and particularly to help Joan and her mother each to find her own voice. The way Joan, the mother and grandmother used language to disqualify each other, to obscure differences, and to confuse the other person was a constant challenge. It required a counterpoint focusing on concrete, specific issues which could be clearly demonstrated with behaviors and transactions occuring within the hour.

The consultant set a necessary process in motion by recommending hospitalization. Though this was difficult for me, it was clearly not as hard for the family. Joan protested mildly and Mrs. M. was greatly relieved. The situation had truly become too chronic to proceed without such a structured separation.

But most significant in the consultation was an affirmation of the intrinsic support that exists within confrontation. Support, as we usually think of it, can be experienced as "help to the handicapped." If we support somebody we imply they need to be held up. On the other hand, confrontation denotes expectation, which is a different kind of support. Nothing, I am convinced can feel so right to people as to be told"you're wrong—now do it differently," especially when you know, deep down, that you must have done something wrong, or else why would you be here? Therapists need to criticize in the context of acceptance. In a way this is our art—to warmly accept someone as part of the human race while telling them how much they've mucked up their humanity.

Clearly, this is but a first step. If we say, you're wrong, we must of course be prepared to offer alternatives for setting it right. We must know what to do, how to intervene in ways that will create new options for a family.

A week after the consultation, Joan was hospitalized. In the family session preceeding her admission we began the long, hard process of working towards disengagement.

Mrs. M: I am beginning to see the picture now, sometimes you just plain want too much for your children. You think you know their potential and want them to succeed in everything. And I am on her back about school.

Ther: I know it's important to you, but I think that that should be the first task for both of you. Joan says she is 15. A 15 year old needs to fail in school or succeed in school; that is her task at 15. School should be *her* thing. If she fails she fails. So that is the first growing up. (To mother) And your first growing up is to let her fail!

Mrs. M: Keep my hands, my mouth, my feet out of it!

Ther: (To mother) Your growing up is to let her fail.(To Joan) If you fail mother will not tell you not to fail again. She will not say anything about school and if you fail you fail. It will not be mother's fault. What do you think about that?

Mrs. M: I am beginning to see what you all are saying now.

Ther: Can you grow up?

Mrs. M: Yes.

Ther: Okay, very good.

Joan remained in the in-patient unit for two months, returning to her own school after three weeks. Weekly family sessions focused on developing a means of negotiation between mother and daughter, using specific issues and incidents as they arose during the week, and during the interviews. We worked to establish rules and turf boundaries, to reconstitute skills of direct communication with each other, and to demystify their interaction. As mother began to step back, to disengage, Joan tried to pull her in again. Mother had so little tolerance for frustration with Joan that she would quickly escalate confusing, contradictory, angry communication. The therapy required consistent monitoring of this process. Sometimes the sessions were very heavy indeed; sometimes we were able to relate with humor to the issues between them.

Joan: I don't know, I don't see anything wrong with me.

Mrs. M: Nobody said there is something wrong with you.

Joan: I know, but I don't see any faults with myself.

Mrs. M: That is a fault right there.

Ther: You like yourself?

Joan: Yeah.

Ther: So that's great.

Mrs. M: But you're supposed to see your faults, too. I think I'm a great mother, but Dr. M. said, horrible, horrible! (Laughing).

Ther: (To Joan) So why are you being so good now? Agreeing to everything Mom wants? Are you obeying the rules just because Mom says you should?

Joan: No.

Ther: So...?

Ms. M: Speak up.

Joan: I don't know.

Mrs. M: I think she wants to get out from under this ... what do you call that thing that smooths the road?

Joan: Steam-roller...

Mrs. M: Steam-roller, mother's steam-roller.

Ther: (Laughing with mother) Now you see: I ask Joan a question and you answer! I don't want you to give the answers, because if you do she will then always be free to say, "I don't know."

Mrs. M: Oh, yes ... and you know what, she does that all the time.

Ther: Why not? You answer for her. You give her all the answers, all the reasons. You don't need to do that.

Mrs. M: You want me to step back?

Ther: No, no, I don't want you to step back, because I know you can control this.

Mrs. M: Oh, yes ... I will.

Ther: Yes, I know you can control it and I don't want Joan off the hook. I don't want her off the hook. (To Joan) No one is twisting your arm. You need to stand good for what you are doing here, what you are trying to accomplish. If it's getting out from under mother, if it's finding other ways to do things , if ... I don't care what it is. But something. You're what ... sixteen, ... how old?

(Mother starts to answer, stops herself laughingly).

Joan: Fifteen.

Ther: So start using your good head ... I don't want to hear, "I don't know!" anymore.

The most difficult step in the therapy was working towards the separation of Mrs. M. and her mother. This move could only be approached as Mrs. M. felt more in control of her own relationship with Joan, more competent and sure of herself. Still, it was a major effort for her to even begin to think of the possibility of establishing a separate living situation for herself and Joan. She went back and forth on this; she could not bring herself to make a decision. Even more agonizing for her was the prospect of actually facing her mother with such a decision. Several separate sessions were held with Mrs. M. and her mother. Fortunately, there were systems of support available to the grandmother through family and peer networks, that I could activate as I worked with them to agree to separate living situations.

Continuous treatment ended when Mrs. M. moved into her own apartment, about three months after they first came to the Clinic. However, before Joan could be discharged to her mother Mrs. M. was hospitalized once again. Joan was temporarily placed in a group home. She came regularly during this time to visit friends at the Clinic, and for brief follow-up sessions.

In one of these interviews I asked Joan how she thought it would be different for her now when she was able to return to live with her mother. Before answering seriously, she got a wicked gleam in her eye and grinning broadly said:

"Now I guess she'll be having me do laundry twice a week instead of once a week; cooking three times a week instead of twice a week!"

I thought: When a person can make fun of the things that used to drive them crazy, it's going to be OK.

Several colleagues in reviewing this piece suggested that it would be helpful to my readers to know if Joan had really attacked her mother in the middle of the night. Within this seemingly minor suggestion lies the thread of a continuing theoretical debate in the family field. It was not simply to satisfy curiosity that they suggested the addition of this information. It was in the interest of including what they considered a significant piece of information, the knowledge of which would be useful for purposes of both assessment and treatment. I questioned if knowing "the truth" would be useful to a therapist for treatment planning or intervention; although conceding its possible value for diagnosis. But even in relation to the latter, I have reservations. In fact, in this case I felt that knowing the truth too soon, or perhaps at all, could well handicap a therapist by turning her attention to individual pathology rather than current interaction between people. For if the therapist knew that Joan had secretly attacked her mother (and grandmother) and was lying about it; or, on the other hand, if the mother and grandmother were lying or indulging in a mutual fantasy, the therapist would be faced with the awful dilemma of villain, and victim, rather than a system that was creating and maintaining such behaviors. For the truth of whether or not Joan did in fact assault her mother is far less significant for a therapist to know than the fact that both mother and grandmother were acting as if she had. That is useful information in family therapy.

12

"Sometimes Its Better For The Right Hand Not To Know What The Left Hand Is Doing."

Richard Fisch, M.D.

Mrs. S. called me. She said her son needed help. He was 12 years old and was having trouble with other children at school and at home. She wasn't sure how to set up the appointment but would leave it to my decision. I asked her if her son would be resistant to coming in and she replied that she wasn't sure but that he had no trouble relating to adults. When she began to elaborate on that I told her it would be best to leave any further description of the problem till we met in my office. I further suggested that it might " be better in the long run " for me to meet only with her and her husband, at least for that first session. She was agreeable to that.

(I discourage patients from giving me much information on the phone. I do this because I want to convey that treatment is a "getting down to business," not a casual affair to be discussed over a phone. I also want to convey a separation between my office and their lives outside of it. This helps set the stage when, later in treatment, I can further convey that, while discussion may be needed, it is action in their lives that is more important. As for whom I see in an initial session, this will often be determined by my assessment as to who, in the family, is the complainant and not, necessarily, by who is the identified patient. In a child-centered problem, it is almost always the parents who are the complainants, not the child, and since they are also the power in the family, I usually anticipate I will be doing the greater bulk of the work with them. Thus, having the parents come in initially conveys that *they* are initiating treatment and are asking my help in *their* dealings with *their* child. On occasion, I may see the child with his or her parents in the first interview, but I will never see a child alone the first time.)

Session 1.

Mr. and Mrs. S. arrived on time. She is thirty-seven years old and he thirty-eight. They are an attractive couple; both are slim, youthful and athletic looking. Both are engineers working in the electronics field, although Mrs. S's job is part-time. In addition to their 12-year-old son, Billy, they have an 8-year-old boy, Larry. Mrs. S. reiterated her concern about Billy.

The principal problem had to do with his difficulty in socializing with children, especially with those his own age. In school, he often got into fights and seemed to be generally hostile to the other children. The problem had reached its peak about two years ago when he got into a "rage reaction" at school and had to be sent home. While the problem had subsided some in the last two years, it was still considerable and treatment was precipitated by a recent call from his teacher; that he had had another "outburst" in class and was sent home for mis-behavior at school, although not all of it for "outbursts" or "rage reactions." They added that Billy's difficulties were not limited to school. He had no friends in their neighborhood either and he would spend "75 percent" of his time watching television. They would scold him for spending so much of his time in front of the TV set; would try to limit the hours of watching and urge him to go outside and meet with other children, but this was to no avail. When I asked how he got along with Larry, they said they frequently squabbled with each other but did not identify this as any particular problem; it was not excessive in their minds, did not reach uncontrollable levels, and it appeared to be a mutual bickering rather than any harrassment by Billy, per se.

Then they launched into a rather pessimistic picture. Billy was "neurologically and physically handicapped." At about 4 or 5 years of age he was diagnosed as having psychomotor epilepsy and through the years had been maintained on anti-convulsive medications. This had markedly limited his seizures so that in the last year or two he had had only four episodes. These, they described, came on only at night and while he was asleep. However, he had also been diagnosed as having a "porencephalic cyst" and that this lesion had left him with spasticity of the left hand. For this he had also been receiving physical therapy and while function had improved he still had noticeable spasticity and difficulty with fine touch movement. But this was not the end of his "neurological" problems. Later, during his schooling, he had been diagnosed by school personnel as having "dyslexia" and because of this diagnosis had been placed in special education classes for the last two years. It seemed that such placement was also determined by his hostile behavior in class and the decision to transfer him was precipitated by his "rage reaction" and the teacher fearing she could no longer control him. Finally, Mrs. S. said that because of all the problems Billy presented she had been able to look back and realize that from birth he was "hyperactive" and difficult to handle.

In asking for Mr. S.' views, he echoed much of what his wife had said. However, he added that Billy also suffered from some kind of frustration he was unable to put into words. They would often question him—"Why are you upset? What really bothers you?" And they would be dismayed when he responded in a self-denigrating way: "I always botch things up. Why is everything I do a boo-boo?" They attempted to help him by giving him "environmental support"—trying to find things for him to do he could feel good about himself in accomplishing, taking him on special trips skiing, golfing, bicycle riding, picnics. When the parents went out they made a special effort to find sitters who would be "supportive" such as male college students. They acknowledged this tended to limit their social life since such sitters were hard to come by. Finally, they would make "contracts" with Billy and give him special rewards for being a "nice kid."

(I made no comments throughout this narrative. My sole activity was to raise questions to clarify the points they were making: what they regarded as the problem, what had precipitated their decision to seek treatment, how they had attempted to deal with or help Billy overcome his problem and what kind of outcome of therapy they wanted. I had gotten a rather clear picture of the problem and how they had been attempting to "solve" it. My principal uncertainty was how to evaluate the neurological picture and how to find the leverage to deal with the parent's implicit pessimism about their son. As for the former, I was more concerned about the epilepsy and the spasticity than I was the "dyslexia." I do not regard "dyslexia," "minimal brain damage" or "learning disability" as valid or constructive ways of explaining a child's school difficulties. In addition, I know that these diagnoses can be very loosely used and are resorted to by some schools to protect their own educational philosophies of hidden coercion— much as "schizophrenia" is used to obscure parental or social agency mismanagement. But I also knew that these parents had firmly accepted this definition of Billy's trouble and that this enlarged their pessimistic expectations of him. These expectations were then manifested in the numerous "helping" efforts they had described which had turned the school and the home into treatment centers for him and could, at the very least, only add to his one-down self-consciousness. I anticipated that, whatever else I would do, I would want to get the parents to move away from that position. I, therefore, anticipated with them that I might have to work with Billy through them, explaining that since he had been subjected to such a profusion of special services it could be counter-productive for me to work with him directly while he struggled with the additional stigma of having to see a "shrink.")

Before ending the session, I said that as a next step I felt it important to see

Billy but that after that I might ask to see them again. They were agreeable to that and we stopped.

(In seeing Billy, I had in mind to check out the report of his gross neurological problem as well as get my own appraisal of his general demeanor and his accounting for his difficulty with other children. Seeing him alone could have another use. Should I need some rationale for supporting any advice to the parents they might question, I could refer to "material" that presumably came up in the session with Billy, material that could not be challenged because of the privacy of the session and my own "expert" interpretation of that material.)

Session 2. (Four days later.)

Billy was a pleasant looking boy and more outgoing than I had anticipated. He was slightly small for his age but in the course of discussion it never came up as a consideration on his part and did not seem to be any problem to him. I told him that his parents had seen me because they were concerned about his not having friends at school or at home. I asked him if this was a problem for him or were his parents being overly concerned? He appeared slightly uncomfortable in answering that question and said that he did have some friends at home. He acknowledged that he had no friends at school and did little with the friends he had at home, but on further elaboration about what he did do with his friends he implied that he had no dealings with them and that he did spend most of his free time watching television.

(I did not make any point of this "confession" nor confront him with it, but merely accepted his statements as helping me to be clearer on things. With children, as with adults, initial sessions are devoted to data seeking and are conducted matter-of-factly but with specific questions designed to elicit special information. My principal goal at that stage is to get a clear, concise picture of the significant transactions in the patients' lives, especially those revolving around the problem. Also, I am always looking for "leverages"—what is important and meaningful to the patient which I can use to get them to accept suggestions from me; suggestions which redefine a situation or ones which influence them to take some necessary action in their lives and regarding their problem. Since my highest priority is on action and little or none on "insight," "confrontation" plays a minimal role in my therapy.)

I shifted in my questioning. I said that while his parents might be concerned about his not having friends, it might not be of any concern to him; was there something different *he* was concerned about. He readily answered that his biggest complaint was that he has been "bugged all my life." He explained that he has been made fun of and harrassed about his left hand. I told him that his parents had mentioned his left hand to me but that I would appreciate it if he would show me what kind of trouble he had with it. He then demonstrated by slowly and jerkily picking up a nearby ashtray, holding it between his thumb and forefinger and explaining while he did so how much trouble he was having and that I should notice how his "fingers didn't work right." I moved my chair closer to his and watched with apparent curiosity as he performed this spastic task. When he put the ashtray down, I told him that I found that a very intriguing way to pick up the ashtray and would he please show me again just how he did that. He seemed pleased to oblige me and as he repeated the task I made my own comments on the complexity of movements required by his hand and fingers to be *able* to pick it up in just that fashion. I asked him to perform other tasks with his hand and marvelled, each time, at the way his hand performed it. Then I began trying to imitate his hand's movements but I always failed and expressed frustration that I couldn't do with my hand what he so easily could do with his left hand. He was surprised at my failure and this allowed me to tell him that I would bet his father couldn't do it either. When he challenged this I said, "I'll tell you what. I bet that even your right hand can't imitate your left." He tried, but as I anticipated, he was unable to do it. For some moments, then he looked at his left hand wonderingly and admiringly.

(Since for him, perhaps not his parents, the most meaningful problem was focussed on his left hand, I decided to see what I could do with that. I had not anticipated this before seeing him nor even in the earlier part of the session. But since I am always looking to use whatever is thrown my way I began to formulate a way of working with his hand to redefine his one-down position to a one-up. I began this redefinition by expressing interested curiosity in his hand, then by referring to its spastic movements as worthy of further, greater attention, then by referring to the movements as an *ability*, and finally as an ability that was unique and implicitly superior to those of mine, his father and even his stronger hand. His response to that indicated his acceptance of the redefinition and rather than labor the point, I shifted to a slightly different area.)

I asked him, as if it were a new and sudden thought, "Are there any kids at school who *don't* bug you about your hand?" He said there were. I said, "You know, you don't have to just wait for some kid to bug you, you can be in charge of some of the bugging." Since he appeared intrigued by that thought, I challenged him to see if he could pick out one kid who had never bugged him and, *without saying a word*, see if he could get that kid to bug him about his hand. He was quite agreeable, almost gleeful about the idea and we ended the session on that note.

(I was assuming that Billy's apprehension about being "bugged" would, through his defensive and withdrawn posture, invite harrassment and recreate a self-fulfilling prophecy. I was, therefore, attempting to interdict that cycle by getting him to be *curious* about the "bugging" and, at the same time, even less defensive by defining it as something he could control—not simply be victimized by.)

Session 3. (Six days later.)

Mr. and Mrs. S. came at my request. I said that I had had a most instructive and enlightening session with Billy. They commented that something of some significance must have happened since he had gone around for several days after showing them what he could do with his left hand. Before he had tended to keep it hidden. I told them I had shown great curiosity in his hand but I expressed surprise that it had made such an impact on him. In passing, I attributed this welcome change in Billy to their innate curiosity and patience.

(When I have had any beneficial impact on a child, I attempt to minimize my own influence and, instead, attribute progress to some quality or effort of the parents. I always want to strengthen the idea that it is *their* ability to positively influence their child and, thereby, enhance their optimism and willingness to take further steps.)

I told them that in that session I was able to get a handle on what might be underlying Billy's poor self-esteem, his unhappiness and, therefore, his asocialization. I explained that with his disability and all the years of doctors' appointments, treatments, special programs and the attention that has surrounded his difficulties he had become fearful of being in the omnipotent position of reordering his parents' lives; that while he had some concern about his own possible fragility, he was more concerned that his parents were too fragile and intimidated by him and his disability and that he was in control. This fear, I continued, held him back from risking approaching other children. As could be seen, all their well meant urgings, encouragements, special outings, and the like, were seen by Billy as evidences of their intimidation and he was unable to profit from them.

(The above explanation to the parents regarding Billy's "fear of omnipotence" is an example of a type of framing I often find necessary. In this case I had already formed some general idea of what I wanted the parents to do, principally to stop the well meant campaign of intrusiveness in his life through their questioning, exhortations, "special programs" and the like. I believed that all that could only add to his self-consciousness and therefore his difficulty in socializing.

However, it is one thing to know what the parents should do, it is another to get them to do it. I could have simply told them what I believed, that he is essentially a normal boy despite his left-handed motor problem but a boy made self-conscious by their well intended help. But this would have run counter to all their beliefs about him; they saw the problem as starting almost from birth, over the years their lives revolved more and more around his problem and they viewed him as having deficits—neurologically and psychologically—that set him apart from other "normal" children. To have ignored their views would have run the risk of their discounting any further input I could provide and, worse, set them to seek a more pathology-oriented therapist for their son. Thus, I felt it necessary to frame any further advice by an explanation which incorporated their own belief system but with some elaboration of my own that would make any ensuing suggestions "logical" in their minds.

In its essence, they were seeing Billy as having some significant psychological problem which led him to have a poor image of himself and in turn contributing to his difficulty making friends. Since I was the "expert" I was then free to describe what, in my "expertise" had come to light regarding the exact nature of that psychological problem. It was not too difficult to refer to "a fear of omnipotence." I had reason to use that framing before for parents who needed to treat their child matter-of-factly, at times punitively, but who were intimidated by the notion the child was "mentally ill" or "sick." To tell parents, then, that their child's "sickness" requires a departure from "egg-shell" handling allows them to shift more easily to a matter-of-fact management. In this case, as in many cases, the parents are overly conscientious and this reframing also allows them something to *do* for their child. In any case, it is more certain that people will back off from some traditional position if they are given something to do that requires a 180 degree shift.)

They said this made a lot of sense but confirmed their own suspicions that they were not handling Billy right. Since their implied sense of ineptness might interfere with their getting on with what they needed to do I said that most of what they had done for Billy was neccessary and should not have been different and that I was commenting on those *few* things that might not, *at this point*, be useful to continue. In any case, what they did was born from their sincere desire to help him and for most children would be logical. Since they seemed to relax on hearing that I proceeded to detail what they now could do.

I reminded them that what I was about to suggest might still seem strange, but they were to keep in mind that it stemmed from my awareness of Billy's need to overcome his feared omnipotence. To begin with there needed to be a separation between Billy's world at school and his world at home; that whatever difficulties he had at school should not intrude itself into the activities and routines of his parents. Therefore, the school should be notified that whatever problems they encountered with Billy were to be handled by them and under no circumstances should he be sent home for any misbehaviors. I said that it would help the school authorities relax if they were also told they could use their own judgement in handling Billy in any way they deemed appropriate. In keeping with this, I further suggested that they not punish him for any delinquencies that occurred at school; this would not only avoid reduplicated penalties but, more importantly, convey to him that he is not in a position any longer to "force" them to go out of their way to impose disciplinary measure simply by acting up at school. Finally, I asked them that they not only discontinue urging him to get out of the house and make friends but that they actively discourage it. I suggested this might best be done by telling him that they prefer he stay home as much as possible since it's easier to keep track of him and avoids the possibility of his bringing home some noisy children. Instead, he could "watch those nice shows on TV." Mrs. S. agreed quite readily and seemed to sense some humor in it. She smiled and said, "Well, at least that will be some switch." However, Mr. S., while agreeing to the plan, expressed concern that Billy might simply follow their instructions. I said that was possible, but since they had already made a concerted effort to get him out of the house with no success, there was nothing to lose by shifting tack. I added that what I was suggesting might not initially aid Billy's socialization, but that it was directed to a first or more basic step, their conveying to him that his friendlessness was not a burden to them. This seemed to reassure Mr. S. and we ended the session with the plan to meet in two weeks.

(As the reader can tell, all these suggestions and comments were designed to aid the parents in backing away from a management of their son which I felt could only be confirming and adding to his self-consciousness and difficulty in socializing. In effect, I was attempting to get them to stop *creating* a problem. For further elaboration of this rationale, the reader is referred to "Change— Principles of Problem Formation and Problem Resolution" by Watzlawick, Weakland and Fisch. W. W. Norton. 1974.)

Session 4. (Twelve days later.)

When they came in, Mrs. S. began right away saying that they had done what I asked and a few days later Billy had brought home two friends. She laughed as she said that he had even made lunch for them and she didn't mind the mess he had made in the kitchen. He hadn't repeated that since but she expressed amazement that their new tack would have such rapid and definite results. I expressed amazement also; that while I had hoped for some sign of less tension on Billy's part, I was surprised that it went further and I indicated that I was disconcerted that improvement had gone so fast.

(When patients or parents come in and announce a definite improvement, an improvement they are clearly acknowledging, I am most likely going to take the position that "things have moved too fast" and that, therefore, no further improvement should take place "for the time being." I may offer various rationales for this position but most often will simply say that in my experience, there is more danger changing things too fast than too slow. There is little, if any, error in this strategy since it is my general view that problems are more likely to arise when people are working too hard at things rather than at a leisurely pace. While patients are encouraged by initial success, it is too easy for them to become apprehensive lest the improvement isn't sustained. Their intensified and urgent efforts can often be counter-productive and produce a demoralizing retrogression. If, on the other hand, their therapist looks a bit worried about the unexpected efficiency of their efforts, it underscores the potential for change and, at the same time puts them in the more relaxed position of not having to keep up the effort. Often, I may not only suggest that things should not improve further, but I will suggest that they make an effort to have things slide back a "peg or two." Thus, should any retrogression occur, this is not demoralizing since it is "according to plan." In actuality, it is rare for things to retrogress, and more often than not patients come in and smilingly tell me they had "failed" in their efforts to hold things back.)

They also reported that the school was quite willing to cooperate with their request, in fact almost seemed relieved. They said they couldn't add much more since "things have been quiet" on the school front since then. As we were about to end Mr. S. said that they had been planning to send Billy to a special school for dyslexic children sometime in the fall and what did I think about that. I attempted to discourage it by saying that while it might be necessary this school semester had just begun and there wasn't enough time to evaluate Billy's potential for progress; that it might be better to wait further. I added that while such a special school could have its advantages in meeting some of Billy's needs, it would have the disadvantage of gearing his educational experience even further away from the more regular context than the special classes he was in. This could have a bearing on the very problem they were coming in about, his difficulty in socialization and the marginal position he has been in vis-a-vis other children. I then asked that we meet again in about three weeks.

Session 5. (Three weeks later.)

Mrs. S. came in by herself. She said that her husband had wanted to come in but since he was starting a new job they both felt it best he not take too much advantage of working hours. She said that Billy was "still holding his own." He had had friends over again, was spending more of his time out of the house and consequently less time watching television. She also reported that one morning when he had missed the school bus he simply took his bicycle and got himself to school. She regarded that as significant since characteristically he would ask her to drive him to school. She said he is still reluctant to attend school and she feels it necessary to get him up in the morning, urge him to speed up in getting ready so he won't miss the bus and the like. I suggested that his slowness in preparing for school was another facet of the overall problem—his fear that his own difficulties could push the parents around, and that it could be dealt with as they had done the school and his getting out of the house after school. I therefore suggested that at least on one morning she make an effort to get him to be late and we discussed some ways of implementing that—not setting the alarm, being slow in serving breakfast, etc. However, I told her that while I thought this might be helpful to him, on second thought, it might be taking things a little too fast again. I wasn't sure so she should think it over but not feel she should rush into it, beneficial as it might be. I ended the session and, again, suggested we meet in three weeks.

(As mentioned previously, I feel there is more danger in attempting to move patients on after there has been a report of improvement than in taking the position of "go slow." At the very worst, should I underestimate the confidence of the patient in moving ahead, he will make it clear to me that he is quite impatient and the impetus for change will all the more come from him. Therefore, while Mrs. S. was describing another facet of Billy's problem, she was defining it as a lesser one and the previous improvement he had shown was still holding up. I felt it important not to press it further but to appear to withdraw my suggestion. In implying that it would, nevertheless, be a beneficial move, I could allow her to go ahead with it but in a relaxed way since I was attaching no importance or urgency to it.)

Session 6. (Three weeks later.)

Mr. and Mrs. S. came in together. Mrs. S. said that Billy was coming along fine, especially with friends. His contacts with children in the neighborhood were now more and more frequent and there had evolved some visiting at each other's houses. She seemed quite pleased but Mr. S., while acknowledging those gains, looked uncomfortable and tense. He expressed concern that, while things seemed to be going well, they might not be *fully* attending to Billy's needs, for example, his need to be more responsible. On further exploration, it turned out that Billy's "irresponsibilities" were minimal and Mr. S. acknowledged that they weren't any problem. He explained that the *real* problem for him was his anxiety that they weren't doing their best; that he was not carrying out my suggestions *correctly* and that they were making mistakes that would show up sooner or later. Since Mrs. S. didn't seem bothered by this, I directed my comments to her husband. I told him that since Billy's trouble had as one element a lack of confidence, it would be greatly beneficial if his father could convey that by making mistakes himself even in his handling of Billy. This might now be his most beneficial effort with Billy, while his wife could continue the previous tack we had discussed. Therefore, I urged him to make sure he made some mistakes with Billy, at least from "time to time." He relaxed on hearing that and I concluded the session by saying that I felt we should meet in two weeks.

(On hearing the mother's report, that gains in Billy's socialization had been maintained, even elaborated on, I anticipated that this might be a terminating session. While the reader may feel this is rather precipitous, I believe there are fewer risks in terminating treatment after a small, but strategic, change has occurred. Billy's asocialization had been a rather long-standing business and in a matter of a short space of time he had done quite well. The leap from no friends to one friend is a much greater one than from one friend to two friends. Much of the business of doing therapy briefly is knowing what *not* to meddle with. However, the father's reaction discouraged me from bringing up the offer of termination. I therefore decided to redefine his "incorrectness" as a therapeutically beneficial and neccessary feature of the overall treatment. Although he showed some visible relaxation following that, I thought it would help to plan the next session sooner than we had been accustomed to.)

Session 7. (Two weeks later.)

Mr. and Mrs. S. came in and said that things were going quite well with Billy. Both were visibly pleased. Neither could think of any complaints about his deportment and as far as they could tell analagous improvement had taken place in the school setting. They said that they had some unexpected trouble, not from Billy, but from his brother, Larry. He had taken some money from a younger child. On learning of it they had taken him over to that child's home, had him apologize to the boy and his parents, return the money and, after some brief discussion with the boy's parents, took Larry back home.

Again, Mr. S.' main concern was not that Larry was becoming a problem, but wondering whether they had handled the incident thoroughly and correctly enough. Since I felt they had handled it quite well, I limited my comments to predicting that the only error I could be sure they would make at any time in the future would be to underestimate their beneficial handling of situations that arose with the kids. I would never fear they hadn't done enough, only that they would never feel they had. They acknowledged that this had been an old Achilles heel of theirs, especially his. Mrs. S. then said she felt confident enough about the kids and their handling of them that she was planning to quit her part-time job and divert her time to endeavors of a more leisurely sort; things she had been looking forward to for many years.

I then took the opportunity of suggesting that we either stop treatment or, at least, take a long vacation from it. They said they were really quite pleased, even amazed, at the progress Billy had made and they preferred to stop treatment at this point; perhaps leave things ad hoc should anything come up.

Follow up. (Two months later.)

Mrs. S. called and said that things had been going quite well. Billy was doing fine in school, not getting into fights, making friends there as well as in the neighborhood. They were having no further trouble with Larry. She added that she and her husband were quite pleased with the outcome of treatment and thanked me for "what almost seems a miracle." I said that I appreciated their thanks and that while I needed all the credit I could get, I knew they deserved a major portion of it for the efforts they had made, the willingness to try out some "crazy stuff" and the way they went about it. I promised her, though, that since I did need the credit, I wouldn't divulge to anyone that they had had any part in Billy's improvement. Mrs. S. recognized my facetiousness and we ended the telephone conversation.

(As I mentioned in the opening of this case, I always want to convey that it's the parent's child and their effort that will count. I do not back away from this position because a case has gone well or has terminated. In my final rejoinder on the phone, I simply used humor, to convey that message.)

(From a case report by Richard Fisch, M.D., 467 Hamilton Ave., Palo Alto, Calif.)